# STEPPER MOTORS
## Fundamentals, Applications and Design

# STEPPER MOTORS
## Fundamentals, Applications and Design

**V.V. ATHANI**
*Dean, Cummins College of Engineering for Women, Pune*
*Formerly, Senior Professor, Department of Electrical Engineering*
*Indian Institute of Technology, Bombay*

PUBLISHING FOR ONE WORLD

**NEW AGE INTERNATIONAL (P) LIMITED, PUBLISHERS**

New Delhi • Bangalore • Chennai • Cochin • Guwahati • Hyderabad
Jalandhar • Kolkata • Lucknow • Mumbai • Ranchi

Visit us at **www.newagepublishers.com**

Published by New Age International (P) Ltd., Publishers
First Edition : 1997
Reprint : 2008

---



**ISBN : 81-224-1006-5**

**Rs. 595.00**

**C-07-11-2107**

**6 7 8 9 10**

Printed in India at Nisha Enterprises, Delhi.

PUBLISHING FOR ONE WORLD

**NEW AGE INTERNATIONAL (P) LIMITED, PUBLISHERS**
4835/24, Ansari Road, Daryaganj, New Delhi - 110002
Visit us at **www.newagepublishers.com**

*In Loving Memory of My Father*

***The Late Vasudeo Anant Athani***

# Preface

Stepper motors have become quite popular even in a developing country such as India. Growth of indigenous manufacture of computer peripherals and office equipment has provided an impetus to stepper motors in India. As a result, more and more industries are entering into fray of stepper motor manufacturing.

Stepper motors have become increasingly popular in India, especially in the last decade. Indigenous manufacture of computer peripheral devices, such as printers, floppy and hard disc drives, *etc.*, has gained momentum. Electronic typewriters and fax machines are being manufactured in ever-increasing numbers. Engineering industries, especially the export oriented units, have woken up to the fact that, unless they adopt such sophisticated production techniques as CNC machines and robots, they cannot survive in intense international competition. All these applications, alongwith a host of others, employ stepper motors. This has increased the awareness of stepper motors in India. However, users of stepper motors, both students and practising engineers, are facing the difficulty of lack of adequate reference material on stepper motors. Hence there exists a need for an authoritative book on stepper motors at an affordable price. The present monograph is meant to meet this need.

This monograph covers all aspects of stepper motors : construction, principle of operation, characteristics, applications, analysis and design. It also covers electronic controllers without which the stepper motor cannot operate.

## SPECIAL FEATURES

Some of the special features of this monograph are worth mentioning:

1. Chapter 7, on applications stepper motors, discusses in detail the question of *how to select a stepper motor* for a given application. This discussion will be particularly useful to practising engineers in their work. Students and hobbyists will also benefit from this discussion.
2. Chapter 9 deals with the principles of *design of stepper motors*, especially of PMH (permanent magnet hybrid) type. Such a discussion appears, perhaps for the first time, in a monograph of this type.
3. In Chapter 2, on construction of stepper motors, the latest *REMP Disc Rotor type* (*i.e.*, DM) stepper motor has been presented, again, perhaps the first time in a monograph of this type.
4. In Chapter 5 on microprocessor control of stepper motors, following three outstanding Indian contributions to stepper motor control technology have also been discussed:

(a) *ASIC for Stepper Motor Control* being developed by VLSI group of Central Electronic Engineering Research Institute (CEERI) Pilani, India.

(b) *4-20 mA Serial Link for Remote Control of stepper motors* developed again at CEERI-Pilani, and

(c) *Low Cost Intelligent Controller* developed at Indian Institute of Technology (IIT) Bombay by the author.

The *author* hopes the reader finds the monograph in general and above mentioned special features in particular, useful and interesting.

Pune V.V. Athani

# *Acknowledgements*

The author has received help, advice and guidance from numerous sources, so that it is not possible to individually thank them all. The author hereby acknowledges their help and assistance. However, the author would particularly like to express his heart-felt thanks to:

1. Dr. Hi Dong Chai to permit the use of his publications in Chapter 8 on modelling of stepper motors.
2. Dr. A. Hughes, Dr. G.C. Verghese whose publications have been used in Chapter 8 on stepper motor modelling.
3. Warner Electric Brake & Clutch Co., material from whose *Guide to Selecting and Controlling Step Motors* has been used in our discussion on drive circuits, damping methods and applications of stepper motors.
4. Dr. R.P. Soni of CEERI-Pilani for preparing both the first draft and the revised final draft of more than half the chapters of this monograph.
5. Mr. B.D. Deshpande and his colleagues at M/s Srijan Control Drives, Pune (India) for their active collaboration in the development of indigenous technology in the area of stepper motors.

Pune

V.V. Athani

# Contents

# CHAPTER - 1

# *Introduction to Stepper Motors*

This chapter starts with the definition of the stepper motor. It then presents a brief historical review of the development of stepper motors.

## 1.1 DEFINITION OF A STEPPER MOTOR

On account of its unusual construction, operation and characteristics, it is difficult to define a stepper motor. The best course seems to be to state the definition given in British Standard Specifications [1]: "A stepper motor is a brushless DC motor whose rotor rotates in discrete angular increments when its stator windings are energised in a programmed manner. Rotation occurs because of magnetic interaction between rotor poles and poles of the sequentially energised stator windings. The rotor has no electrical windings, but has salient and/or magnetised poles."

From this definition, it is clear that a stepper motor is a digital actuator whose input is in the form of programmed energization of the stator windings and whose output is in the form of discrete angular rotation. It is, therefore, ideally suited for use as an actuator in computer control systems, digital control systems, etc. Control systems employing stepper motor as actuators are known as incremental motion control systems (IMCS).

## 1.2 HISTORY OF STEPPER MOTOR DEVELOPMENT

We present below a brief account of the development of the stepper motor with a view to placing the modern stepper motor in proper perspective.

History of the stepper motor can be traced back to the 19th century; they were then referred to as electromagnetic engines [2]. Two important inventions pertaining to the variable reluctance (VR) stepper motors, which took place in the 20th century, are worth mentioning. The first one was the invention of salient tooth structure on both the stator and rotor of the VR stepper motor, for which Walker [3] was awarded a British patent in 1919. The second one was the invention, by Chicken and Thain, [4] of the sandwich structure for producing large torques in a small volume, for which an American patent was granted in 1920.

As far as application of stepper motors are concerned McCelland [5] described application of the stepper motor in British warships. Kieburtz followed suit with an account of stepper motor usage in US Navy [6].

The modern stepper motor was first described by Thomas and Fleischauer in 1957 [7]. This was the VR type motor, whose commercial production commenced in the USA in the early '60's [8, 9]. The permanent magnet hybrid (PM) stepper motor was invented by Feirtag and Donahoo of General Electric Co. (GEC) in 1952 [10]. GEC started its production in 1952. Superior Electric Co. improved upon the existing design of the PM stepper motor and commenced its manufacture in the early '60's under the brand name *Slo-syn.* Superior Electric Co. introduced their *Industry standard M-series* stepper motors in 1970; these motors were specifically designed for application in IMCS's. Sigma Instruments Co. came out with an ingenious stepper motor, called *cyclonome* motor, in 1952. However, it was not successful in the market; it was consequently withdrawn in 1969, and PM stepper motors were introduced by Sigma Instruments Co.

Sanyo Denki was the first to manufacture stepper motors in Japan in the early '70's. The finest Japanese stepper motors were from Fujitsu Fanuc for application in their world famous Fanuc series of CNC systems. These motors were capable of running at a fantastic speed of more than 16,000 steps/sec, and of providing static torques of upto 100 kg-cm. They were, however, discontinued in the '80' when Fanuc replaced them by high performance DC servomotors in their Fanuc CNC systems.

As far as India is concerned, Automatic Electric Ltd. of Bombay pioneered introduction of the stepper motor in India in 1967. The author was entrusted with design of electronic controller for it [11]. However, the largest manufacturer of stepper motors in India is Srijan Control Drives, Pune, which was started by a former engineer from Automatic Electric. Another firm, called Katragadda Electronics Ltd. of Hyderabad has entered the stepper motor market in a big way, with French collaboration. In addition, there are a number of small manufacturers of stepper motors in India. All these are PM type motors. VR stepper motors are *not manufactured* in India.

Indigenous production of computer peripherals and electronic typewriters on the one hand, and of CNC systems on the other, has given a powerful boost to stepper motor market in India. In fact, it is expected that stepper motor production in India will double in the next five years. In view of their growing importance, stepper motors have been identified as a *thrust area* for development of indigenous technology by the Department of Science and Technology, Government of India. The author has carried out an important research project involving generation of indigenous know-how in stepper motor design [12], and development of a low cost intelligent stepper motor controllers [13].

With such a rapid development of stepper motors in India, there will be a need for an indigenous standard reference book on stepper motors. This monograph is meant to satisfy this need.

## REFERENCES


1. British Standard Specification No. BS5000, Part 60, 1982.
2. J.V. Byrne, and J.C. Lacy, "Characteristics of saturated stepper and reluctance motors", IEE Conf. Publn. No.136, pp. 93-93, 1976.
3. C.L. Walker, "Improvements in and connected with electromagnetic step-by-step signalling and synchronous rotation", UK Patent No. 137, 150, 1919.
4. C.B. Chicken, and J.H. Thain, "Electrical signalling apparatus", US Patent No. 1, 353, 025, 1920.
5. W. McCelland, "The application of electricity in warships", JIEE (USA), Vol. 65, pp. 829-871, 1927.
6. R.B. Kieburtz, "The step motor – the next advance in control systems", IEEE Trans. on Auto Control, Vol. AC-9, pp. 98-104, 1964.
7. A.G. Thomas, and Fleischauer, "The power stepping motor – a new digital actuator", Control Engg., Vol. 4. pp. 74-81, 1957.
8. S.J. Bailey, "Incremental Servos: Part IV", Control Engg. Vol. 8, pp. 133-135, 1961.
9. J. Proctor, "Stepping motors move in", Product Engg., Vol. 4, pp. 74-188, 1963.
10. K.M. Feirtag, and J.T. Donahoo, "Dynamoelectric machine", US Patent No. 2, 589-999, 1952.
11. V.V. Athani, and L.R. Subramanyam, "Study of step servo systems", Proc. Symp. on Control Theory, Ind. Instt. of Science, Bangalore, Vol. 3, pp. 425-445, 1968.
12. V.V. Athani, "Design of permanent magnet hybrid (PMH) stepper motors", Proc. Int. Conf. on Electrical Rotating Machines, Taj Mahal Hotel, Bombay, Vol. 2, pp. VA8 – VA13, 1992.
13. V.V. Athani, "Development of stepper motors and controllers", DST Sponsored Project, Final Project Report, 1992.

# CHAPTER - 2

# *Construction and Oreration of Stepper Motors*

As far as construction is concerned, stepper motors may be divided into two major groups: (i) without permanent magnet (PM), and (ii) with PM. Each group may be further subdivided as shown below:

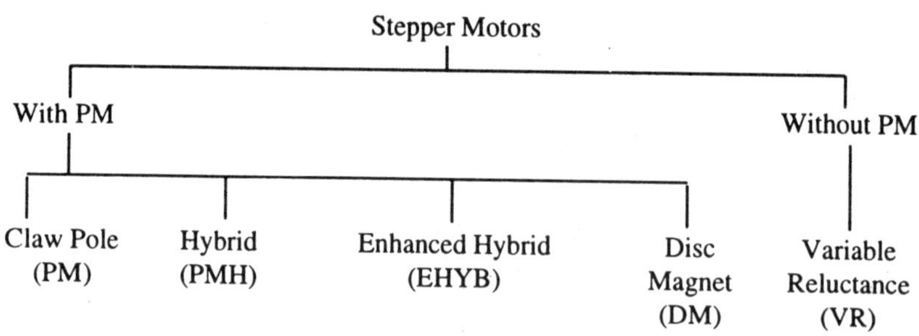


Construction and operation of these stepper motors are explained below:

## 2.1 VARIABLE RELUCTANCE (VR) STEPPER MOTOR

The VR stepper motor is characterized by the fact that there is no permanent magnet either on the rotor or the stator. The rotor carries no windings either. The rotor is of salient pole type and is made entirely of soft iron stampings. The stator is also made of soft iron stampings. This also has salient poles, which carry stator windings. The number of poles on the stator is an even multiple of the number of phases for which the stator windings are wound. The number of phases on the stator must be at least 3 for bidirectional control of the stepper motor. The maximum number of phases on the stator is limited to 5.

The construction of a 3-phase VR stepper motor, with 12 poles on the stator and 8 poles on the rotor is shown in Fig. 2.1.

When phase *A* winding is energized, the rotor moves to the position in which the rotor teeth align themselves with teeth of phase *A*. This is the position in

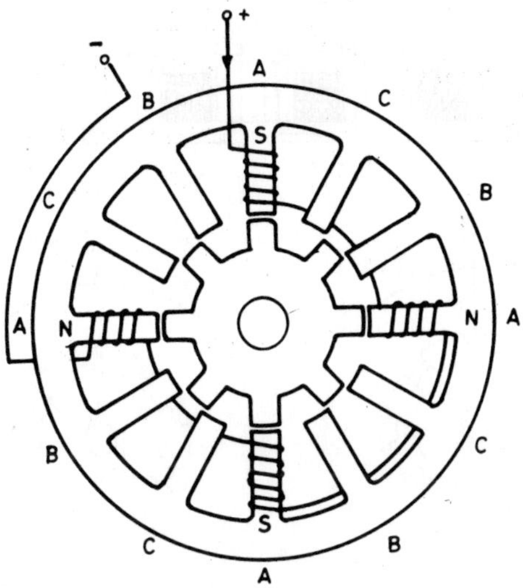


**Fig. 2.1** Schematic Diagram of a Three Face Single Stack Variable Reluctance Step Motor. Only the '*A*' Face Windings are shown for Clarity

which the reluctance of the magnetic circuit is the minimum. When phase *A* is de-energized and phase *B* is energized, the rotor moves through 15° in CW direction so as to align its teeth with those of phase *B*. Next, de-energizing *B*-phase and energizing *C*-phase causes the stator to move through a further 15° in CW direction; in this position the rotor poles are aligned with *C*-phase teeth.

The construction, shown in Fig. 2.1 is a single stack motor. In order to increase the torque exerted by the motor, multiple stack construction is adopted as shown in Fig. 2.2.

## 2.2 PERMANENT MAGNET STEPPER MOTOR WITH CLAW POLES

This is a permanent magnet rotor motor. It is also known as can-stack motor and is shown in Fig. 2.3. Its main advantage is its low manufacturing cost. It finds use in applications such as paper feed motor of a printer or head drive motor of a floppy disk drive.

## 2.3 HYBRID (PMH) STEPPER MOTORS

This is the most popular type of stepper motor. Its construction and operation are explained below.

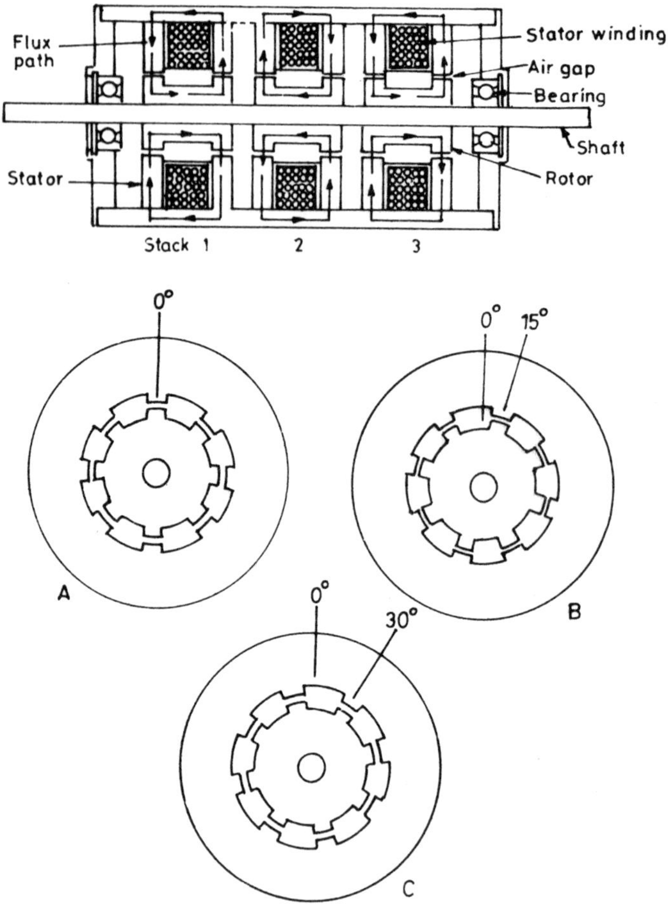


**Fig. 2.2** 3-Phase, 3-Stack, *VR* Stepping Motor

### 2.3.1 Construction of PMH Motor

The simplest type of PMH stepper motor is shown in Fig. 2.4. The stator has four poles. Each pole carries a winding. Windings on poles 1 and 3 are connected in series to form phase *A* winding. Similarly windings on poles 2 and 4 are connected in series to form *B*-phase winding. The axes of these windings are perpendicular to each other in space. The rotor is a bar magnet having N and S poles as shown in Fig. 2.4.

### 2.3.2 Operation of PMH Stepper Motor

The principle of operation of the PMH stepper motor can be explained by referring to Fig. 2.4. Let us start with Fig. 2.4 (a). Suppose that a voltage + V is applied to *A*-phase winding. As a result let stator pole 1 be N-pole and pole 2 be S-pole.

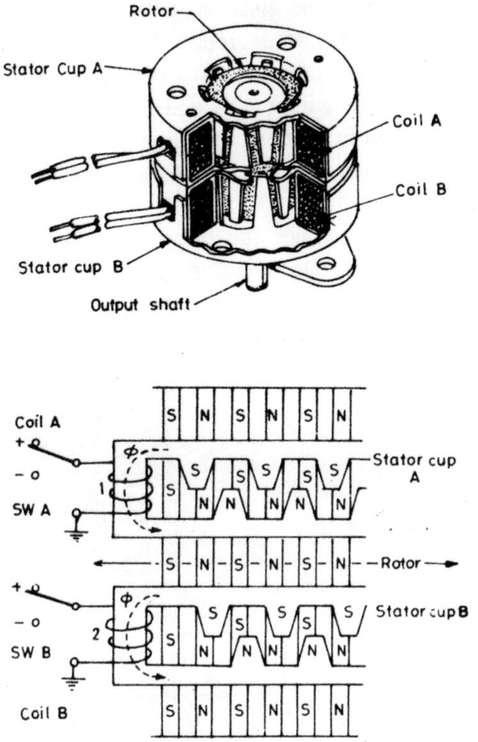


**Fig. 2.3** Cutaway 2 ϕ Permanent Stepper Motor

This gives rise to a stator magnetic field vector $F_a$, as shown in Fig. 2.4 (a). The rotor will position itself in such a way as to lock its N-pole to stator S-pole, and vice-versa.

With winding $A$ energised as before, let a voltage + V be applied to winding $B$, causing pole-2 to be an N-pole and pole-4 to be S-pole. This produces another stator magnetic field vector $F_b$ as shown in Fig. 2.4 (b). The resulting stator magnetic field vector $F$ will be at + 45 degrees from its former position. Hence the rotor will move through a fixed angle of + 45 degrees, as shown in Fig. 2.4 (b).

With winding $B$ energised as before, let winding $A$ be deenergised. $F_a$ becomes zero, leaving $F_b$ as before. The rotor, therefore, will move through another 45 degrees to align itself with $F_b$ as shown in Fig. 2.4 (c).

With phase $B$ energised as before, let a voltage –V be applied to phase $A$. This reverses the stator magnetic field vector $F_a$ as shown in Fig. 2.4 (d). The resulting stator field vector $F$ shifts by another 45 degrees, causing the rotor to follow suit as shown in Fig. 2.4 (d).

Proceeding thus from Fig. 2.4 (e) to Fig. 2.4 (h), it becomes clear as to how every change in the pattern of energisation of stator windings causes the stator field vector to shift by a further 45 degrees.

Fig. 2.4 illustrates a number of important aspects of stepper motor operation.

(1) As long as the stator windings *A* and *B* are energised in a particular manner, the rotor stays put in the corresponding position.

The rotor will move further only when the pattern of energisation of the stator windings is changed.

(2) Fig. 2.4 (a to h) illustrates the meaning of the term "programmed sequence" of energisation of stator windings.

(3) Fig. 2.4 (a to h) contains, in fact, three programmed sequences of energisation of stator windings.

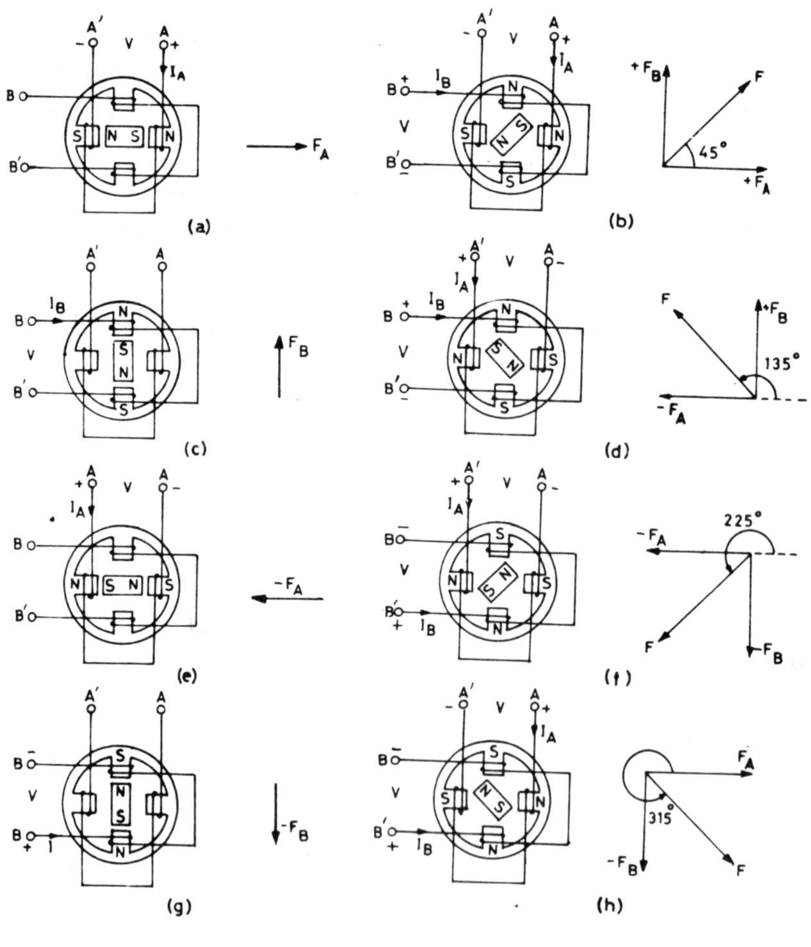


**Fig. 2.4** Principle of Operation of Hyprid Stepper Motor

(i) Fig. 2.4 (a, c, e, g), constitutes single phase energisation (1-1) sequence inasmuch as only one stator winding is energised at any time.

(ii) Fig. 2.4 (b, d, f, h), on the other hand, form two phase energisation (2-2) sequence, because both the *A* and *B* phases are energised either with + V or – V at any time.

Both of the above sequences are "*four step sequences*", since the rotor moves through 90 degrees per step. The difference between them is in the equilibrium position of the rotor. With single phase sequence, the rotor positions are 90, 180, 270 and 360 degrees, while the rotor positions are 45, 135, 225 and 316 degrees in the case of two phase sequence.

(iii) Fig. 2.4 (a to h) constitutes an "*8-step sequence*" in which the rotor moves through 45 degrees per step. Here one and two phases are alternatively energised. This sequence is known as mixed, hybrid or (1-2) sequence.

The sequence shown in Fig. 2.4 is for CCW rotation. The direction of rotation can be reversed by reversing the energisation sequence; e.g. if you are at step "*c*", then go to "*b-a-h...*" instead of "*d-e-f...*" in order to reverse the motor.

### 2.3.3 1.8 Degree Rotation Hybrid Stepper Motor

Fig. 2.4 is meant for explaining the principle of operation of PMH stepper motor only.

The construction of a commercial 1.8 degree rotation per step PMH motor is illustrated in Fig. 2.5. Notice that the rotor carries a cylindrical permanent magnet which is sandwiched between two soft iron laminated and toothed rotor discs. Cross sections of the two rotor discs are shown in Fig. 2.5 (b, c). Each rotor disc has 50 teeth. The stator is also made up of soft iron stampings. It has 8 poles, each pole having 5 teeth. Thus there are 40 poles on the stator. Careful observation of Fig. 2.5 (b, c) reveals that the rotor teeth are in perfect alignment with stator teeth in Fig. 2.5 (b). On the other hand, the rotor teeth are in alignment, not with stator teeth but with stator slots as in Fig. 2.5 (c). This is a position perfect misalignment of stator and rotor teeth. This is described by stating that the rotor teeth in the two cases are offset by half a tooth pitch.

### 2.3.4 Bifilar Wound Hybrid Stepper Motor

Observe from Fig. 2.4 that each of the phase windings *A* and *B* are connected to + V and – V DC supply during certain stages while they are de-energised during certain stages. This requires a centre-tapped bipolar DC supply having outputs + V, 0, – V volts DC. Single pole-three position Switches are required to connect each winding to + V, – V volts DC or to de-energise it as shown in Fig. 2.6 (a). Such an arrangement is often inconvenient in practice.

As an alternative, the construction of the motor is modified as shown in Fig. 2.6 (b). Herein each phase winding is split into two equal section A1, A2, and B1, B2. The two sections are differentially wound as shown by the polarity dots in Fig. 2.6 (b).

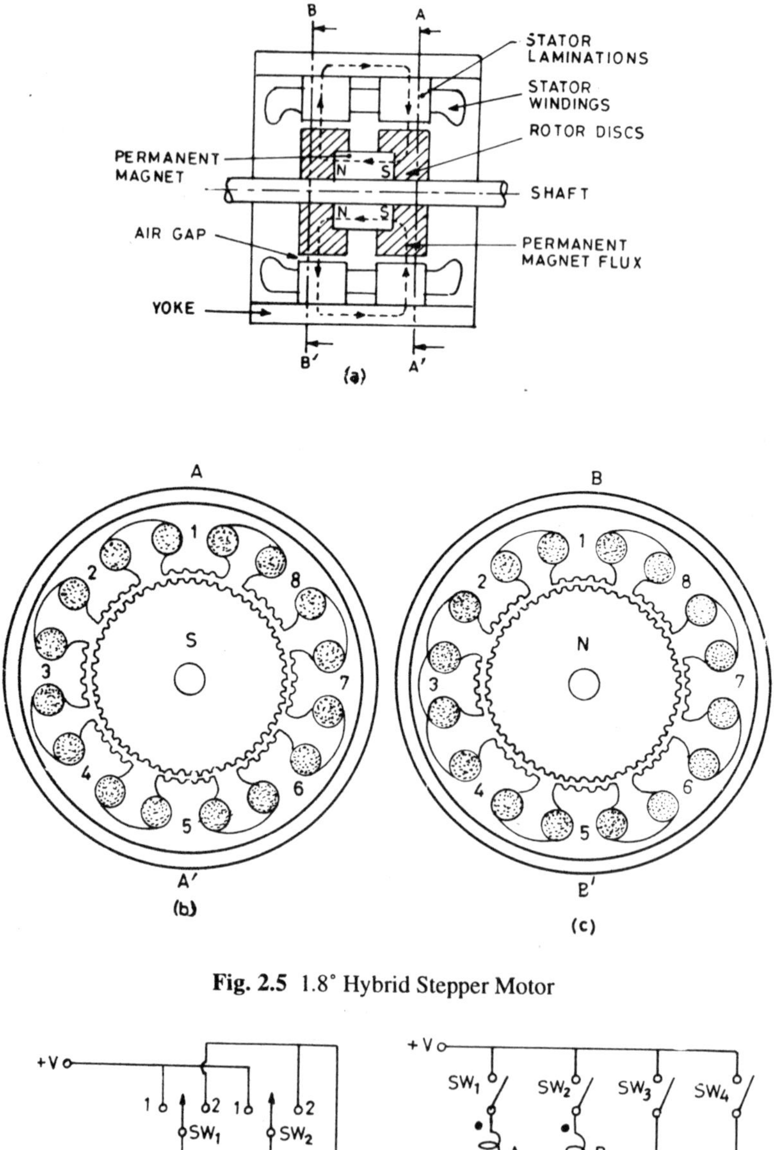


**Fig. 2.5** 1.8° Hybrid Stepper Motor

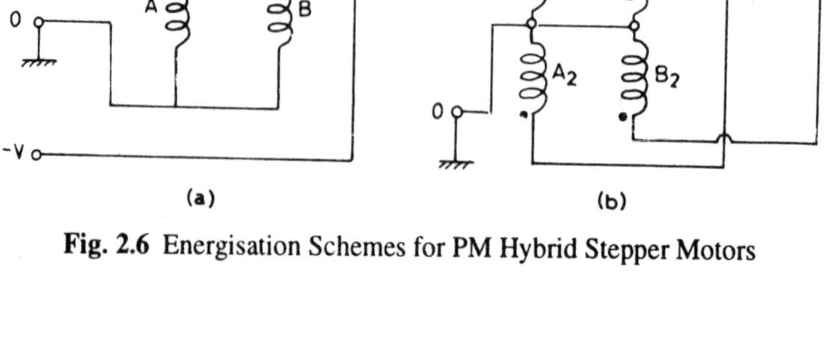


**Fig. 2.6** Energisation Schemes for PM Hybrid Stepper Motors

The significance of this is that a positive current flowing through winding A2 will give rise to a stator field vector which is 180 degrees out of phase with stator field produced by flow of positive current through winding A1. This construction is known as "Bifilar Wound Hybrid Stepper Motor".

With bifilar windings, a unipolar supply alongwith four on-off switches is sufficient for yielding 4-step or 8-step sequence of operation, as shown in Fig. 2.6 (b).

A 1.8 degree hybrid stepper motor with bifilar windings is shown in Fig. 2.7.

## 2.4 ENHANCED PMH STEPPER MOTOR

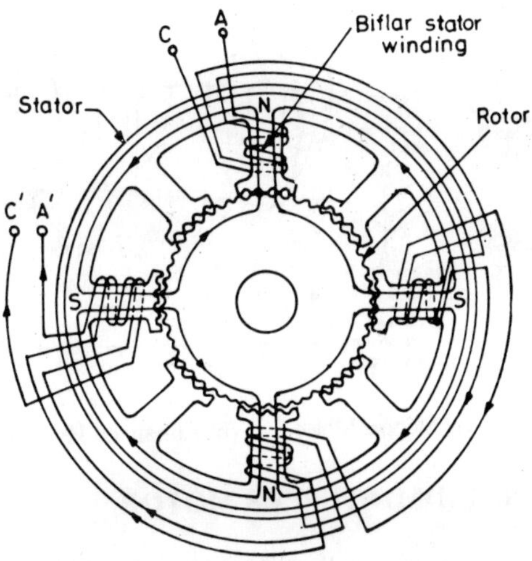


**Fig. 2.7** 1.8° Bifilar Wound Hybrid Stepper Motor

This is a modification of the PM hybrid stepper motor. It was introduced into the market by M/s Sigma Instruments in 1985.

The modification to the standard structure of the PMH stepper motor of Fig. 2.8, consists of insertion of rare earth cobalt (REC) or NdFeB permanent magnet pieces into stator slots as shown in Fig. 2.5. Mark the polarities of the REC magnet pieces with respect to the polarities of the rotor teeth.

The presence of REC magnets in the stator slots forces the airgap flux to cross over from rotor teeth directly to stator teeth. The airgap flux is prevented from leaking. As a consequence, there is a significant reduction in flux leakage, and hence a significant increase in the static torque available from the stepper of a given size. In fact, Horber [8] has reported an almost 100% increase in static torque as a result of insertion of REC magnets into stator slots of the standard PMH stepper motor. He has, therefore termed these motors as enhanced stepper motors.

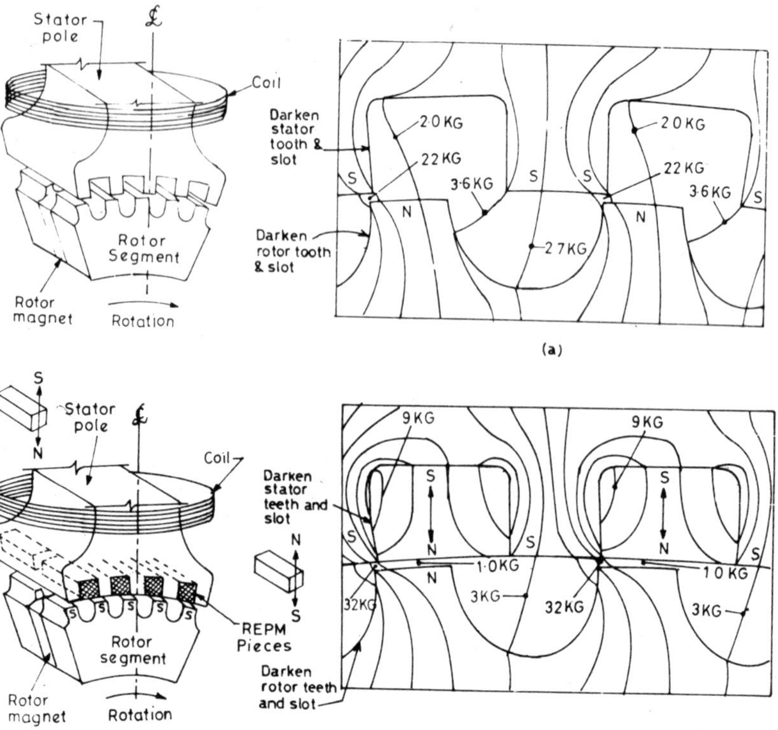


**Fig. 2.8** (a) Standard Hybrid Stepper Motor (b) Enhanced Hybrid Stepper Motor

## 2.5 DISC MAGNET (DM) STEPPER MOTOR

A new type of stepper motor, called *Disc Magnet (DM) stepper motor* was introduced in 1981 by M/s. Portescap of Switzerland [ ] since it represents a significant advances in stepper motor technology, the construction and operation of DM stepper motors are explained below.

The origin of the DM stepper motor can be traced to the early 60's when M/s Portescap developed a tiny single phase stepper motor for driving the hands of a quartz controlled electronic watch. This watch motor was characterized by (i) minimum size and weight, (ii) lowest power consumption, and (iii) highest efficiency. It employed a tiny rare earth $SmCo_6$ [REC] magnet piece as rotor. From this basic design of the "watch motor" was evolved the present multiple pole, multiple phase (2-5 phase) high torque high speed DM stepper motor, which can compete with a DC servo motor.

### 2.5.1 Construction of Disc Magnet (DM) Stepper Motor

The basic construction of a DM stepper motor is shown in Fig. 2.9. Its rotor consists of a thin disc of REC. By means of a selective magnetization process, a large number of alternate N and S poles are impressed as shown in Fig. 2.9.

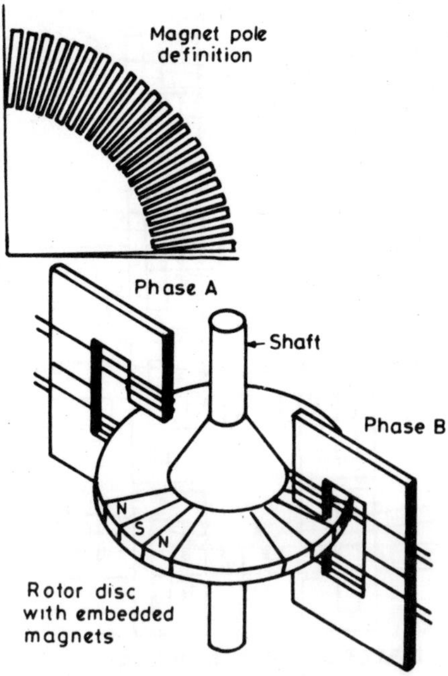


**Fig. 2.9** DM Stepper Motor Construction

The stator is made up of CRGO steel laminations and has a number of poles. The stator poles may be divided into 2-4 phases. The simplest two phase, two poles per phase construction is shown in Fig. 2.9. The axes of the two phases are in space quadrature. Windings are placed on the tips of the stator poles.

### 2.5.2 Operation of the DM Stepper Motor

Fig. 2.10 explains the operation of the DM stepper motor. Let us suppose that initially both *A* and *B* phases are "off". When phase *A* is connected to + V with phase *B* "off", N and S poles are produced on phase *A* as shown in Fig. 2.10 (a). The rotor moves to the right by half a pole pitch so as to lock its N and S poles with *A*-phase S and N poles respectively, as shown in Fig. 2.10 (a).

In the second stage, phase *A* is turned off, while the *B* phase is connected to – V, giving rise to stator N and S poles as shown in Fig. 2.10 (b). The rotor moves through 1/2 a pole pitch to the right so as to lock its S and N poles with the stator N and S poles respectively.

In the third stage, *B* phase is turned off while – V is connected to *A* phase. This causes the rotor to moves by one more 1/2 pole to the right.

Finally, de-energization of phase *A* and connection of phase *B* to + V causes a still further motion of the rotor to the right by 1/2 pole.

This completes one cycle of the 4-step sequence of operation of the DM stepper motor. Figs. 2.9 and 2.10 show only the basic construction and operation of the DM stepper motor. The exploded view of a commercial, 1.8° step

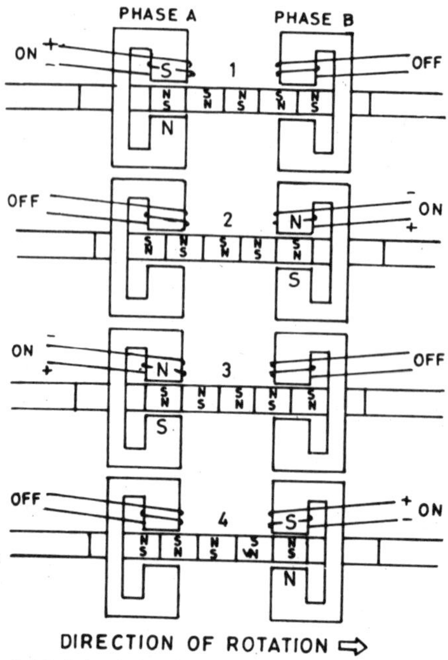


**Fig. 2.10** Principle of Operation of DM Stepper Motor

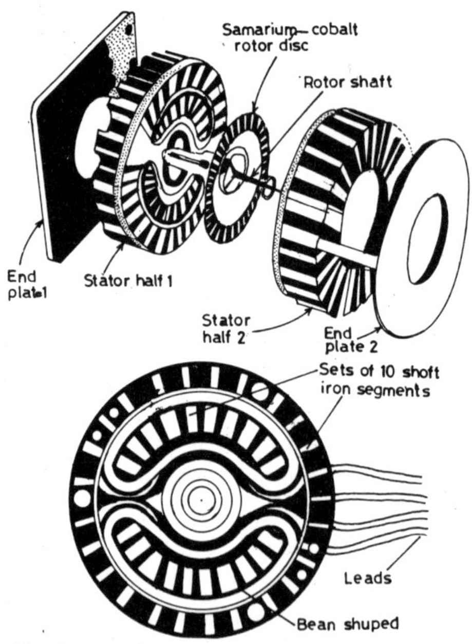


**Fig. 2.11** Exploded view of DM stepper motor

angle, DM stepper motor is shown in Fig. 2.11. The thin DM rotor as well as the two halves of the stator are seen in this figure.

### 2.5.3 Characteristics of DM Stepper Motor

Phase windings *A* and *B* are placed at the tips of the stator poles. Rotor magnets also face the airgap directly. This results in maximum flux in the airgap and hence maximum torque. Consequently, the DM stepper motor has the highest torque/weight and torque/size ratios. Power/size and power/weight ratios are also the highest.

The magnetic circuit of each phase is independent of the others. Hence mutual flux and therefore mutual inductance are low.

On account of short flux paths, the stator magnetic circuits may be designed to operate at below the knee point on the *B-H* curve of the magnetic material. This results in low harmonic distortion and negligible higher harmonic torque components. Finally, there is little variation of inductance with angular rotation of the shaft.

The above characteristics render the DM stepper motor the best suited for microstepping. They also result in the availability of significantly higher dynamic torque at high stepping rates, compared to the PMH stepper motor.

A comparison of the performance of DM stepper motor, PMH stepper motor and DC servomotor is shown in Fig. 2.12 [11]. Superiority of the DM stepper motor is clearly seen.

### 2.5.4 Typical Applications of DM Stepper Motors

By virtue of above characteristics, DM stepper motors are particularly suitable for high performance high volume applications such as computer peripherals, robotics, CNC systems for machine tools, etc. They can out perform even DC servo motors in some of these applications.

DM stepper motors are often equipped with speed sensing coils, so that the same motor may operate as DC servo motor [10].

## 2.6 ELECTROHYDRAULIC STEPPER MOTOR

The EH motor consists of a PMH or VR stepper motor connected to a hydraulic servo motor in a closed loop system shown in Fig. 2.13. When the electric stepper motor moves through one step, it rotates a pilot valve. The pilot valve causes high pressure fluid to be admitted into the cylinder of a hydraulic motor.

As the hydraulic motor rotates, the spool moves in such a way as to close the pilot valve. Due to the hydraulic motor used, this stepper motor is capable of developing very high torques, of the order of several Nm, and also of running at high stepping rates, of the order of 1000 to 2000 steps/sec. They are, therefore, suitable for heavy applications like numerical control of large machine tools.

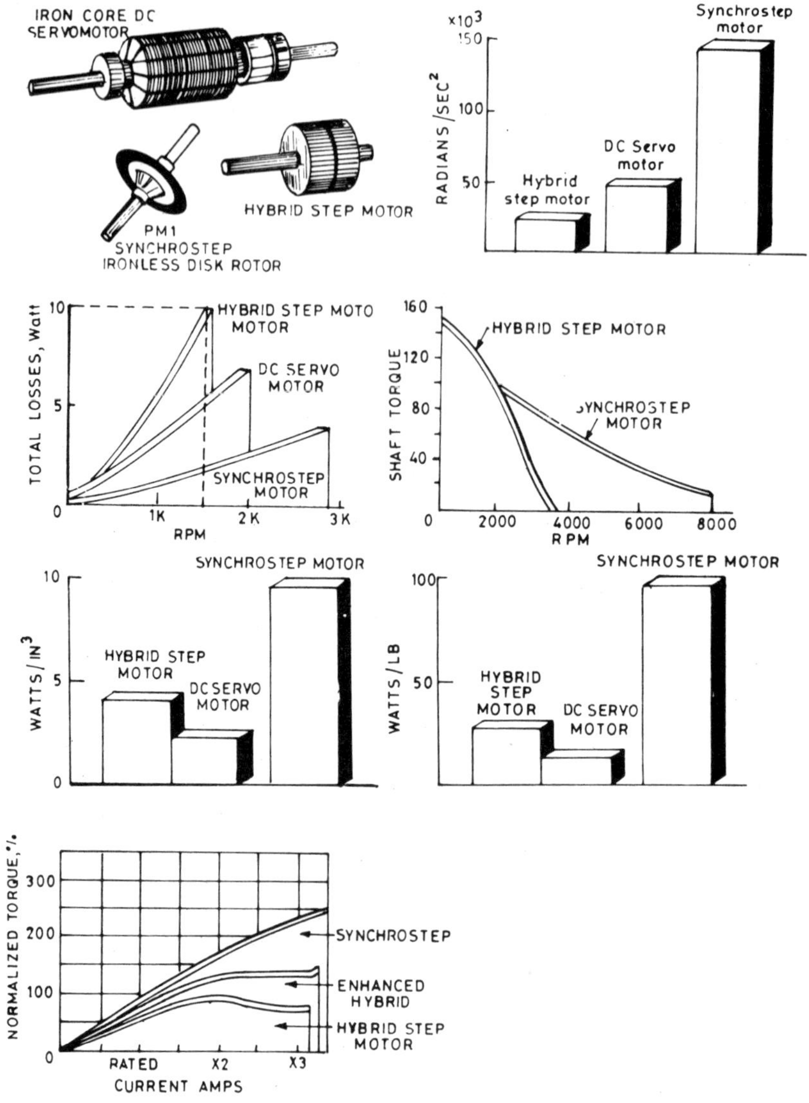


**Fig. 2.12** Comparison of DM Stepper Motor with Hybrid Stepper Motor and DC Servomotor

## 2.7 CONCLUSION

The construction and principle of operation of various types of stepper motors have been discussed in this chapter. A comparison of these stepper motors is given in Table 2.1. Readers may refer to Kuo [1, 2] and for further details.

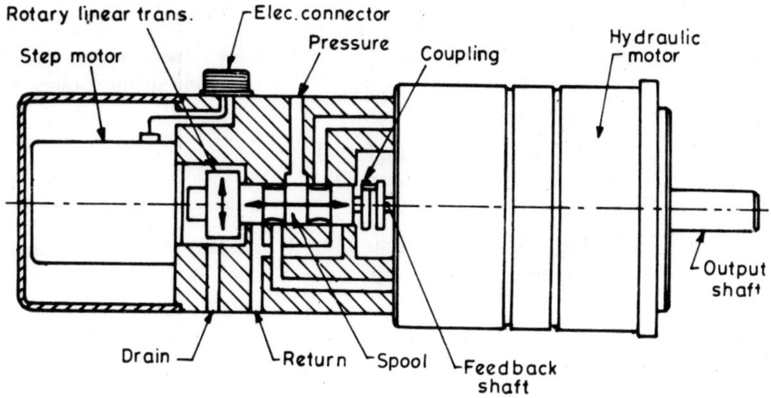


**Fig. 2.13** Schematic Drawing of Electro-hydraulic Stepper Motor (EHSM)

**Table 2.1** Comparison of stepper motors

| *Motor Type* | *Advantages* | *Disadvantages* |
|---|---|---|
| Stepper Motors | 1. Can be driven open loop without feed-back. | 1. Fixed step angle; no flexibility in step resolution. |
| | 2. No accumulative position error. | 2. Low efficiency with ordinary controller. |
| | 3. Responds directly to digital control signals; so stepper motors are natural choice for digital computer control. | 3. High overshoot and oscillation in step response |
| | 4. Mechanically simple; requires little or no maintenance. | 4. Limited ability to handle large inertia load. |
| | 5. Free from contamination. | 5. Friction load increases position error, but error is not accumulative. |
| | 6. Can be repeatedly stalled without damage. | 6. Limited power output and sizes available. |
| | 7. Relatively rugged and durable. | |
| Variable Reluctance Stepper Motors | 1. High torque to inertia ratio. | 1. No detente torque available with windings de-energized. |
| | 2. Low rotor inertia. | 2. Exhibits mid-range resonance at some stepping rates under some drive conditions. |
| | 3. Capable of high stepping rate; high speed slewing capability. | 3. Normally available in 3.6 to 30 deg. step angles |

| *Motor Type* | *Advantages* | *Disadvantages* |
|---|---|---|
| | 4. Ability to freewheel. | 4. Low efficiencies at low voltages and stepping rates. |
| | 5. Light weight. | |
| | 6. 3, 4 and 5 phase, single and multi-stack models available. | |
| Permanent Magnet Hybrid Motors | 1. Provides detente torque with windings de-energized. | 1. Higher inertia and weight due to presence of rotor magnet. |
| | 2. Less tendency to resonate. | 2. Performance affected by change in magnet strength. |
| | 3. Higher holding torque capability. | |
| | 4. Better damping due to presence of rotor magnet. | |
| | 5. High stepping rate capability. | |
| | 6. High efficiency at lower speeds and lower stepping rates. | |
| Electro-hydraulic Motor | 1. Very high holding torque capability. | 1. Requires high pressure hydraulic supply in addition to electric supply. |
| | 2. Very high torque-to-inertia ratio. | 2. More complex construction and operation. |
| | 3. Can handle high inertia load well. | |
| | 4. Capable of high stepping rates. | |
| | 5. Less tendency to oscillate and resonate. | |

## REFERENCES


1. Kuo, B.C. "Theory and application of step motors", West Pub. Co., St. Paul, 19 Chap. 1.
2. Kuo, B.C. "Step motors and control systems", SRL Pub. Co., Champaign, IL, 19 Chap. 1.
3. Acarnley, P.P., "Stepping motor : a guide to modern theory and practice", IEE Press, Series No. 19 (2nd Edn). 199 Chap. 1.
4. Kenjo, T., "Stepping motors and their microprocessor controls", Clarendon Press, Oxford, 1985, Chap. 2.
5. Gopal, M., "Digital control engineering", Wiley Eastern Ltd., New Delhi, 1988, Chap. 9.

6. Del Toro, V., "Electrical machines and power systems", Prentice Hall of India, New Delhi, 1985, Chap. 9.
7. "Stepping motors and associated electronics", Philips Data Handbook No. C17, 1986.
8. Horber, R.W., "A method of influencing the fundamental torque components in hybrid stepping motors", Proc. 14th Annual Symp. on IMCSD, 1985, pp. 369-373.
9. "Stepper motor drives", Think ESCAP, No. 5, Portescap, La Chaux-de-Fonde, Switzerland, Chap. 3.
10. Veignat, N., "Advances in stepper motors: the disk magnet technology", Portescap, La Chaux-de-Fonde, Switzerland, Oct. 1991.
11. "Step into the future with Synchro Step", PMI Motion Technologies, Commack, NY, 8186 No. 123.
12. Coon, W.R. Brodsky, K.F., and Lobsinger, IL, " Variable reluctance vs. hybrid: a guide to selection of stepper motors", Proc. 15th Annual Symp. on IMCSD. 1986, pp. 303-30.
13. Athani, V.V., "Microprocessor control of stepper motors", (Part 1), Electronics for You, Vol. 22, No. ... 1990, pp....

# CHAPTER - 3

# *Characteristics of Stepper Motors*

This chapter is devoted to the study of characteristics of stepper motors, which may be divided into two groups: static and dynamic characteristics.

## 3.1 STEP ANGLE AND ACCURACY

### 3.1.1 Step Angle $\theta_s$

Is angle through which an unloaded stepper motor rotates for every step of the energisation sequence shown in Fig. 3.1. It is determined by the number of teeth on the rotor and stator, as well as the number of steps in the energisation sequence.

### 3.1.2 Steps/Revolution (Z)

Is given by

$$Z = 360°/\theta_s \tag{3.1}$$

For *permanent magnet hybrid (PMH)* step motors,

$$\theta_s = 360°/(N_r \, . \, K_{ws}) = 360°/Z \tag{3.2}$$

where $N_r$ = no. of teeth on rotor discs

and $K_{ws}$ = 4 for 4-step sequence (i.e. 1 phase on and 2 phase on)
= 8 for 8-step (i.e. 1-2 or hybrid) sequence
of energisation of stator windings.

Table 3.1 gives $N_r$ required to yield various step angles when $K_{ws} = 4$ and $K_{ws} = 8$.

For *Single Stack Variable Reluctance* (*VR*) stepper motors, the step angle $\theta_s$, is governed by the following relations:

$$N_s = m.p. = Nr \pm p \tag{3.3}$$

$$Z = 1/(|\,(1/N_r) - (1/N_s)\,|) = N_s \, . \, N_r/(|\,N_s - N_r\,|) \tag{3.4}$$

$$Z = p.m\,(m-1) \text{ for } N_s > N \tag{3.5}$$

$$= p.m\,(m+1) \text{ for } N_s < N_r \tag{3.6a}$$

**Table 3.1** Relation between $\theta_s$ and $N_r$ for PMH stepper motor

| $N_r$ | $K_{ws} = 4$ | | $K_{ws} = 8$ | |
|---|---|---|---|---|
| | Z | $\theta_s$(°) | Z | $\theta_s$ (°) |
| 6 | 24 | 15.0 | 48 | 7.5 |
| 9 | 36 | 10.0 | 72 | 5.0 |
| 12 | 48 | 7.5 | 96 | 3.75 |
| 15 | 60 | 6.0 | 120 | 3.0 |
| 25 | 100 | 3.6 | 200 | 1.8 |
| 30 | 120 | 3.0 | 240 | 1.5 |
| 50 | 200 | 1.8 | 400 | 0.9 |
| 75 | 300 | 1.2 | 600 | 0.6 |

$$\theta_s = 360°/Z \quad (3.6b)$$

where $N_s$, $N_r$ = no. of teeth on stator, rotor respectively
$m$ = no. of phases (minimum 3)
$p$ = no. of teeth per phase (minimum 2)

Table 3.2 lists combinations of $N_s$, $N_r$, $m$ which yield a particular step angle $\theta_s$.

### 3.1.3 Step Angle Accuracy

Is usually ± 5% of $\theta_s$; in a few cases, we can get accuracy of 3%. In certain exceptional cases, it is possible to get an accuracy of ± 1%.

Accuracy is determined by manufacturing tolerances and the properties of the magnetic and other materials used.

Typical accuracy curve for a stepper motor is shown in Fig. 3.1. Observe that the positioning error is non-cumulative. Consequently positioning error at the end of $N$ step will still be the same as that for a single step, viz. ± 5% of $\theta_s$. Further as the motor is loaded, the positioning error increases.

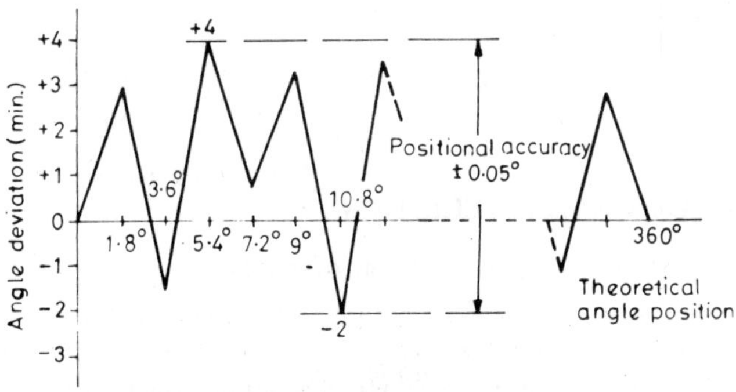


**Fig. 3.1** Positional Accuracy

**Table 3.2** Relation between $\theta_s$, $N_s$, $N_r$, $m$ and $p$ for VR stepper motor

| $Z$ | $\theta_s$ | $m$ | $p$ | $N_s$ | $N_r$ |
|---|---|---|---|---|---|
| 24 | 15 | 3 | 4 | 12 | 8 |
| | | 4 | 2 | 8 | 6 |
| | | 3 | 2 | 6 | 8 |
| 30 | 12 | 3 | 5 | 15 | 10 |
| 48 | 7.5 | 3 | 8 | 24 | 16 |
| | | 4 | 4 | 16 | 12 |
| | | 3 | 4 | 12 | 16 |
| 60 | 6.0 | 3 | 10 | 30 | 20 |
| | | 4 | 5 | 20 | 15 |
| | | 5 | 3 | 15 | 12 |
| | | 3 | 5 | 15 | 20 |
| | | 4 | 3 | 12 | 15 |
| | | 5 | 2 | 10 | 12 |
| 100 | 3.6 | 4 | 5 | 20 | 25 |
| | | 5 | 5 | 25 | 20 |
| 120 | 2.0 | 3 | 20 | 60 | 40 |
| | | 4 | 10 | 40 | 30 |
| | | 5 | 6 | 30 | 24 |
| | | 3 | 10 | 30 | 40 |
| | | 4 | 6 | 24 | 30 |
| | | 5 | 4 | 20 | 24 |
| 200 | 1.8 | 4 | 10 | 40 | 50 |
| | | 5 | 10 | 50 | 40 |
| 300 | 1.2 | 3 | 50 | 150 | 100 |
| | | 4 | 25 | 100 | 75 |
| | | 5 | 15 | 75 | 60 |
| | | 3 | 25 | 75 | 100 |
| | | 4 | 15 | 60 | 75 |
| | | 5 | 10 | 50 | 60 |

## 3.2 STATIC CHARACTERISTICS

Two characteristics in this category are of interest:

*Torque-Angle Curve:* of a step motor is shown in Fig. 3.2. It is seen that the torque increases, almost sinusoidally, with angle $\theta$ from equilibrium position.

*Holding Torque ($T_H$):* is the maximum load torque which the energized stepper motor can withstand without slipping from equilibrium position. If the

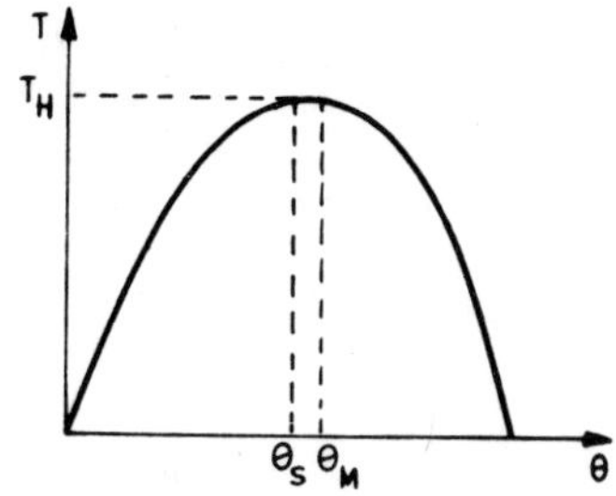


**Fig. 3.2** Torque Angle Curve

holding is exceeded, the motor suddenly slips from the present equilibrium position and goes to the next stable equilibrium position.

*Detente Torque ($T_D$):* is the maximum load torque which is unenergized stepper motor can withstand without slipping.

Detente torque is due to residual magnetism, and is, therefore, available only in PM and hybrid stepper motor. It is about 5-10% of holding torque. It is typically a fourth harmonic torque as shown in Fig. 3.3. It is also known as *cogging torque*.

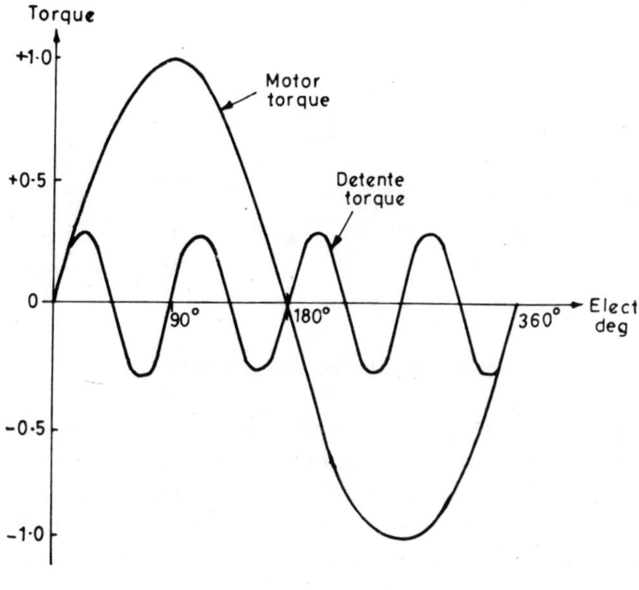


**Fig. 3.3** PM Hybrid Motor Torque and Detente Torque Profiles

*Torque Current Curve:* A typical torque current for a stepper motor is shown in Fig. 3.4. It is seen that the curve is initially linear but, later on, its slope progressively decreases as the magnetic circuit of the motor saturates.

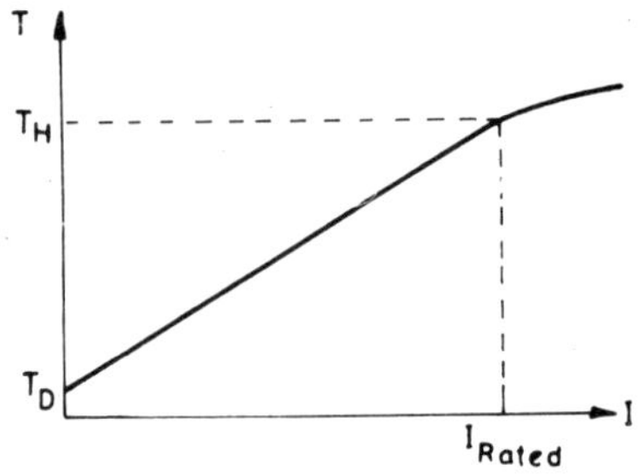


**Fig. 3.4** Torque-Current Curve

*Torque Constant* $(K_t)$: of the stepper motor is defined as the initial slope of the torque-current (*T-I*) curve of the stepper motor. It is also known as torque sensitivity. Its units are N-m/A, kg-cm/A, or oz-in./A.

## 3.3 DYNAMIC CHARACTERISTICS

These are represented by torque-stepping rate curves for the motor as shown in Fig. 3.5. Note that two torque-stepping rate curves as shown Fig. 3.5: pull-in and pull-out curves. Their significance is as follows.

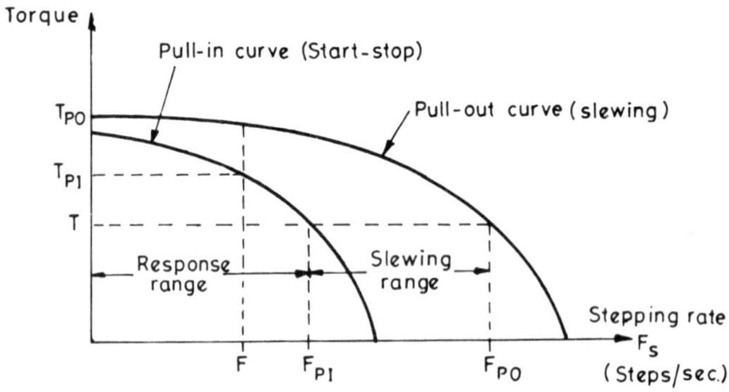


**Fig. 3.5** Torque-Speed Characteristics

*Pull-in-Curve:* Corresponds to the so-called *start-stop* or *single stepping mode* of stepper motor operation as shown in Fig. 3.6 (a). Note that, in this mode, the rotor comes to rest after moving through one step. Consequently, the rotor will not move any further as soon as you stop energizing the motor winding in the given programmed sequence. The motor can, therefore, start or stop with each individual pulse. *i.e.*, respond to each individual pulse.

*Pull-out Curve:* Corresponds to *slewing mode* of stepper motor operation as shown in Fig. 3.6 (b). Note that, in this mode, the rotor is still moving in response to the previous pulse when the next pulse comes. Consequently, the motor can run at a much faster rate in slewing mode than in start-stop mode. However, the motor cannot start slewing from rest; nor can it stop immediately

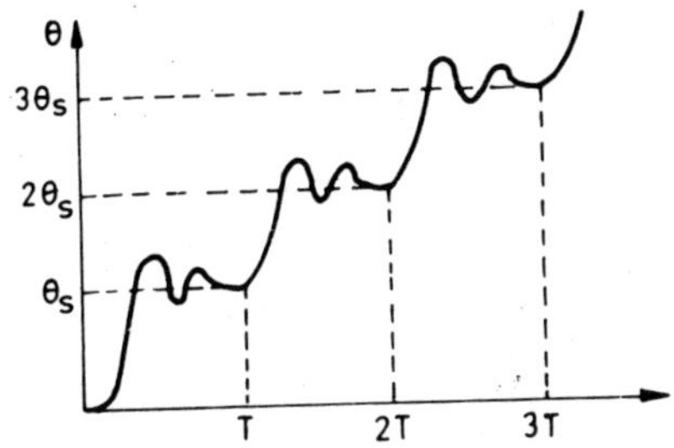


(a) Start-Stop Mode

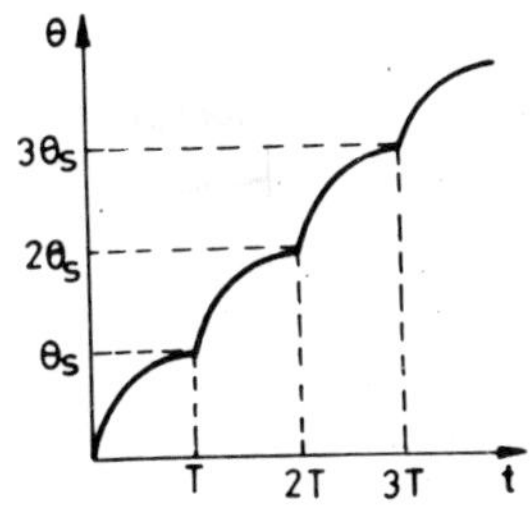


(b) Slewing Mode

**Fig. 3.6** Modes of Operation

when you stop applying pulses. The motor will, in fact, over-run by several steps before it comes to rest.

The following characteristics of the motor are defined on the basis of pull-in and pull-out curves shown in Fig. 3.5.

*Pull-in Torque ($T_{PI}$):* Is the max. torque that the stepper motor can develop in the start-stop mode at a given stepping rate $F_s$ (steps/sec), without losing synchronism.

*Pull-out Torque ($T_{PO}$):* Is the max. torque the stepper motor can develop at a given stepping rate $F_s$ (steps/sec), in the slewing mode, without losing synchronism.

*Pull-in-Rate ($F_{PI}$):* Is the max. stepping rate at which the stepper motor will start or stop, without losing synchronism, against a given load torque $T$.

*Pull-out Rate ($F_{PO}$):* Is the max. stepping rate at which the stepper motor will slew, without missing steps, against a load torque $T$.

*Response Range:* Is the range of stepping rates at which the stepper motor can start or stop, without losing synchronism, at a given torque $T$. Response range spans stepping rates $F_s \leq F_{PI}$, the pull in rate.

*Slewing Range:* Is the range of stepping rates $F_{PI} < F_s \leq F_{PO}$ at which the stepper motor can run in the slewing mode against a given load torque $T$ without losing synchronism.

*Synchronism:* This term means a strict one-to-one correspondence between the number of pulses applied to the stepper motor controller and the number of steps through which the motor has actually moved.

Synchronism is of utmost importance in the design of control systems employing stepper motors.

*Mid-frequency Resonance:* It is practical experience that the pull-in curve of a stepper motor suddenly dips very low in a particular range of stepping rates as seen in Fig. 3.7. This phenomenon is known as mid-frequency resonance. This phenomenon is a manifestation of instability of motor operation. This phenomenon has been analyzed by various researchers [12]. However, no definite reason has been identified. It would be better to avoid it in the selection of speed of operation of the motor.

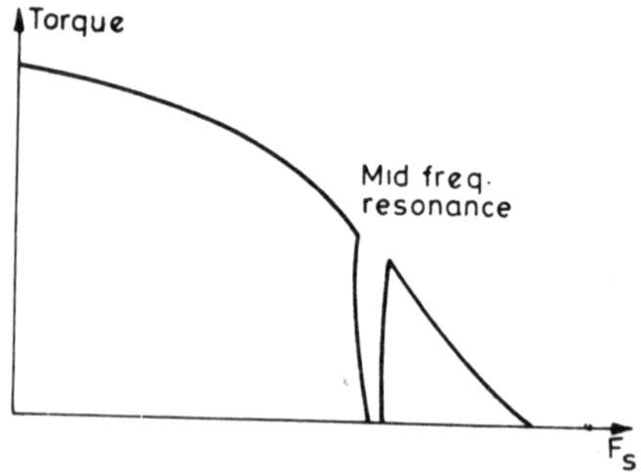


**Fig. 3.7** Mid Frequency Resonance

## 3.4 FIGURES OF MERIT (FM's)

Figures of merit (FM's) are performance indices which give quantitative information on certain aspects of performance and design of actuators such as stepper motors, DC or AC servomotors, and electrohydraulic or electro-pneumatic servomotors. FM's are employed for comparison between various actuators, so as to enable selection of the best type of actuator for a particular application. Furthermore, certain FM's such as power rate, can be used for sizing the actuator [6]. Finally, Taft has shown [7] how FM's are related to the main dimensions of various types of actuators.

In this section, various FM's are introduced and their relationship to actuator performance and design are explained. The reader is referred to Arnold [8] for further information.

### 3.4.1 Electrical Time Constant ($T_e$)

$$T_e = L_m/R_m \tag{3.7}$$

where $L_m$ and $R_m$ are inductance and resistance of the motor winding. $T_e$ governs the rate at which current rises when the motor winding is turned on. It also determines how quickly the current decays when the winding is turned off. Fig. 3.8 shows the rise and decay of current through the motor winding.

The torque is proportional to current and acceleration, in turn, is proportional to torque. Thus the rate of rise of current determines how quickly the motor can develop torque and, consequently, how fast it can accelerate the load to its final position. In motion control, the speed of response is of paramount importance. Hence, the electrical time constant $T_e$ must be minimized.

The electric time constant is dependent upon the inductance and resistance of the motor winding. The inductance is determined by the magnetic circuit, i.e. by magnet iron volume as well as by the volume of copper used in the motor design. Once these have been fixed by design, neither reducing conductor size nor increasing the number of turns will reduce the electric time constant. The magnetic circuit itself has to be redesigned.

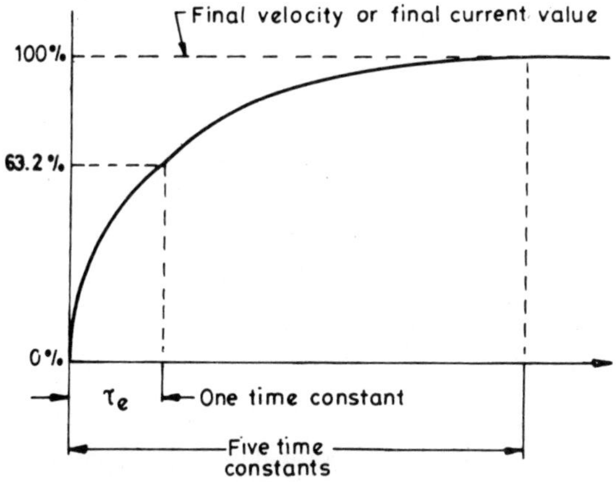


**Fig. 3.8** Definition of Electrical Time Constant ($T_e$)

### 3.4.2 Motor Time Constant ($T_m$)

$$T_m = J/(K_e \cdot k_t/R_m) = J \cdot R_m/K_e \cdot k_t \tag{3.8}$$

where $J$ = moment of inertia of the motor (kg-m$^2$), $R_m$ = resistance of the motor winding (ohms), $K_e$ = back emf constant (volts-sec/rad) and $k_t$ = torque constant (Nm/A).

Motor back emf and torque constants are determined by magnetic circuit and phase winding design. Winding resistance is also the result of winding design. Moment of inertia is determined by mechanical design.

In this way, motor time constant $T_m$ combines all the three aspects of motor design, viz. magnetic circuit, electric circuit and mechanical design. Achieving a low $T_m$ requires excellence in motor design. High torque must result from a low resistance and low inertia design.

In a motor, the motor time constant $T_m$ is in series with the electric time constant $T_e$. This means that how fast the motor reaches its final velocity or position depends, firstly, on how fast the current rises in the motor winding and develops torque, and secondly on how fast the motor speed increases. As a rule of thumb, the ratio of $T_e/T_m \approx 0.1$.

### 3.4.3 Initial Acceleration ($a_0$)

$$a_0 = T/J \text{ (rad/s}^2) \tag{3.9}$$

where $T$ = rated torque (N-m) and $J$ = moment of inertia (kg-m$^2$).

$a_0$ gives a quantitative idea of how fast the motor accelerates to its final velocity or position. Maximization of $a_0$ calls for good magnetic circuit design to produce high torque, in conjunction with good mechanical design to minimize rotor inertia. The moment of inertia of the load coupled to the motor also determines $a_0$. In this way, $a_0$ is a figure of merit which can be used for comparing motors.

### 3.4.4 Motor Constant ($K_m$)

$$K_m = T/\sqrt{W} \tag{3.10}$$

where $T$ = rated motor torque (N-m), whereas $W$ = rated power ($W$) of the motor.

The above expression for $K_m$ can be manipulated to yield

$$K_m = T/\sqrt{W} = K_t \, . \, I/\sqrt{I^2R} = \sqrt{K_e^2/R} = \sqrt{K_t \, K_e/R} \tag{3.11}$$

This shows that maximizing $K_m$ entails minimizing $R$, while maximizing $K_t$ and $K_e$. Maximizing $K_e$ and $K_t$ calls for optimization of magnetic circuit design. However, decreasing $R$ increases electrical time constant $T_e$, which is undesirable. A trade-off between electrical and magnetic circuit design is necessary to achieve a good $K_m$.

This figure of merit was evolved with a view to comparing frameless DC torque motors with respect to the efficiency of copper usage. Torque motors are essentially static or low speed motors. Hence how useful $K_m$ will be in comparing high speed stepper motors is a mute point.

### 3.4.5 Power Rate

Is a figure of merit evolved by Arnold [9] and is defined as $dP/dt$ (Watts/s). An expression for $dP/dt$ can be derived as follows:

$$\frac{dP}{dt} = \frac{d}{dt}\left(T \cdot \frac{d\theta}{dt}\right) = T \cdot \frac{d^2\theta}{dt^2} = T \cdot \frac{T}{J} = \frac{T^2}{J} \tag{3.12}$$

Now $T = K_t \, . \, I$, so that

$$\frac{dP}{dt} = \frac{K_t^2 \, I^2}{J} \cdot \frac{R_m}{R_m} = \frac{K_t^2}{JR_m} \cdot I^2 \, R_m = I^2 \, R_m/T_m \tag{3.13}$$

where $T_m = JR_m/K_t^2 = JR_m/K_e \, J_t$ = motor time constant.

The power rate is thus a ratio of copper loss to motor time constant. It is thus the best figure of merit in as much as it encompasses mechanical design, magnetic circuit design and electric winding design. It can be used to compare different types of stepper and servo motors. Every motor technology has a limited range of power rates as shown in Fig. 3.9. The power rate can also be used for selection of motor for a particular application, as explained in Section, 7.11.

### 3.4.6 Static Stiffness (S)

Is a measure of the ability of the actuator to resist disturbing torques and forces and thereby to maintain position. It is defined as

$$S = \text{Torque/rad} \tag{3.14}$$

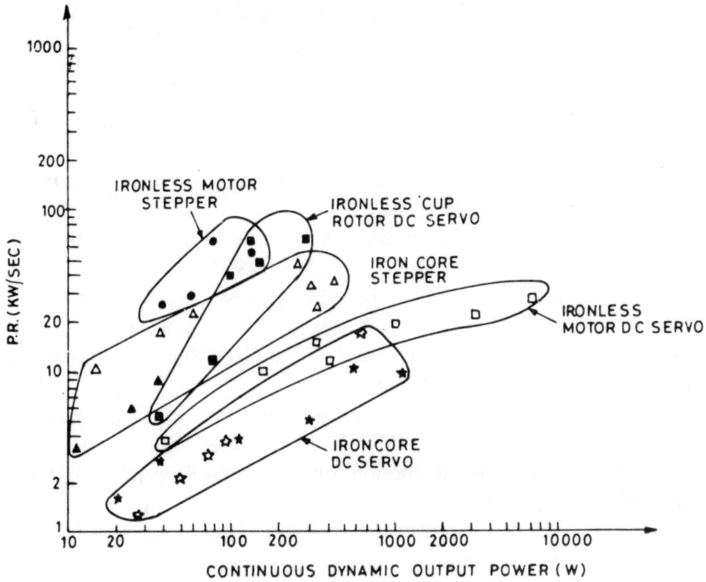


**Fig. 3.9** Power Rate vs. Power Output Curve

It is related to natural frequency of oscillations, $\omega_n$ (rad/sec), moment of inertia $J$ (kg-m$^2$) static torque $T$ (N-m) and the no. of pole pairs $N$ by

$$\omega_n = (1/2\,\pi)\,\sqrt{S/J} \tag{3.15}$$

$$\therefore \quad S = 4\pi^2 \,.\, \omega_n^2 \,.\, J = T \,.\, N \tag{3.16}$$

Alternatively $S$ can also be defined as the slope of the static torque $T_{ws}$. $\theta$ curve as it passes through 0° (See Fig. 3.1).

On account of high number of pole pairs (usually 25-100) the stepper motor has an inherently large stiffness, $S$.

### 3.4.7 Bandwidth (BW)

Is a measure of the frequencies upto which the actuator or servo system can respond. DC or AC servo system have bandwidth in the 50-100 Hz range, whereas a stepper motor has bandwidth in 150-250 Hz range. The bandwidth is usually 60-80 per cent of the natural frequency, $\omega_n$.

Bandwidth is a measure of the speed of response. Hence it might appear at first sight that the higher the bandwidth, the better the system. However, this is not so, because the higher the bandwidth, the more suceptible is the system to external disturbances. Hence the bandwidth has to be set as a compromise between speed of response and noise.

## REFERENCES

1. Kuo, B.C., "Step motors and control systems", SRL Publishing Co., Champaign, 11, U.S.A., 1979. Chap. 1.
2. Kenjo, T., "Stepping motors and their microprocessor controls" Oxford University Press, Oxford, 1985, Chap. 2.
3. Acarnley, P.P., "Stepping motors: a guide to modern theory and practice", IEE Press, Series No. 19, 1984, Chap. 1.
4. "Warner Electric's Guide to Selecting and Controlling Step Motors", Warner Electric Brake and Clutch Co., Beloit, WI, 1980.
5. British Standard Specifications BS 5000: Part No. 60, 1982.
6. Arnold, F. and Floresta, J.G., "Power rate : most important figure-of-merit to incremental motion designer", Proc. 13th Annual Symp. on IMCSD, pp. 11-18, 1984.
7. Taft, C.K. and Prina, S.R., "Motor figures of merit as a function of motor size", Proc. 18th Annual Symp. on IMCSD, pp.155-162, 1989.
8. Arnold, F., "Understanding motion control figure-of-merit", Proc. 17th Symp. on IMCSD, pp.1-12, 1988.
9. Arnold, F., "Use power rate to match motors to applications", EDN, Oct. 4, 1984 issue, pp. 225-232, 1984.
10. Arnold, F., "Designing incremental motion systems with power rate", Proc. 14th Annual Symp. on IMCSD, pp.37-50, 1985.
11. Arnold, F., "Some precautions on the use of power rate as a reliable figure of merit, Control Eng., Vol., No.11, pp. 137-138, 1987.

## CHAPTER - 4

# *Drive Circuits for Stepper Motors*

In this chapter, we will study electronic drive circuits for hybrid stepper motors such as logic sequence generators, power drivers, current suppression circuits, pulse generators, and ramping circuits.

## 4.1 BLOCK DIAGRAM OF STEPPER MOTOR CONTROLLER

Fig. 4.1 shows the block diagram of a typical controller for hybrid or variable reluctance stepper motor. It consists of the following blocks:

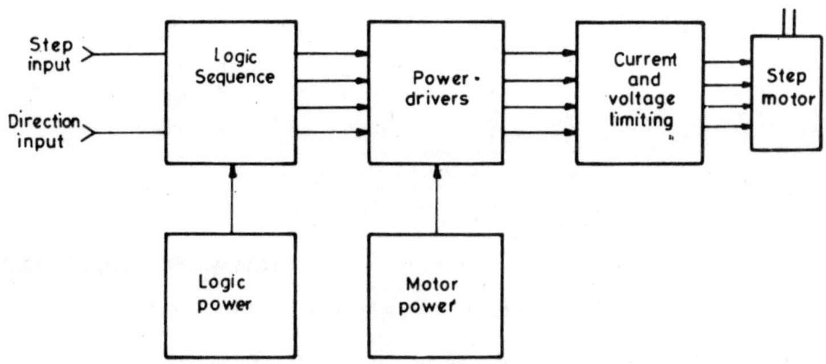


**Fig. 4.1** Block Diagram of a Typical Step Motor Control

**(a) Logic Sequence Generator.** Generates programmed logic sequences required for operation of a stepper motor. Table 4.1 lists the logic sequences for 'one phase on', 'two phases on' and hybrid logic sequences for a PM hybrid stepper motor. Logic sequences required for operation of 3-phase, 4-phase and 5-phase VR stepper motors are given in Table 4.2.

**(b) Power Drivers.** These are power switching circuits which ensure a fast rise of current through the phase windings which are to be turned on at a particular step in the logic sequence.

**Table 4.1** Logic Sequences for PM Hybrid Stepper Motors

| *Sequence* | *4-Step* | | | | | | | | *8-Step* | | | |
|---|---|---|---|---|---|---|---|---|---|---|---|---|
| | *Single Phase 'on' (1-1)* | | | | *Two Phase 'on' (2-2)* | | | | *Hybrid (1-2)* | | | |
| *Step No.* | *A1* | *A2* | *B1* | *B2* | *A1* | *A2* | *B1* | *B2* | *A1* | *A2* | *B1* | *B2* |
| 1 | 1 | 0 | 0 | 0 | 1 | 0 | 1 | 0 | 1 | 0 | 1 | 0 |
| 2 | 0 | 0 | 1 | 0 | 0 | 1 | 1 | 0 | 0 | 0 | 1 | 0 |
| 3 | 0 | 1 | 0 | 0 | 0 | 1 | 0 | 1 | 0 | 1 | 1 | 0 |
| 4 | 0 | 0 | 0 | 1 | 1 | 0 | 0 | 1 | 0 | 1 | 0 | 0 |
| 5 | | | | | | | | | 0 | 1 | 0 | 1 |
| 6 | | | | | | | | | 0 | 0 | 0 | 1 |
| 7 | | | | | | | | | 1 | 0 | 0 | 1 |
| 8 | | | | | | | | | 1 | 0 | 0 | 0 |

**Table 4.2** Logic Sequences for VR Stepper Motors

| *Sequence* | *3-Step* | | | | | | *6-Step* | | |
|---|---|---|---|---|---|---|---|---|---|
| | *Single phase 'on' (1-1)* | | | *Two phase 'on' (2-2)* | | | *Hybrid (1-2)* | | |
| *Step No.* | *A* | *B* | *C* | *A* | *B* | *C* | *A* | *B* | *C* |
| 1 | 1 | 0 | 0 | 1 | 1 | 0 | 1 | 0 | 0 |
| 2 | 0 | 1 | 0 | 0 | 1 | 1 | 1 | 1 | 0 |
| 3 | 0 | 0 | 1 | 1 | 0 | 1 | 0 | 1 | 0 |
| 4 | | | | | | | 0 | 1 | 1 |
| 5 | | | | | | | 0 | 0 | 1 |
| 6 | | | | | | | 1 | 0 | 1 |

(a) 3-Phase VR Stepper Motors

| *Sequence* | *4-Step* | | | | | | | | | | | | *8-Step Hybrid* | | | | | | | |
|---|---|---|---|---|---|---|---|---|---|---|---|---|---|---|---|---|---|---|---|---|
| | *Single phase 'on' (1-1)* | | | | *Two phase 'on' (2-2)* | | | | *Three-phase 'on*'* (3-3)* | | | | *1-2* | | | | *2-3** | | | |
| *Step No.* | *A* | *B* | *C* | *D* | *A* | *B* | *C* | *D* | *A* | *B* | *C* | *D* | *A* | *B* | *C* | *D* | *A* | *B* | *C* | *D* |
| 1 | 1 | 0 | 0 | 0 | 1 | 1 | 0 | 0 | 1 | 1 | 1 | 0 | 1 | 0 | 0 | 0 | 1 | 1 | 0 | 0 |
| 2 | 0 | 1 | 0 | 0 | 0 | 1 | 1 | 0 | 0 | 1 | 1 | 1 | 1 | 1 | 0 | 0 | 1 | 1 | 1 | 0 |
| 3 | 0 | 0 | 1 | 0 | 0 | 0 | 1 | 1 | 1 | 0 | 1 | 1 | 0 | 1 | 0 | 0 | 0 | 1 | 1 | 0 |
| 4 | 0 | 0 | 0 | 1 | 1 | 0 | 0 | 1 | 1 | 1 | 0 | 1 | 0 | 1 | 1 | 0 | 0 | 1 | 1 | 1 |
| 5 | | | | | | | | | | | | | 0 | 0 | 1 | 0 | 0 | 0 | 1 | 1 |
| 6 | | | | | | | | | | | | | 0 | 0 | 1 | 1 | 1 | 0 | 1 | 1 |
| 7 | | | | | | | | | | | | | 0 | 0 | 0 | 1 | 1 | 0 | 0 | 1 |
| 8 | | | | | | | | | | | | | 1 | 0 | 0 | 1 | 1 | 1 | 0 | 1 |

(b) 4-phase VR stepper motors

| Sequence | 5-Step | | | | | | | | | | | | | | | | | | | | 10-Step Hybrid | | | | | | | | | | | | | | |
|---|---|---|---|---|---|---|---|---|---|---|---|---|---|---|---|---|---|---|---|---|---|---|---|---|---|---|---|---|---|---|---|---|---|---|---|
| | *Single-phase 'on' (1-1)* | | | | | *Two-phase 'on' (2-2)* | | | | | *Three-Phase 'on'** *(3-3)* | | | | | *Four-Phase 'on'** *(4-4)* | | | | | *1 – 2* | | | | | *2 – 3* | | | | | *3 – 4** | | | | |
| *Step No.* | *A* | *B* | *C* | *D* | *E* | *A* | *B* | *C* | *D* | *E* | *A* | *B* | *C* | *D* | *E* | *A* | *B* | *C* | *D* | *E* | *A* | *B* | *C* | *D* | *E* | *A* | *B* | *C* | *D* | *E* | *A* | *B* | *C* | *D* | *E* |
| 1 | 1 | 0 | 0 | 0 | 0 | 1 | 1 | 0 | 0 | 0 | 1 | 1 | 1 | 0 | 0 | 1 | 1 | 1 | 1 | 0 | 1 | 0 | 0 | 0 | 0 | 1 | 1 | 0 | 0 | 0 | 1 | 1 | 1 | 0 | 0 |
| 2 | 0 | 1 | 0 | 0 | 0 | 0 | 1 | 1 | 0 | 0 | 0 | 1 | 1 | 1 | 0 | 0 | 1 | 1 | 1 | 1 | 1 | 1 | 0 | 0 | 0 | 1 | 1 | 1 | 0 | 0 | 1 | 1 | 1 | 1 | 0 |
| 3 | 0 | 0 | 1 | 0 | 0 | 0 | 0 | 1 | 1 | 0 | 0 | 0 | 1 | 1 | 1 | 1 | 0 | 1 | 1 | 1 | 0 | 1 | 0 | 0 | 0 | 0 | 1 | 1 | 0 | 0 | 0 | 1 | 1 | 1 | 0 |
| 4 | 0 | 0 | 0 | 1 | 0 | 0 | 0 | 0 | 1 | 1 | 1 | 0 | 0 | 1 | 1 | 1 | 1 | 0 | 1 | 1 | 0 | 1 | 1 | 0 | 0 | 0 | 1 | 1 | 1 | 0 | 0 | 1 | 1 | 1 | 1 |
| 5 | 0 | 0 | 0 | 0 | 1 | 1 | 0 | 0 | 0 | 1 | 1 | 1 | 0 | 0 | 1 | 1 | 1 | 1 | 0 | 1 | 0 | 0 | 1 | 0 | 0 | 0 | 0 | 1 | 1 | 0 | 0 | 0 | 1 | 1 | 1 |
| 6 | | | | | | | | | | | | | | | | | | | | | 0 | 0 | 1 | 1 | 0 | 0 | 0 | 1 | 1 | 1 | 1 | 0 | 1 | 1 | 1 |
| 7 | | | | | | | | | | | | | | | | | | | | | 0 | 0 | 0 | 1 | 0 | 0 | 0 | 0 | 1 | 1 | 1 | 0 | 0 | 1 | 1 |
| 8 | | | | | | | | | | | | | | | | | | | | | 0 | 0 | 0 | 1 | 1 | 1 | 0 | 0 | 1 | 1 | 1 | 1 | 0 | 1 | 1 |
| 9 | | | | | | | | | | | | | | | | | | | | | 0 | 0 | 0 | 0 | 1 | 1 | 0 | 0 | 0 | 1 | 1 | 1 | 0 | 0 | 1 |
| 10 | | | | | | | | | | | | | | | | | | | | | 1 | 0 | 0 | 0 | 1 | 1 | 1 | 0 | 0 | 1 | 1 | 1 | 1 | 0 | 1 |

(c) 5-phase VR stepper motors

* These sequences are possible but *not* preferred.

**(c) Current Suppression Circuits.** These are meant to ensure a rapid decay of current in the phase winding that is turned off at a particular step in the logic sequence.

## 4.2 LOGIC SEQUENCE GENERATOR

This is a finite state sequential logic circuit which generates the particular logic sequence, from among those given in Tables 4.1 and 4.2, selected by the user for operation of his stepper motors. The selected logic sequence is treated as a truth table, and is implemented with the help of flip-flops and logic gates.

### 4.2.1 Logic Sequencers for Hybrid Stepper Motors

Hybrid stepper motors can be operated with three logic sequence as shown in Table 4.1. The corresponding timing diagrams are shown in Fig. 4.2. A logic

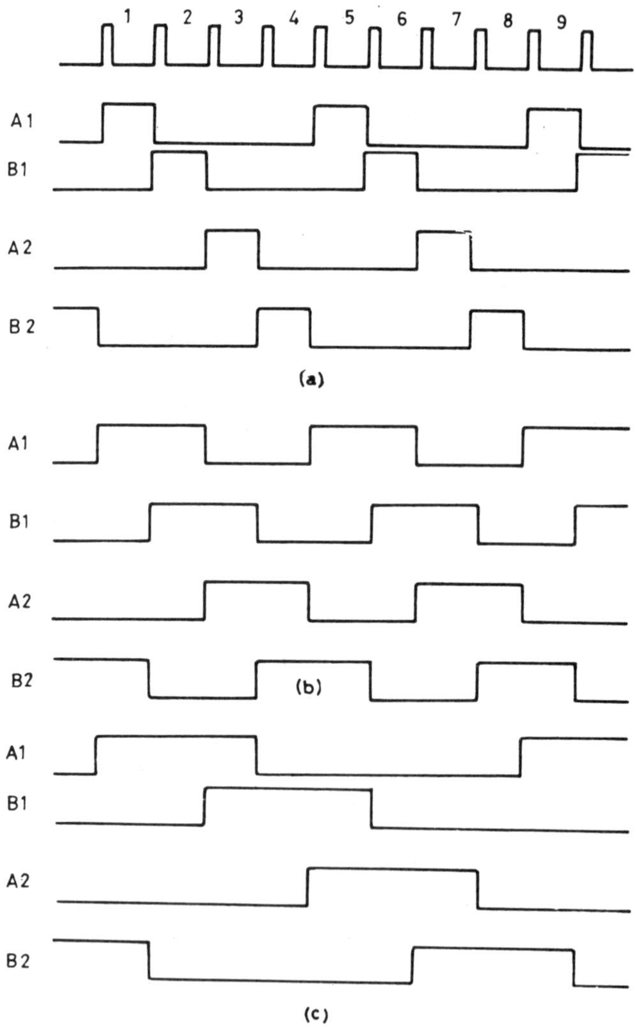


**Fig. 4.2** Timing diagrams for logic sequences of PMH

sequencer for generating the most popular 'two phases on' sequence is shown in Fig. 4.3. Fig. 4.4 shows the 'one phase on' logic sequence. These are 4-step logic sequences. On the other hand, the 8-step 'hybrid' (i.e. 1-2) logic sequence can be generated by circuit shown in Fig. 4.5.

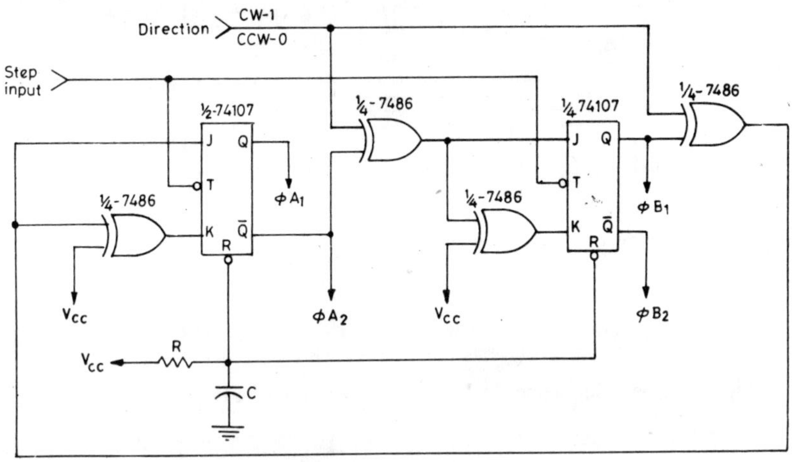


**Fig. 4.3** Sequencer for 2-Phases "on" Sequence

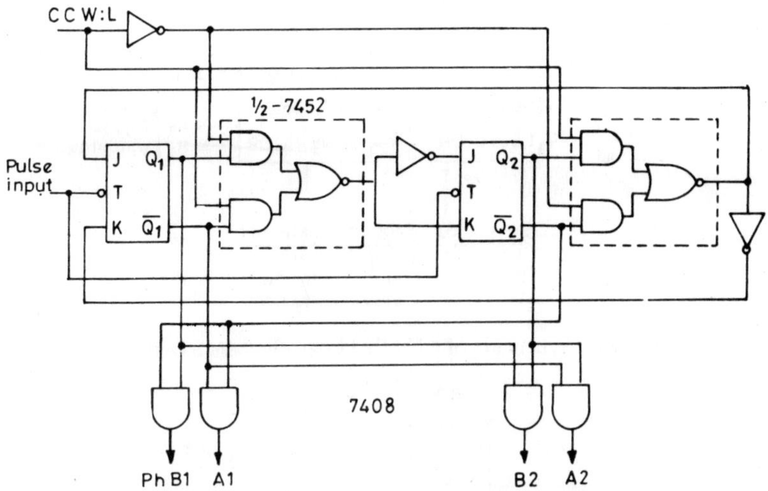


**Fig. 4.4** Sequencer for 1-Phases "on" Logic

### 4.2.2 Unified Logic Sequencer for Hybrid Stepper Motors

A single, unified logic sequencer which can generate all the three logic sequences of Table 4.1 for hybrid stepper motors has been developed by Athani and Riswadkar [8]. This circuit is shown in Fig. 4.6 (a). It consists of (i) synchronous 3-bit counter that generates the 8 logic states corresponding to

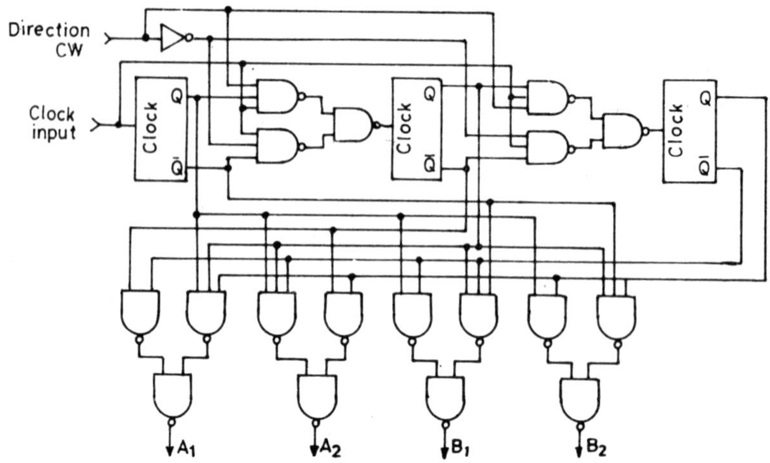


**Fig. 4.5** Logic Sequencer for Half-step Operation of a PM Stepping Motor

the 8-step logic sequence given in Table 4.1; (ii) sequence selector having two sequence bits $S_1$, $S_2$ for selecting the desired sequence; (iii) sequence generator for outputting the selected sequence. Details of these blocks are, shown in Figs. 4.6 (b), (c) and (d) respectively. This single circuit thus replaces all the

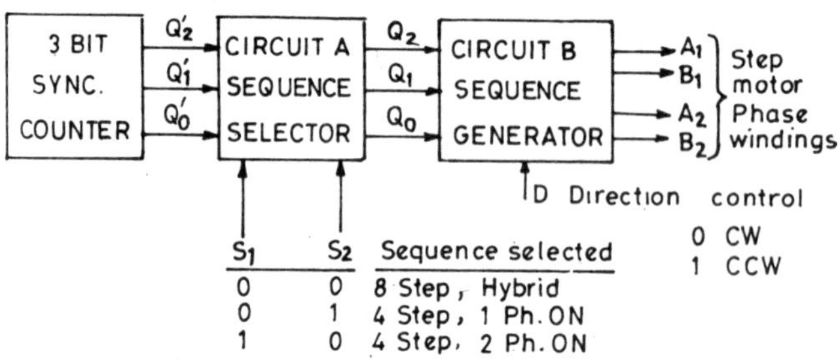


**Fig. 4.6(a)** Schematic of a Unified Logic Sequence Generator

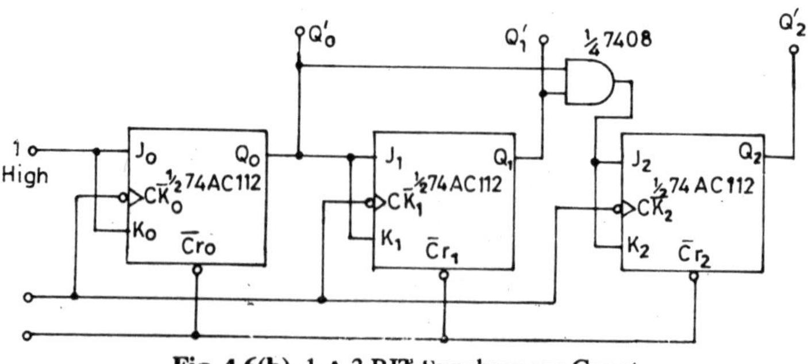


**Fig. 4.6(b)** 1 A 3 BIT Synchronous Counter

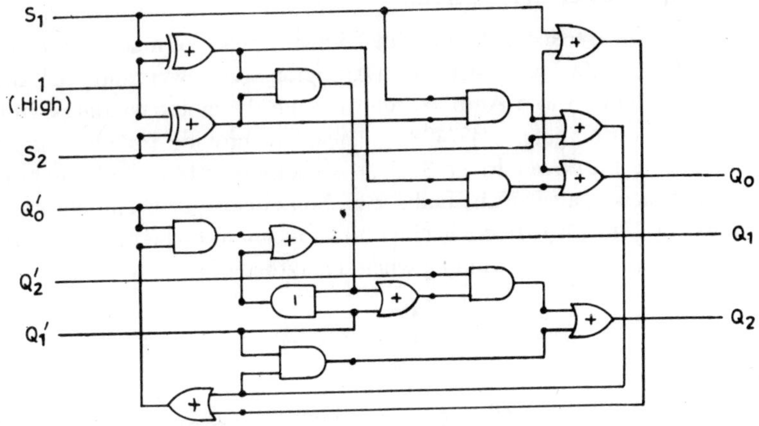


**Fig. 4.6(c)** Sequence Selector

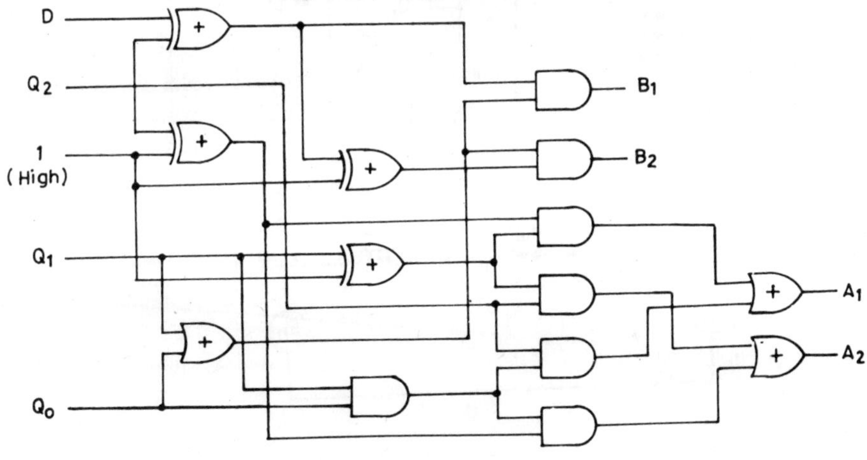


**Fig. 4.6(d)** Sequence Generator

three circuits of Figs. 4.2-4.5. It uses 2 numbers of 74AC112 flip flops, 4 numbers of 7408 quad NAND gates, 3 numbers of 7432 NOR gates and 2 numbers of 7486 EX-OR gates. It is thus compact, economical, and programmable. It is very useful for students, hobbyists, experimenters, etc. doing work on hybrid stepper motors.

## 4.3 POWER DRIVERS

The signals output by the logic sequence generators are low level signals which are too weak to energize stepper motor windings. Consequently, switching power amplifiers have to be used to raise the voltage, current and power levels of the logic sequence outputs sufficiently high to drive the rated currents through stepper motor circuits. These are called power driver circuits and are discussed below.

### 4.3.1 Simple Power Drive Circuit

A typical power transistor driver circuit for one phase of a stepper motor is shown in Fig. 4.7 (a). It consists of a Darlington pair power amplifier, and is capable of driving 3 to 5 Amp. current through the motor windings. In this circuit, an invertor gate, 1/4-7408, is meant to provide isolation of logic sequencer from the power driver. Such an isolation *must* be provided to protect the logic sequencer against any faults, e.g. short circuits, open circuits, switching transients, etc. $D_3$ is free wheeling diode meant to maintain continuity of current through the motor winding when it is turned off.

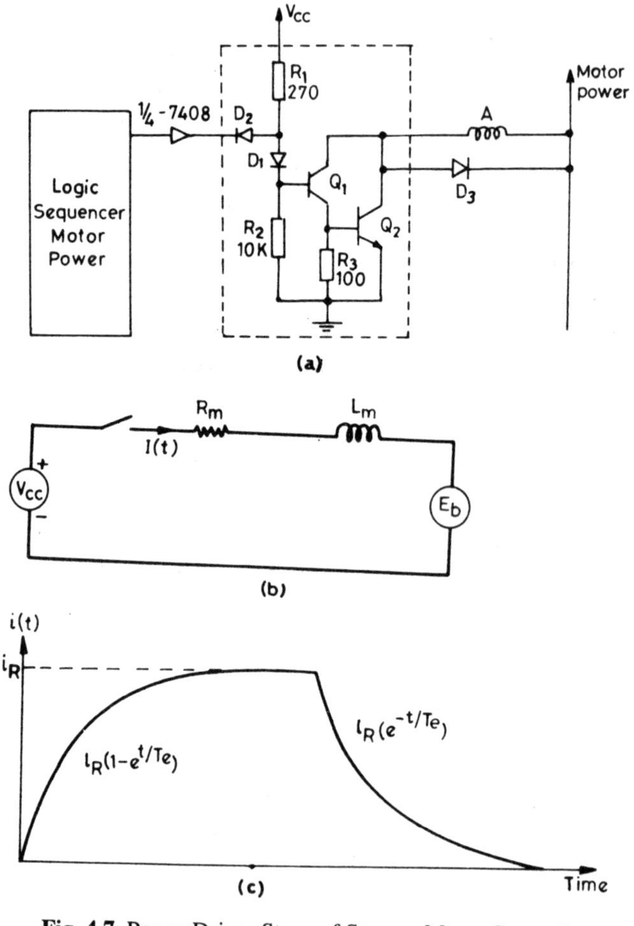


**Fig. 4.7** Power Driver Stage of Stepper Motor Controller

There are two problems with this simple power driver circuit. They can be understood from the equivalent circuit as shown in Fig. 4.7 (b). When the concerned motor winding is turned on, the rise of current through the motor winding is governed by

$$V = iR_m + L_m\,(di/dt) + E_b \qquad (4.1)$$

where $R_m$ and $L_m$ are the resistance and inductance of the motor winding and $E_b$ is the back emf induced in the motor winding.

The solution of Eqn. (4.1) is shown in Fig. 4.7 (c) and is characterized by

$$i\,(t) = I_R\,(1 - e^{-t/\tau_e}) \qquad (4.2)$$

where $I_R = V/R_m$ = rated current (4.3)

and $\tau_e = L_m/R_m$ = electrical time constant of the motor winding. (4.4)

This time constant limits the rise and fall of current in the motor winding. At very low stepping rate, the interval between input pulses is large enough to permit rise of current in the motor winding to its rated value, as shown in Fig. 4.8 (a). When the winding is de-energized, the current has sufficient time to decay to zero value, as shown in Fig. 4.8 (a). However, as the input pulse rate increases, the current has time neither to rise to its rated value, nor to decay to zero value, as shown in Fig. 4.8 (b) and (c). This reduces the 'swing' (i.e. difference between max. and min. value) of current through the motor winding. Consequently the dynamic torque of the motor decreases as the stepping rate increases, as seen from Fig. 3.3. This is layman's explanation. A mathematical expression for dynamic torque has been derived in Section 8.12. This section also discusses the factor affecting the dynamic torque of the motor.

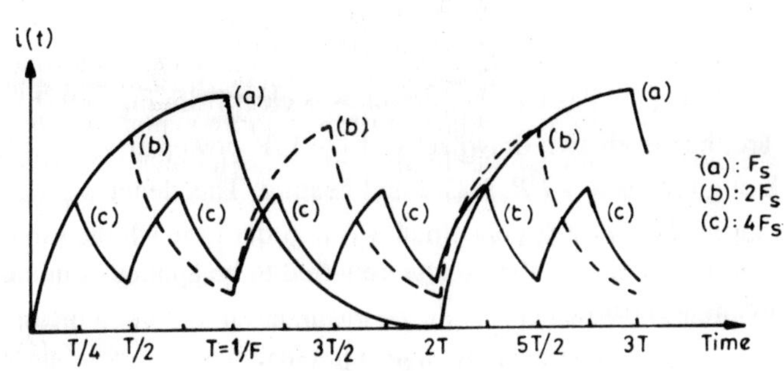


**Fig. 4.8** Effect of Increasing Stepping Rate on Current Swing

In order to remedy this situation, special power driver circuits have been developed to cause the current to rise fast even at high stepping rates.

Similarly current suppression circuits have been designed to ensure rapid decay of current through the motor winding upon its being turned off. These circuits are presented in the next two sections.

### 4.2.2 L/R Drive

In this drive, a resistance $R_s$ is connected in series with the motor winding as shown in Fig. 4.9 (a), and higher voltage $V'$ is applied. Thereby the time constant of the motor winding is reduced to

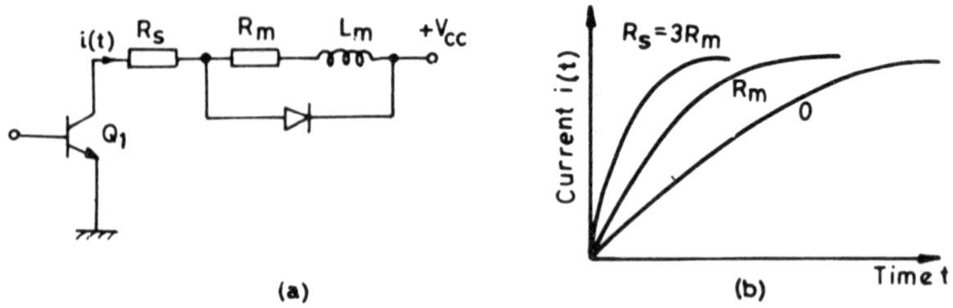


**Fig. 4.9** L/R Drive

$$\tau_e' = L_m/(R_m + R_s). \tag{4.5}$$

The reduction in time constant $T_e'$ for various values of $R_s$ is shown below:

| $R_s$ | $R_m$ | $3R_m$ | $4R_m$ | $9R_m$ |
|---|---|---|---|---|
| $\frac{\tau_e'}{\tau_e} = \frac{L_m/(R_m+R_s)}{L_m/R_m} = R_m/(R_m+R_s)$ | 0.5 | 0.25 | 0.2 | 0.1 |

As a result of reduction of electrical time constant, the motor current rises much more rapidly and hence the motor develops much greater torque at high stepping rates than the basic power driver as is clear from Fig. 4.9 (b).

There are, however, two drawbacks of the L/R power driver: (a) Flow of current through $R_s$ causes $I^2R_s$ losses and heating. This denotes a wastage of power as far as the motor is concerned; (b) in order to reach the same steady state current, $I_R$, as before, the voltage required to be applied is much higher than before, as seen from

$$V' = V_R\,(R_s + R_m)/R_m \tag{4.6}$$

Consequently, *L/R* drive is limited to small instrument stepper motor whose rated current is a few hundred mA/phase.

### 4.3.3 Bilevel Drive

This circuit is shown in Fig. 4.10 (a). We turn on both $Q_1$ and $Q_2$ at $t = 0$. This applies a high voltage $V_H = (4 \text{ to } 10).\ V_R$ to the motor winding, where $V_R$ = rated voltage. The motor windings current, $i\,(t)$, increases as per relation

$$i\,(t) = I_H\,(1 - e^{-t/\tau_e}) \tag{4.7}$$

where $I_H = V_H/R_m$ and $\tau_e = L_m/R_m$ = electrical time constant.

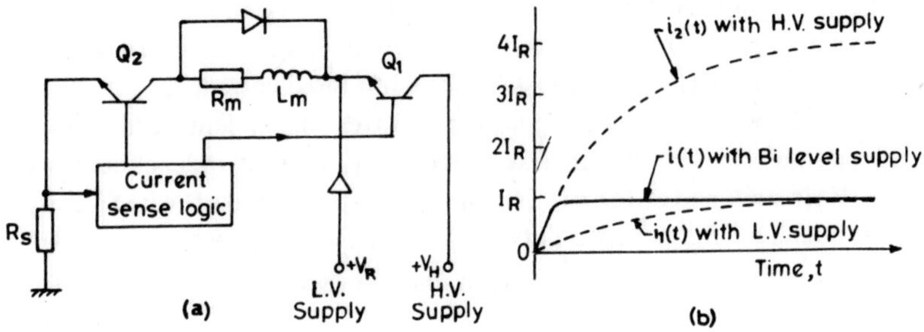


**Fig. 4.10** Bilevel Drive

As soon as $i$ ($t$) = $I_R$, where $I_R$ = rated current = $V_R/R_m$, $Q_1$ is turned off, so that rated voltage $V_R$ is applied through diode $D_1$. $i$ ($t$) thereupon settles to $I_R$ immediately.

This circuit is good and energy efficient. However, it is more complex inasmuch as it requires (i) two regulated power supplies $V_H$ and $V_R$, two power transistor switches $Q_1$ and $Q_2$, and current sensor $R_s$, and complex switching logic. Hence, it is not very popular.

### 4.3.4 Chopper Drive

Herein, a high voltage $V_H$ = (4 to 10) $V_R$ is applied to the motor winding, as shown in Fig. 4.11 (a). As a result, the motor current rises very fast as per Eq. (4.7). When the winding current goes slightly (typically 2 to 5%) above rated current $I_R$, $V_H$ is switched off. Thereupon the current decreases exponen-

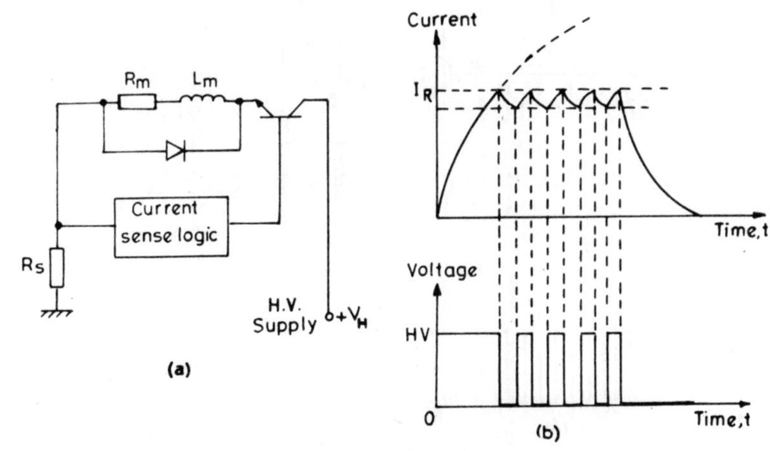


**Fig. 4.11** Chopper Drive

tially. When it falls slightly (again 2 to 5%) below the rated value $I_R$, $V_H$ is switched on again. This causes current to oscillate around the rated current $I_R$ as shown in Fig. 4.11(b). However, winding inductance is large enough, so that the winding sees it as almost constant current = rated current $I_R$.

In this scheme, the chopper operation is current dependent. Alternately, we could operate the chopper in fixed frequency, current independent mode. Hence, $V_H$ is switched on at $t = 0$. The first time $V_H$ is turned off when a constant high frequency, $f_{chopper}$, with a duty cycle ratio $x = t_{on}/(t_{on} + t_{off}) = 0.4 - 0.5$. If the chopping frequency $f_{chopper}$, is high enough (8-20 KHz), we get $i\ (t) = I_R$ within 1%.

The chopper circuit is particularly recommended for high torque stepper motors. It is energy efficient like the bilevel drive, but is much simpler than the latter. Hence its popularity.

### 4.3.5 Linear Constant Current Drive

The rate of rise of current through the stepper motor winding is limited by its electrical time constant, $\tau_e = L_m/R_m$ of the motor winding. This limitation can be overcome by energizing the motor winding by a constant current source, rather than by a constant voltage source. Op-amp based constant current sources are available. However, their current ratings are limited to a few hundreds of mA. They can, consequently, be used for driving only small, instrument stepper motors.

A linear constant current source has been developed by Athani and Vinod [5]. This circuit is shown in Fig. 4.12 (a). When the incoming signal goes high, the Darlington pair $Q_1 - Q_2$ turns on, thereby applying voltage $V$ to the motor winding. The motor current $i\ (t)$ increases exponentially as per equation

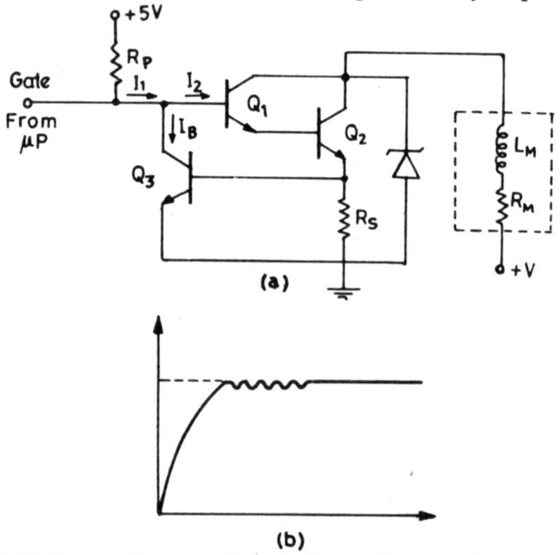


**Fig. 4.12** Linear Constant Current Drive Control of Stepper Motor

$$i(t) = I_L(1 - e^{-t/\tau'_e}) \tag{4.8}$$

where $I_L = V/(R_m + R_s)$ and $\tau'_e = L_m/(R_m + R_s)$ where $R_s$ is a small, current sensing resistor. As $i(t)$ increases towards $I_L$, so does $V_{be}$ of $Q_3$. When $V_{be} = I_L \cdot R_s$, the cut-in voltage of $Q_3$, $Q_3$ turns on, by-passing the base-drive to the Darlington pair $Q_1 - Q_2$. Consequently, $Q_1 - Q_2$ turn off, causing the motor winding current to decrease exponentially, as given by

$$i(t) = I_L e^{-t/\tau'_e} \tag{4.9}$$

When $i(t)$ has decreased to such a low value that $V_{be} = i(t) \cdot R_s$ is less than the cut-off value, $Q_3$ turns-off, and $Q_1 - Q_2$ turns on. The cycle is repeated in rapid succession until $i(t) = I_L$ as shown in Fig. 4.12 (b), as long as the incoming signal from the microprocessor remains high. In this condition, $Q_1 - Q_2$ pair stabilizes in the active region. Hence the name linear constant current circuit (LCC).

### 4.3.6 Variable Voltage Control

This scheme is shown in Fig. 4.13 (a). It consists of a single phase half controlled thyristor bridge circuit, followed by an LC filter to convert the AC mains voltage into a variable DC voltage $V_d$. This is applied to windings A1 or A2 and B1 or B2 by thyristor flip-flops as shown in Fig. 4.13 (b). The flip-flops are set and reset by the logic sequence generator so as to generate the 'two-phase ON' sequence of Table 4.1. The current through the motor windings is sensed by the current sensing resistor, $R_s$. It is compared with rated current by the comparator. The comparator output varies, the firing angle $\alpha$ of the thyristors also varies, thereby varying the DC voltage $V_d$ applied to the motor windings. $V_d$ is so adjusted as to maintain motor current $i(t) = I_R$, the rated current. The result is that a constant current drive is realized. Development of such a variable voltage constant current drive has been reported by Athani and Mundhra [6, 7]. The torque-vs-stepping rate curve obtained for Slosyn M112-FJ25 stepper motor is shown in Fig. 4.13 (c). Two main features of the torque-vs-stepping rate curve are worth noting:

(a) almost constant torque upto 80% of the maximum stepping rate
(b) elimination of mid-range resonances.

### 4.3.7 Bipolar Drives for Stepper Motors

Stepper motor drive circuits studied so far are known as '*unipolar*' drive circuits. The reason is that, with these drive circuits, the current in any particular motor winding flows in one direction only. This means that the current through the motor winding is either $+I_R$ (the rated current) or 0; it never reverses its direction of flow.

There exists another class of drive circuits for stepper motors which cause the current through the motor winding to reverse its direction. Thus, the current through the motor winding will be either $+I_R$ or $-I_R$, and 0. Such drive circuits which cause bidirectional current flow through the motor windings, are known as '*bipolar drives*'. This section is devoted to a study of such bipolar drive circuits for stepper motors.

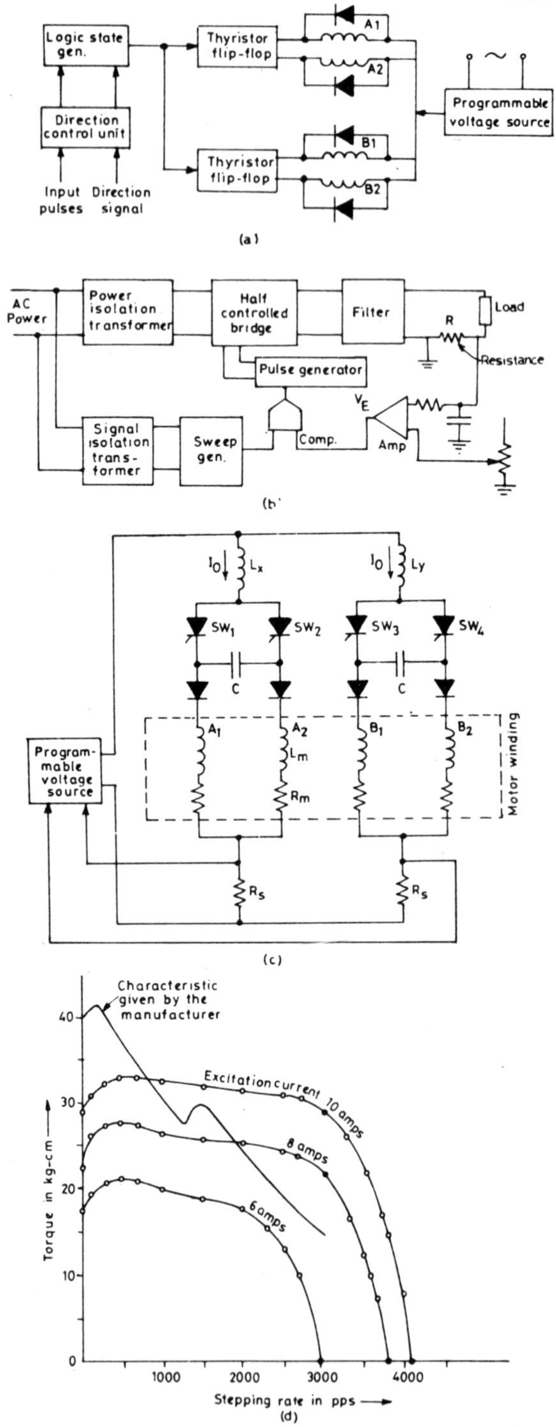


**Fig. 4.13** Variable Voltage Source Stepper Motor Controller

Most of the drive circuits, such as the basic power drive, L/R and chopper drives have their bipolar versions. They have the same characteristics as their unipolar counterparts. These bipolar drive circuits are reviewed below:

### *4.3.7.1 Basic Bipolar Drives*

The basic bipolar drive circuit is shown in Fig. 4.14. The motor winding *A* is connected through transistor switches *Q*1 and *Q*2, to a bipolar DC source having output voltages + V, 0 and – V. When *Q*1 is turned on, current + 1 flows through winding *A*. When *Q*1 is turned off while *Q*2 is turned 'on' the winding current is – 1. Bi-directional current flow thus takes places.

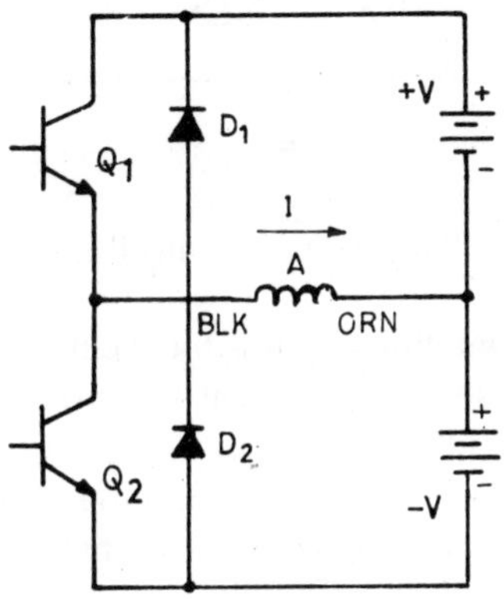


**Fig. 4.14** Basic Bipolar Drive

Practical circuit for bipolar drive of a 4-lead PMH stepper motor, having two stator windings *A*, *B*, is shown in Fig. 4.15. Transistors *Q*1, *Q*3 control the *A* winding, whereas *Q*2, *Q*4 look after winding *B*.

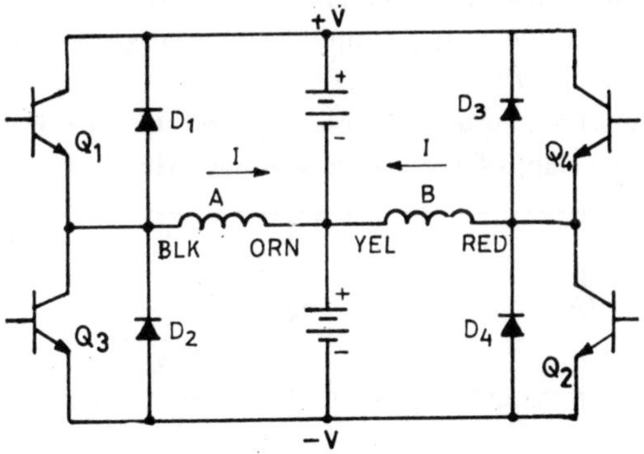


**Fig. 4.15** Practical Bipolar Drive

This drive circuit requires a bipolar regulated DC power supply with + V, 0, – V outputs. It is possible to obtain bidirectional current control using a unipolar power supply, with outputs + V, 0. Fig. 4.16 shows how this can be achieved.

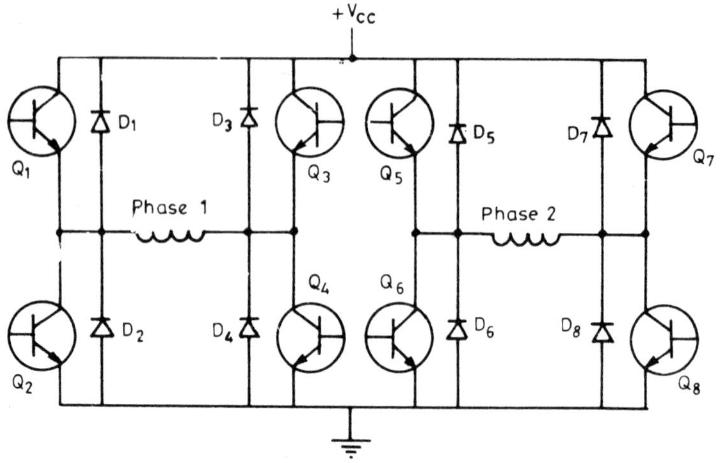


**Fig. 4.16** "H-Type" Bipolar Drive using Unipolar Power Supply

Notice that each motor winding requires four transistors '*H*' circuit. Turning 'on' *Q*1, *Q*4 simultaneously causes current + 1 to flow through winding *A*. On the other hand, turning *Q*2, *Q*3 on reverses the current through *A* winding. Similarly, with *Q*5, *Q*8 'on', current flow through *B* winding is + 1, whereas current – 1 flows through winding *B* upon switching *Q*6, *Q*7 'on'.

*4.3.7.2 Bipolar L/R Drives*

The basic bipolar L/R drive is shown in Fig. 4.17. This circuit is similar to Fig. 4.15, except that resistance $R_s$ is added in series with *A* and *B* windings. Fig. 4.18 shows a variation over Fig. 4.17. Here *A* and *B* windings are in two sections which are connected in parallel. This halves the winding resistance while doubling the current rating. Unipolar power supply version of this current is to be found in Fig. 4.19.

As is the case with their unipolar counterpart, bipolar L/R drives lower the electrical time constant of the motor winding. Hence current rises rapidly

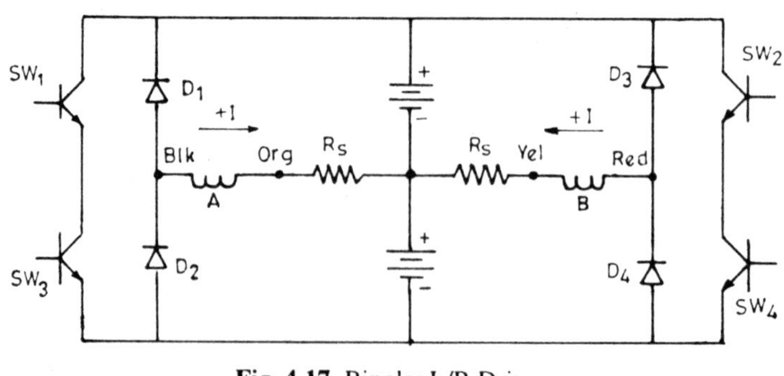


**Fig. 4.17** Bipolar L/R Drive

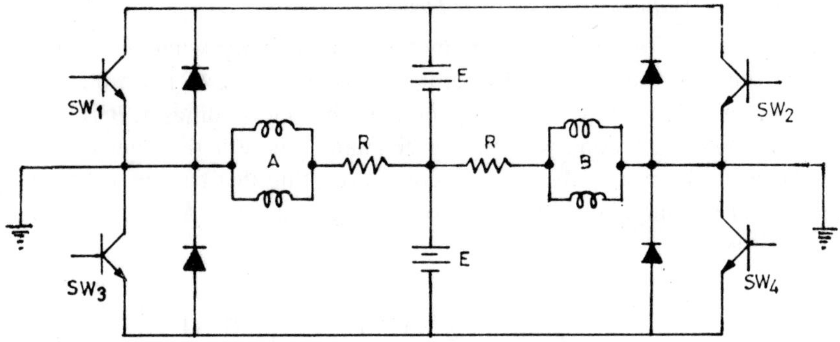


**Fig. 4.18** Simplified Two Power Supply Bioplar Drive Circuit Diagram (L/R Type with Parallel Windings)

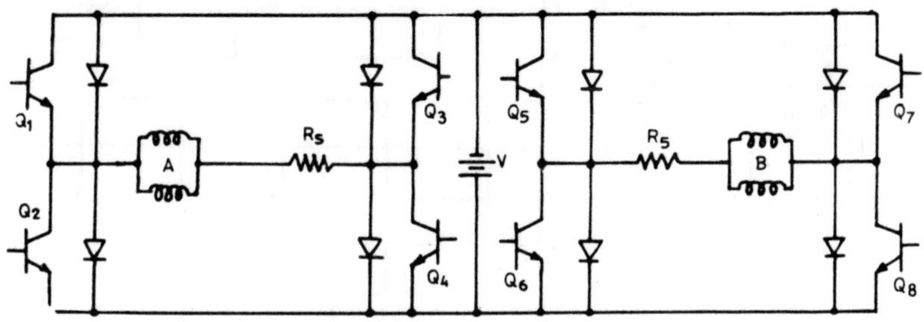


**Fig. 4.19** Bipolar L/R Drive with Unipolar Supply

through the motor winding. Consequently, much higher current and hence torque are available at higher stepping rates.

*4.3.7.3 Bipolar Chopper Drives*

Fig. 4.20 shows bipolar chopper drive for an 8-lead stepper motor. This motor has four stator phases $A$, $B$, $A'$, $B'$ or $A$, $B$, $C$, $D$. This chopper drive requires a much higher voltage from power supply than the rated voltage of the winding. The current rise and hence torque are much higher at stepping rates. The dynamic performance of the motor thus improves considerably.

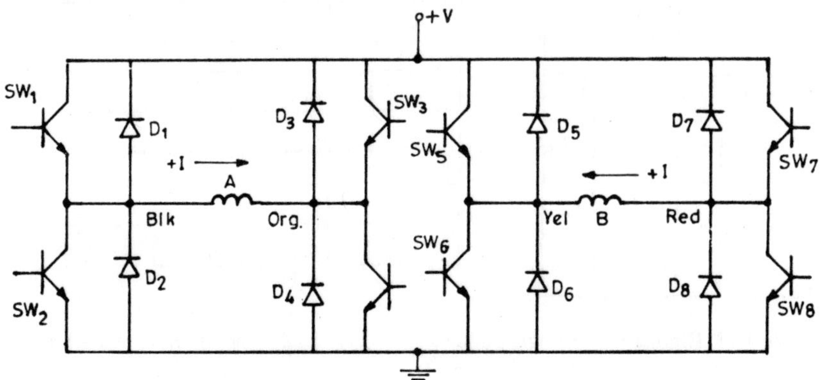


**Fig. 4.20** Bipolar Chopper Drive with Unipolar Supply

#### *4.3.7.4 Logic Sequences for Bipolar Drives*

Logic sequences for a 4-lead stepper motor, with two stator windings $A$ and $B$, and the corresponding timing diagrams are shown in Fig. 4.21. On the other hand, 4-step sequence for 8-lead stepper motor having windings $A$, $B$; $A'$, $B'$ is shown in Fig. 4.22 along with timing diagrams. These logic sequences are similar to those of unipolar drive circuits, excepting that current + 1 in $A2$ winding of the unipolar drive corresponds to current – 1 in $A$ winding of the bipolar drive.

| Step | Motor winding A | B | A′ | B′ |
|---|---|---|---|---|
| (a) Full step seq. | | | | |
| 1 | +1 | +1 | | |
| 2 | +1 | -1 | | |
| 3 | -1 | -1 | | |
| 4 | -1 | -1 | | |
| (b) Half step seq. | | | | |
| 1 | +1 | +1 | | |
| 2 | +1 | 0 | | |
| 3 | +1 | -1 | | |
| 4 | 0 | -1 | | |
| 5 | -1 | -1 | | |
| 6 | -1 | 0 | | |
| 7 | -1 | +1 | | |
| 8 | 0 | +1 | | |
| (c) Dual chopper seq. | | | | |
| 1 | +1 | +1 | +1 | +1 |
| 2 | +1 | -1 | +1 | -1 |
| 3 | -1 | -1 | -1 | -1 |
| 4 | -1 | +1 | 1 | +1 |

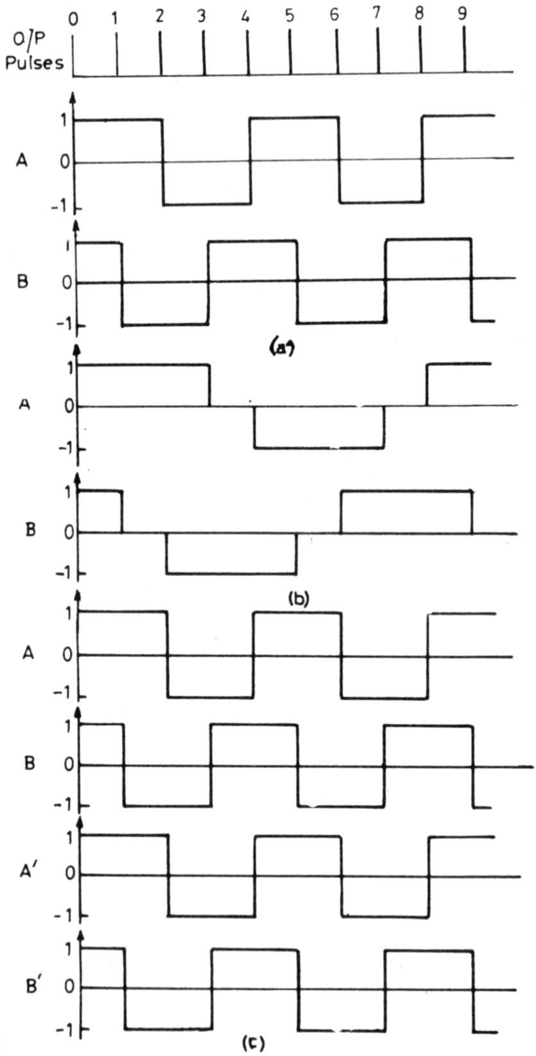


**Fig. 4.21** Bipolar Drive Logic Sequences **Fig. 4.22** Bipolar Drive Waveforms

### 4.3.8 Comparison of Bipolar Drives [9]

The main advantage of bipolar drive lies in the utilization of copper in the motor. In unipolar drive with bifilar windings, current flows through either *A*1 or *A*2 winding at any time. Thus only 50% of *A* winding is utilized at any time. Compared to this, full 100% of *A* winding is utilized in bipolar drives. However, we have to pay for it in terms of higher circuit complexity and larger number of switching transistors.

The second advantage of bipolar drives is that the motor develops much larger torque with bipolar drive owing to much more effective use of the motor winding. However, the time constant of the winding is also increased. As a result, the torque available at higher stepping rates is smaller than with bifilar motor drive as pointed out by Leenhouts [8] (See Fig. 4.23).

The number of phase windings in bipolar is half that of unipolar drive. Hence step angle errors due to manufacturing tolerances of the windings (e.g. resistance, number of turns, etc.) is also halved.

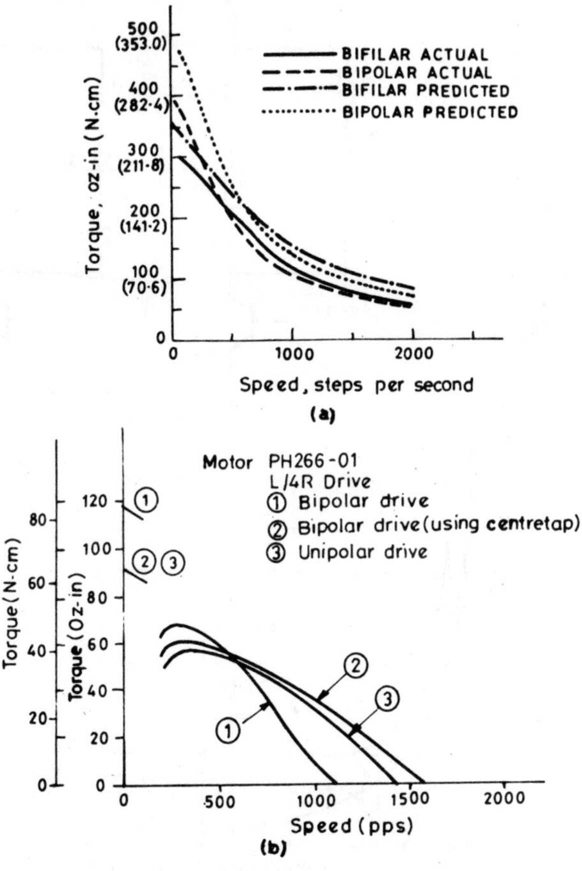


**Fig. 4.23** Comparison of Bipolar and Bifilar Drives

## 4.4 CURRENT SUPPRESSION CIRCUITS

These circuits are needed to ensure fast decay of current through the winding when it is turned off. Common current suppression circuits are shown in Fig. 4.23.

### 4.4.1 Diode Suppression

A free wheeling diode is connected across the motor winding as shown in Fig. 4.24 (a). It not only maintains continuity of current through the motor winding when it is switched off but also provides a low impedance path for the current to decay exponentially according to equation

$$i\,(t) = I_M\, e^{-t/\tau_e} \tag{4.10}$$

where $\tau_e = L_m/R_m$.

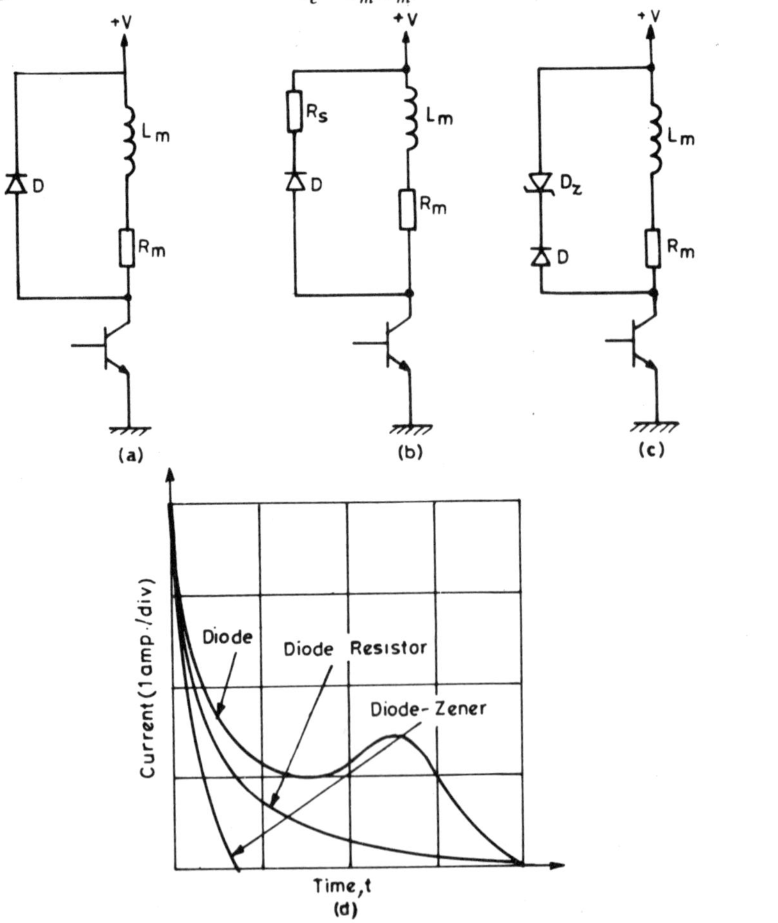


**Fig. 4.24** Current Suppression Circuits for PM Hybrid Stepper Motors

### 4.4.2 Diode-Resistor Suppression

It is shown in Fig. 4.23 (b).

A resistance $R_s$ is connected in series with the diode. It reduces the current decay time constant to $\tau_e' = L_m/(R_m + R_s)$.

Hence current decays much faster than in previous case. This is clearly seen from Fig. 4.24 (b).

### 4.4.3 Diode + Zener Diode Suppression

Is shown in Fig. 4.23 (c). The zener voltage $V_Z$ provides a negative bias which causes the current to decay much faster than with the other two circuits. However, zeners are signal diodes, rather than power diodes. Their power dissipation is limited to 5 W. Consequently, this suppressor can be used for very small instrument stepper motors of typical size 8 to 11.

### 4.4.4 Active Suppression

Is shown in Fig. 4.25. In this circuit, the energy stored in the motor winding is returned to supply instead of dissipating it. $Q_1$ and $Q_2$ are turned on when phase is to be energized. After its specified condition period, $Q_1$ and $Q_2$ are turned off The current in Phase 1 charges the capacitor $C$ via $D_1$ and $D_2$.

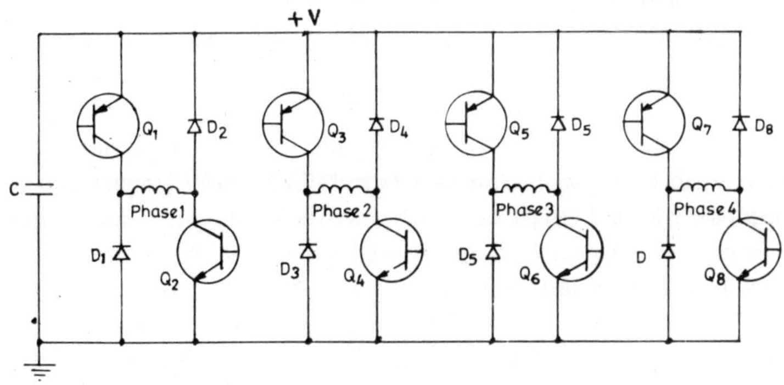


**Fig. 4.25** Simplified Active Suppression Drive with an Energy Storage Capacitor C

The stability and stepping rate of the motor improves with this circuit. Its only drawback is that it requires twice as many power transistors as the conventional drive.

## 4.5 PULSE GENERATORS

For running the stepper at the desired stepping rate, we require a variable frequency pulse generator. A simple pulse generator using the popular 555 chip is shown in Fig. 4.26. A 500 K log taper potentiometer is used to adjust pulse frequency. Pulse width and polarity are set by the one shot multivibrator at the right end. Gate line at the bottom is used to start or stop the pulse generator.

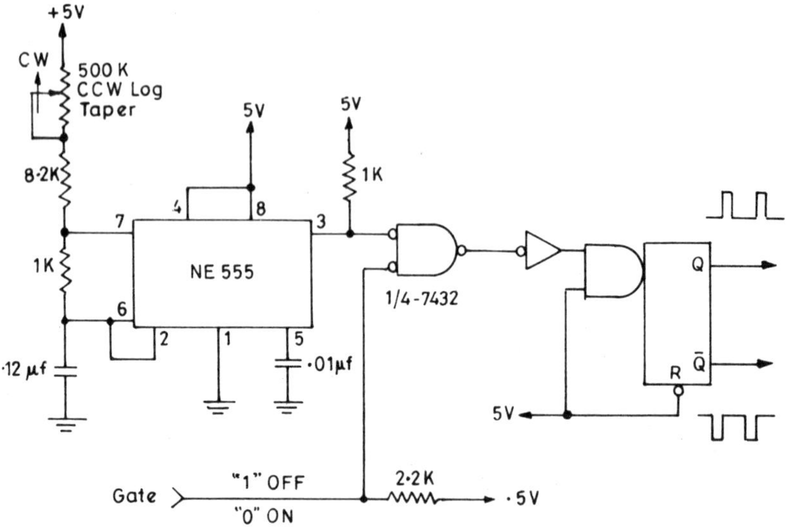


**Fig. 4.26** Circuit Diagram of Pulse Generator

## 4.6 ACCELERATION/DECELERATION CIRCUITS

From Fig. 3.5 (a) we find that the stepping rate is quite low in start-stop or single stepping mode. High stepping rates are possible only when the motor operates in slewing mode. However, the motor will not start if we apply pulses to it at the slewing rate. On the other hand, the motor will overshoot the mark by several steps if we suddenly stop applying pulses when it is slewing.

This shows that, if we wish to run the motor at slewing rate $F_2$ steps/sec., we must start the motor at a rate $F_1$ steps/sec, which is well below the pull-in rate $F_1$ and then accelerate to the slewing rate $F_2$. Similarly, well before we wish to stop, we decelerate from slewing rate $F_2$ to start-stop rate $F_1$, and subsequently stop applying pulses. This exercise is shown in Fig. 4.27 and is called *Velocity profiling*.

Such velocity profiling requires automatic acceleration/deceleration circuits. Four types ot such circuits, called '*ramping*' circuits, are available:

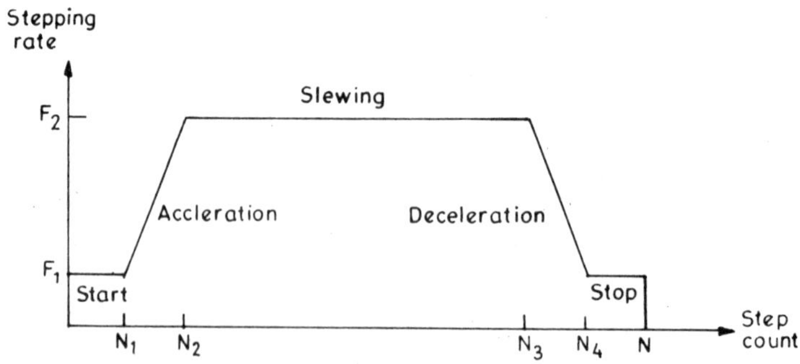


**Fig. 4.27** Velocity Profiling

(i) Linear Ramping
(ii) Exponential Ramping
(iii) R-C Ramping
(iv) Digital Binary Rate Multiplier BRM Ramping

Of these, the linear and exponential ramping circuits are shown in Figs. 4.28 and 4.29. Fig. 4.28 (a) shows linear ramping circuit, while Fig. 4.28 (b) shows associated waveform. Similarly, exponential ramping circuit appears in Fig. 4.29 (a), whereas corresponding waveforms are shown in Fig. 4.29 (b).

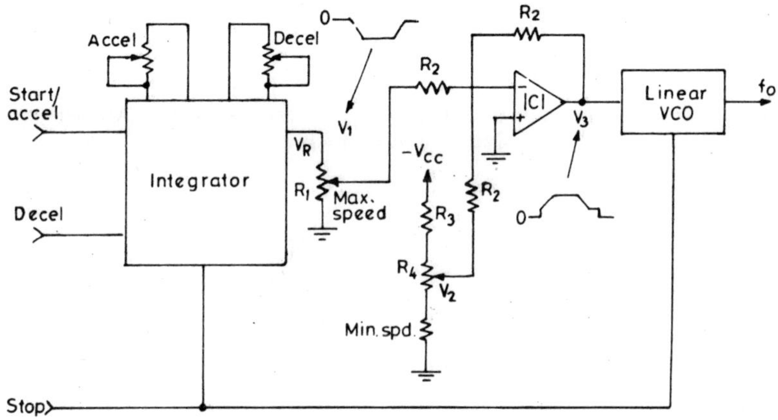


**Fig. 4.28(a)** Circuit Diagram of a Linear Acceleration-Deceleration Control

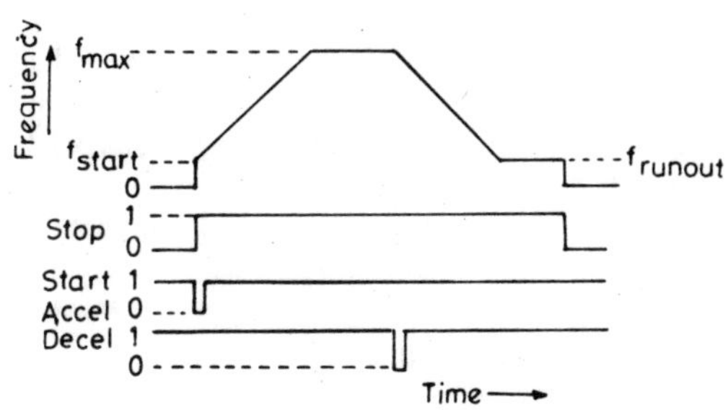


**Fig. 4.28(b)** Linear Acceleration-Deceleration Ramp Profile

## 4.7 CONCLUSION

In this chapter we have discussed electronic circuits employed in logic sequence generation, power drivers, current suppressors, acceleration and deceleration circuits. They are used to start, stop, accelerate and decelerate the stepper motor.

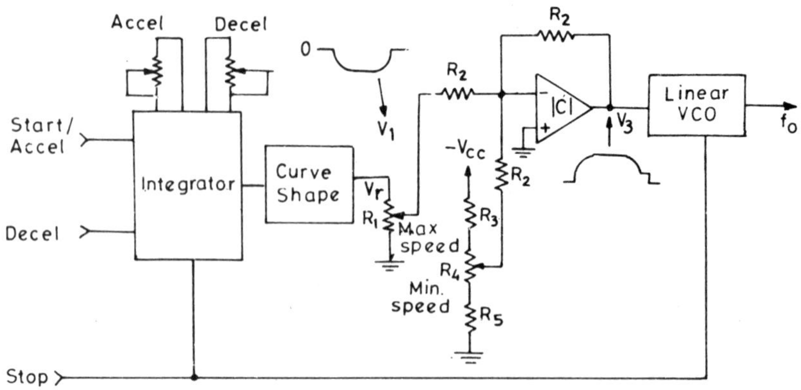


**Fig. 4.29(a)** Circuit Diagram of an Exponential-Inverse Exponential Acceleration-Deceleration Controller

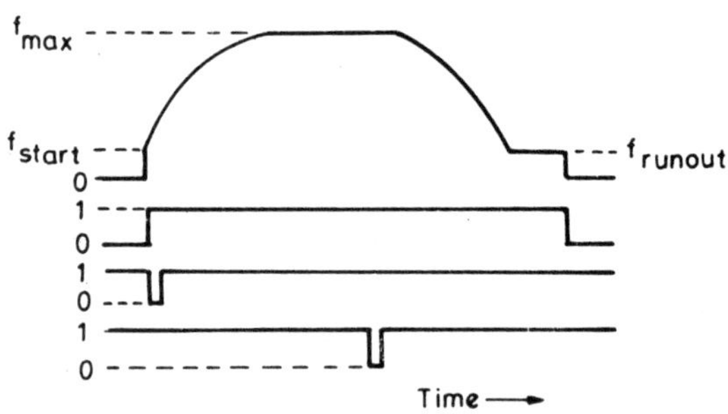


**Fig. 4.29(b)** Exponential/Inverse Exponential Acceleration/Deceleration Ramp.

## REFERENCES

1. .B.C. Kuo, 'Step Motors and Control Systems', SRL Publishing Co., Champaign, IL, USA, 1979, Chap. 4.
2. T. Kenjo, 'Stepper Motors and Their Microprocessor Controls', Clarendon Press, Oxford, 1984, Chap. 5.
3. P.P. Acarnley, 'Stepping Motors: A Guide to Modern Theory and Practice' (3rd Edn.), Peter Peregrinus Ltd., London, 1992, Chap. 2.
4. 'A Guide to Selecting and Controlling Step Motors', Warner Electric Brake & Clutch Co., Belvit, WI, USA., From P-172, 1980.
5. V.V. Athani and H.N. Vinod, 'Linear Current Drive for Stepping Motors', Electronic Engg., Vol. 10, No. 12, p. 28. Dec. 1986.
6. V.V. Athani J.C. Mundhada, 'High Performance Controller for High Torque PM Stepping Motors', IEEE Trans. on Indus. Electron. Vol. IECI-25, No. 4, pp. 343-346, 1978.
7. V.V. Athani and J.C. Mundhada, 'Novel Controller for PM Stepping Motors', Control and Instrum., Vol. 10, p. 9, Nov. 1978.
8. V.V. Athani and A.M. Riswadkar, 'Unified Logic Sequencer for Stepper Motors', Electronics for You, Vol. 28, No. 5, pp. 44-46, May 1996.
9. 'Sigma Stepping Motors Handbook', Sigma Instruments Inc., Braintree, MA, USA, 1972.
10. A.C. Leenhouts, 'A Comparison of Bifilar and Bipolar L/R Drives Performance', Proc. 9th IMCSD, pp. 93-97, 1980.

## APPENDIX

# *Design of Stepper Motor Drives**

## 4A.1 UNIPOLAR L/R DRIVE

A typical unipolar L/R drive is shown in Fig. 4.9 (a).The principle of this drive has already been discussed in Section 4.3.2, and associated waveforms shown in Fig. 4.9 (b). We consider the design aspects of this drive in this section.

For sake of convenience, the unipolar R/L dive is redrawn from Fig. 4.30. The design formulae for this drive are as follows:

Let

$R_m$, $L_m$ = resistance and inductance of the motor phase winding.
$R_s$ = resistance connected in series with the motor phase winding.
$I_{ph}$ = rated current of motor phase winding.
$R_f$ = resistance connected in series with the free wheeling diode.
$D_1$ = free wheeling diode.
$V_s$ = DC supply voltage

1. The electrical time constant covering both the rise and fall of current through the motor winding alone (*i.e.* with $R_s = R_f = 0$) will be

$$\tau_e = L_m/R_m \,. \tag{4.11}$$

2. Let $\tau_{e1}$ and $\tau_{e2}$ be the desired time constants for rise and fall of current through the motor winding. Then

$$\tau_{e1} = L_m/(R_m + R_s) \tag{4.12}$$

$$\tau_{e2} = L_m/(R_m + R_s + R_f) \tag{4.13}$$

Hence

$$R_s = (L_m/\tau_{e1}) - R_m \tag{4.14}$$

$$R_f = (L_m/\tau_{e2}) - R_m - R_s \tag{4.15}$$

3. The supply voltage required to drive the rated current $I_{ph}$ through the motor winding is given by

$$V_s = (R_m + R_s)\, I_{ph} \tag{4.16}$$

4. The power rating of $R_s$ and $R_f$ are given by

---

* Source : Acarnley, P.P., Ref. No. 3

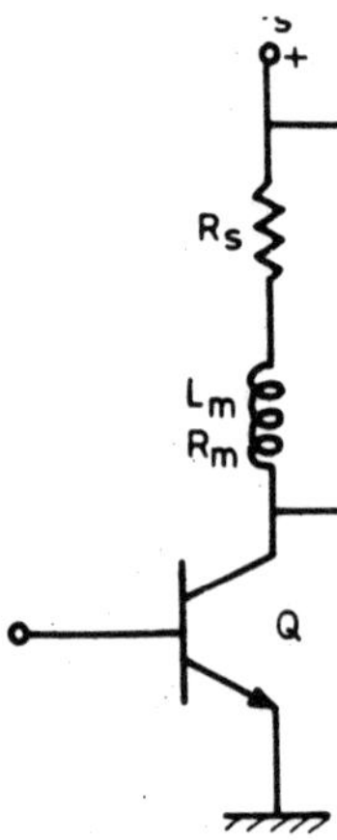


(a) Circuit diagram

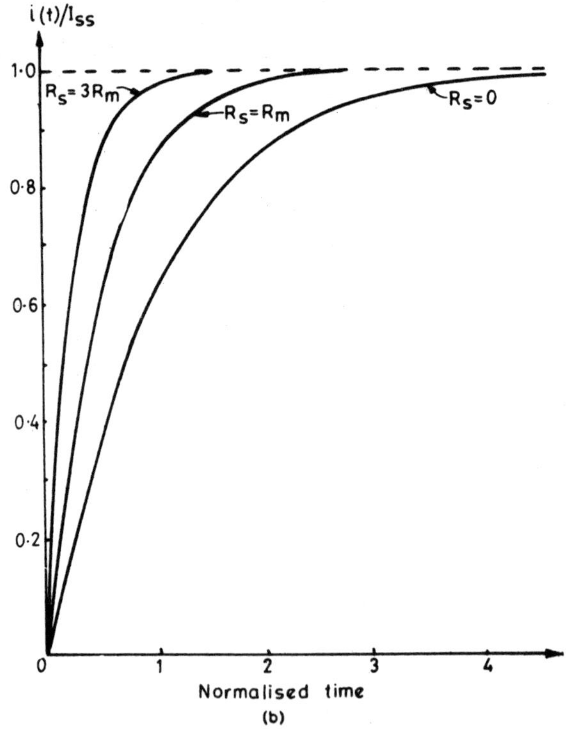


(b) Waveforms

**Fig. 4.30** Unipolar R/L Drive Circuit

$$P_{cus} = I_{ph}^2 R_s$$

$$P_{cuf} = I_{ph}^2 R_f \tag{4.17}$$

These are the peak power dissipations. These could be reduced by a factor of 2 to arrive at the average power dissipation.

5. The peak energy stored in the winding at the time of turn-off is

   stored energy = (1/2) $(L_m I_{ph}^2)$ (4.18)

   This energy is dissipated through $R_m$, $R_s$ and $R_f$ as the winding current decays.

6. The maximum voltage across the power transistor at the time of turn-off will be

$$V_{ce\,(\max)} = V_s + I_{ph} R_f \tag{4.19}$$

   Hence the power transistor must be capable of withstanding $V_{ce\,(\max)}$ and pass $I_{ph}$ through it.

7. The peak reverse voltage across the free wheeling diode $D_1$ is given by $V_s$.

**Ex. 4.1** Design L/R drive for a Slo-syn M093-FC07 stepper motor having the following parameters:

$R_m = 1.23\ \Omega$, $L_m = 7.94$ mH, $I_{ph} = 3.5$ A. Desired $\tau_{e1} = 1$ ms, $\tau_{e2} = 0.5$ ms.

**Sol.** For the stepper motor by itself

$$\tau_e = L_m/R_m = 7.94/1.23 = 6.4 \text{ ms}$$

$$\tau_{e1} = L_m/(R_m + R_s) = 1 \text{ ms} = 7.94/(1.23 + R_s),$$

Hence $$R_s = 7.94 - 1/23 = 6.71\ \Omega \approx 6.7\ \Omega$$

$$\tau_{e2} = L_m/(R_m + R_s + R_f) = 0.5 \text{ ms} = 7.94/(1.23 + 6.71 + R_f)$$

Hence $$R_f = (7.94/2) - (1.23 + 6.71) = 7.94\ \Omega \approx 8.0\ \Omega$$

DC voltage required

$$V_s = (R_m + R_s)\, I_{ph} = (1.23 + 6.72)\,(3.5) = 27.79 \text{ V} \approx 28 \text{ V}.$$

Power rating of $R_s$ and $R_f$ will be

$$P_{cus} = I_{ph}^2\, R_s = (3.5)^2\,(6.7) = 82.1 \text{ W} \approx 100 \text{ W}$$

$$P_{cuf} = I_{ph}^2\, R_f = (3.5)^2\,(8) = 98.0 \text{ W} \approx 100 \text{ W}$$

For the power transistor,

$$V_{ce\,(\max)} = V_s + I_{ph}R_f$$

$$= 28 + (3.5)\,(8) = 56 \text{ V} \approx 60 \text{ V}.$$

Thus the power transistor should be rated for 60 V, 3.5 A. Free wheeling diode $D_1$ is rated for 28 V, 3.5 A.

## 4A.2 BIPOLAR L/R DRIVE

The bipolar L/R drive has been discussed in section 4.3.7.2. in conjunction with Fig. 4.19. The design aspects of this drive are presented below.

A typical bipolar drive for a stepper motor, using unipolar supply, is shown in Fig. 4.31. This is the well known H-bridge circuit. Switching $Q_1$ and $Q_4$ together causes current to flow in positive direction. The current flow is reversed by turning $Q_1$ and $Q_4$ off and turning $Q_2$ and $Q_3$ on. The diodes $D_1$-$D_4$ act as free-wheeling diodes which also serve to return part of the energy stored in the magnetic circuit, back to the DC supply.This makes the bipolar drive more energy efficient than the unipolar drive. Another noteworthy feature of this drive is the current decay in the winding is much more rapid than in unipolar drive, because the current flow in the winding is opposed by supply voltage $V_s$. This is clear from current flow through the circuit when $Q_1$ and $Q_4$ have been switched off, shown by dotted lines. The solid line shows the current flow when $Q_1$ and $Q_4$ are on.

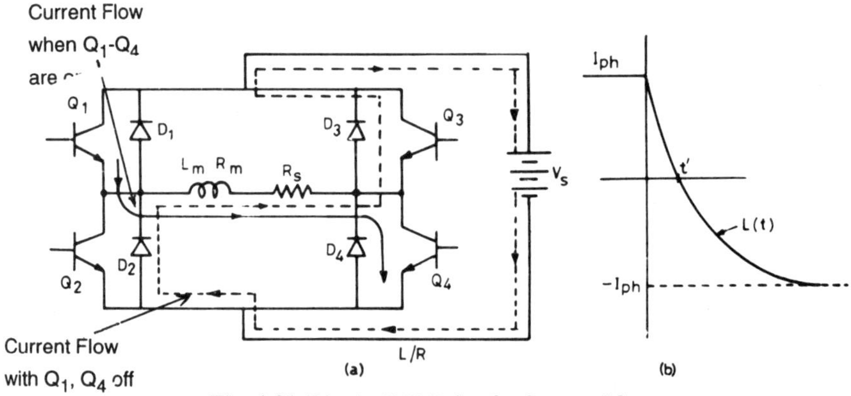


**Fig. 4.31** Bipolar L/R Drive for Stepper Motor

1. When $Q_1$ and $Q_4$ are switched on, the motor winding is connected to supply $V_s$. The rise of current through the motor winding is given by

$$i(t) = I_{ph}(1 - e^{-t/\tau_{e1}})$$

where

$$I_{ph} = V_s/(R_m + R_s) \quad (4.20)$$

$$\tau_{e1} = L_m/(R_m + R_s)$$

2. When $Q_1$ and $Q_4$ are turned off, the current through the motor winding is governed by

$$i(t) = I_{ph}\,e^{-t/\tau_{e1}} - 2I_{ph}(1 - e^{-t/\tau_{e1}})$$

$$= -I_{ph} + 2I_{ph}\,e^{-t/\tau_{e1}} \quad (4.21)$$

where $I_{ph}$ and $\tau_{e1}$ are given by Eqs. (4.20)

Approximating $e^{-t/\tau_{e1}}$ by $(1 - t/\tau_{e1})$, we get from eqn. (4.21)

$$i(t) = -I_{ph} + 2I_{ph}(1 - t/\tau_{e1})$$

$$= I_{ph} - 2I_{ph}(t/\tau_{e1}) \quad (4.22)$$

Hence the time at which $i\,(t) = 0$ is given by

$$t' \approx \tau_{e1}/2 \tag{4.23}$$

3. The energy returned to the supply during this period is given by

$$E_{ret} = \int_0^{t'} V_s\, i\,(t)\, dt$$

$$\approx \int_0^{t'} V_I\, I_{ph}\,(1 - 2t/\tau_{eq})\, dt$$

$$= V_s\, I_{ph}\,(t' - t^2/\tau_{e1})$$

$$= \frac{1}{4}\, V_s I_{ph}\, \tau_{e1}$$

$$= \frac{1}{4}\, I_{ph}\, V_s \frac{L_m}{R_m + R_s}$$

$$= \frac{1}{4}\, L_m\, I_{ph}^2 \tag{4.24}$$

The initial energy stored in the motor winding is $\frac{1}{2}\, L_m\, I_{ph}^2$. Thus,

$$E_{ret} = \frac{1}{2}\,\text{(Initial Stored Energy)} \tag{4.25}$$

4. The max voltage across the power transistor and the diodes will be

$$V_{ce\,(\max)} = \frac{1}{2}\,(V_s + I_{ph}\, R_s) \approx V_s \tag{4.26}$$

and

$$V_{RR} = \frac{1}{2}\, V_s \tag{4.27}$$

Hence the power transistor would be rated for $V_s$ and $I_{ph}$ and the diodes for $\frac{1}{2}\, V_s$ and $I_{ph}$.

**Ex. 4.2** Design a bipolar L/R drive for the same Slo-syn M093-FC07 as in Ex. 4.1.

**Sol.** The series resistance $R_s$ required to yield $\tau_{e1} = 1$ ms is given by

$$R_s = (L_m/\tau_{e1}) - L_m = 7.94 - 1.23 = 6.71\ \Omega$$

The power rating of $R_s$ will be

$$P_{cus} = I_{ph}^2 R_s = (3.5)^2\,(6.71) = 82.1\ \text{W} \approx 100\ \text{W}.$$

The energy returned to supply during current decay

$$\frac{1}{4}\, L_m I_{ph}^2 = \frac{1}{4}\,(7.94 \times 10^{-3})\,(3.5)^2 = 24.32\ \text{mW}.$$

The current in the winding decays to zero in time

$$t' = \frac{1}{2}\tau_{e1} = 0.5 \text{ ms.}$$

The power transistor would be rated for

$$V_s = I_{ph}(R_m + R_s) = (3.5)(1.23 + 6.71) = 27.79 \text{ V} \approx 28 \text{ V}.$$

and $$I_c = 3.5 \text{ A}.$$

The diodes would be rated for $V_{RR} = V_s/2 = 14$ V and $I_f = 3.5$ A.

## 4A.3 CHOPPER DRIVE

The principle of operation of the chopper drive has been explained in section 4.3.4 and Fig. 4.11. The same chopper drive is redrawn in Fig. 4.32. The principle of operation of the chopper is as follows:

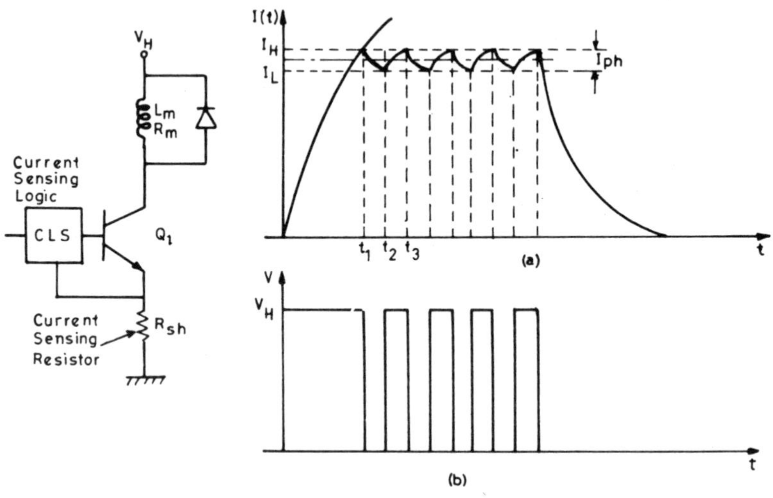


(a) Circuit Diagram (b) Current Dependent Chopping

**Fig. 4.32** Unipolar Chopper (Current Dependent Type)

### 4A.3.1 Unipolar Current Dependent Chopper

We apply a voltage $V_H = 4$ to 10 times $V_{ph}$, the rated voltage of the phase winding. When transistor $Q_1$ is turned on, current in the motor winding is given by

$$i(t) = I_S(1 - e^{-t/\tau_e}) \tag{4.28}$$

where $I_S = 4$ to 10 times $I_{ph}$, the rated current in the motor winding.

When current $i(t) = I_H$, Q1 is turned off. Thereupon current $i(t)$ starts decreasing according to

$$i(t) = I_H\, e^{-t/\tau_e} \tag{4.29}$$

When $i(t)$ falls to $I_L$, $Q_1$ is turned on again. Current $i(t)$ then starts increasing towards $I_S$ in an exponential manner

$$i(t) = I_L + (I_S - I_L)(1 - e^{-t/\tau_e}) \tag{4.30}$$

when $i(t) = I_H$, $Q_1$ is turned off, and the cycle is repeated until such time as the motor winding should remain energized as per the switching sequence and the motor stepping rate.

Usually $I_H = (1.01 - 1.10)\, I_{ph}$, while $I_L = (0.90 - 0.99)\, I_{ph}$, so that the limits of variation of $i(t)$ are ($\pm$ 1%) – ($\pm$ 10%) of $I_{ph}$.

A current sensing device must be employed to sense the winding current $i(t)$. The current sensors usually employed are:

1. Current sensing resistor $R_{sh}$, which is only a fraction of an $\Omega$, and should preferably be a four terminal shunt.
2. DC current transformer based on magnetic amplifier principle.

New generation current sensors based on optro-electronics and optical fiber technologies are now becoming available.

Along with current sensing device. We also require current sensing logic (CSL) to turn $Q_1$ off when $i(t) = I_H$ and on when $i(t) = I_L$. The simplest device that can act as CSL is a Schmitt trigger whose hysteresis could be adjusted to ($\pm$ 1%) – ($\pm$ 10%).

**Ex. 4.3** Design a unipolar chopper drive for Slo-syn M093-FC07 stepper motor, data for which are given in Ex. 4.1.

Take two values of $V_H$, viz. $V_{H1} = 4V_{ph}$ and $V_{H2} = 10\, V_{ph}$, where $V_{ph}$ is the rated phase voltage $= R_m i_{ph}$, $I_{ph}$ being the rated phase current.

**Sol.** (a) $V_{H1} = 4I_{ph}$, so that $I_{S1} = 4I_{ph}$. The design equations are:
The time $t_1$ at which $i(t)$ reaches the value $I_{H1} = 4I_{ph}$ is given by

$$I_{H1} = 1.05I_{ph} = 4I_{ph}(1 - e^{-T/\tau_e})$$

This yields $e^{-T/\tau_e} = 2.95/4 = 0.7375$. Hence

$$t_1 = 0.304\,\tau_e = (0.304)(6.4) = 1.949 \text{ ms}$$

The time $T_2$ required for current to decrease from $I_H$ to $I_L$ is given by

$$I_L = 0.95I_{ph} = 1.05I_{ph}\, e^{-T_2/\tau_e}$$

Hence $$e^{-T_2/\tau_e} = 0.905 \Rightarrow T_2/\tau_e = 0.1001$$

and $$T_2\,(0.1)(6.4) = 0.641 \text{ ms}$$

$$t_2 = t_1 + T_2 \doteq 1.949 + 0.641 = 1.590 \text{ ms}$$

The time $T_3$ for current to rise from $I_L$ to $I_H$ is given by

$$1.05I_{ph} = 0.95I_{ph} + (4I_{ph} - 0.95I_{ph})(1 - e^{-T_3/\tau_e})$$

Hence $$3.05e^{-T_3/\tau_e} = 2.95$$

and $$e^{-T_3/\tau_e} = 0.9672 \Rightarrow t_3/\tau_e = 0.0333$$

This yields $$T_3 = (0.0333)\,(6.4) = 0.2134 \text{ ms}$$

Hence $$T_3 = t_2 + T_3 = 2.590 + 0.2134 = 2.724 \text{ ms.}$$

One cycle of chopper operation takes

$$T_1 = T_2 + T_3 = 0.641 + 0.2134 = 0.854 \text{ ms}$$

This means that the chopper operates at a frequency

$$F_1 = 1/T_1 = 1.172 \text{ kHz}$$

This implies a stepping rate of 1172 steps/s with single phase excitation sequence and 2344 steps/s for two phase excitation sequence.

(b) $V_{H2} = 10\, I_{ph} \Rightarrow I_S = 10\, I_{ph}$. On similar lines as in case (a), we get

$$t_1 = 0.111\, \tau_e = (0.111)\,(6.4) = 0.710 \text{ ms}$$

$$T_2 = 0.1\, \tau_e = (0.1)\,(6.4) = 0.640 \text{ ms}$$

Hence $$t_2 = t_1 + T_2 = 0.710 + 0.640 = 1.350 \text{ ms}$$

$$T_3 = 0.0111\, \tau_e = (0.0111)\,(6.4) = 0.071 \text{ ms}$$

Hence $$t_3 = t_2 + T_3 = 1.350 + 0.071 = 0.711 \text{ ms}$$

$$T_1 = T_2 + T_3 = 0.640 + 0.071 = 0.711 \text{ ms}$$

Hence $$F_1 = 1/T_1 = 1.406 \text{ kHz.}$$

Motor stepping rate = 1406 steps/s or 2812 steps/s for 1-ph and 2-ph excitation sequences respectively.

### 4A.3.2 Fixed Frequency Chopper

In this chopper, we apply voltage $V_H$ to the motor winding as before. However, we switch off the power transistor when $i(t)$ rises to $I_{ph}$ instead of $I_H = 1.05\, I_{ph}$. Thereafter, we operate the chopper at a fixed frequency $F = 1/T$. For safe operation of the power transistor, it is necessary that the duty cycle of the chopper

$$x = t_{on}/(t_{on} + t_{off}) = t_{on}/T < 0.5$$

$x$ usually lies in the range 0.1 – 0.45. this allows the power transistor sufficient time to cool off after one turn-on turn-off cycle as shown in Fig. 4.33.

The design equation of this chopper are as follows:

We start with the transistor turned off at $t = t_1$. Current $i(t)$ decreases exponentially from $I_{ph}$ to $I_L$ for time $t_{off}$. Hence

$$I_L = I_{ph} e^{-t_{off}/\tau_e} \tag{4.31}$$

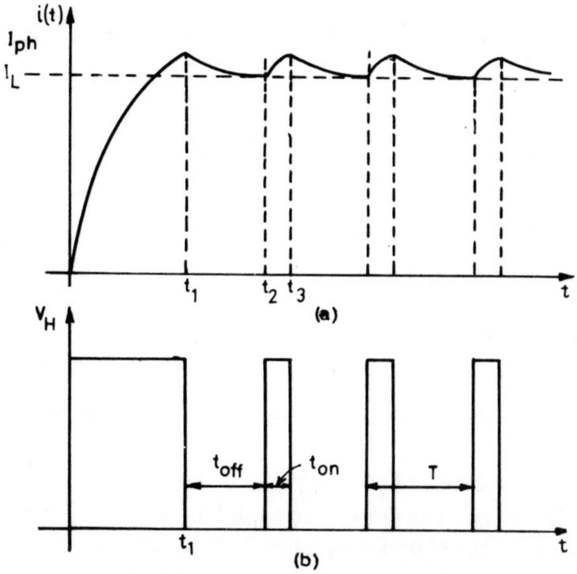


**Fig. 4.33** Fixed Frequency Chopper

At time $t_2 = t_1 + t_{off}$, the power transistor is tuned on. Then current rises exponentially from $I_L$ towards $I_S$. Let the current $i(t) = I_{ph}$ at $t_3 = t_2 + t_{on}$. Then

$$I_{ph} = I_L + (I_S - I_L)(1 - e^{-t_{on}/\tau_e}) \tag{4.32}$$

It is possible to compute $t_{on}$ and $t_{off}$ such that Eqs. (4.31) and (4.32) hold good. Towards this end, we combine Eqs. (4.31) and (4.32) to get

$$I_{ph} = I_{ph}e^{-t_{off}/\tau_e} + (I_S - I_{ph}e^{-t_{off}/\tau_e})(1 - e^{-t_{on}/\tau_e}) \tag{4.33}$$

Next, substitute $t_{on} = xT$, $t_{off} = (1 - x)T$, $I_S = (4 \text{ or } 10)\, I_{ph}$ and simplify of obtain the results

$$\frac{I_S}{I_{ph}} = \frac{1 - e^{-T/\tau_e}}{1 - e^{-xT/\tau_e}} \tag{4.34}$$

**Ex. 4.4** Design a chopper, operating at a fixed frequency of 16 kHz for the Slo-syn M093-FC07 stepper motor of Ex. 4.1. Assume $V_H = 4V_{ph}$ so that $I_S = 4I_{ph}$.

**Sol.** Substituting $I_S = 4I_{ph}$ in Eqn. (4.33) we get

$$I_{ph} = I_{ph}\, e^{-(1-x)T/\tau_e} + (4I_{ph}) - (I_{ph}\, e^{-(1-x)T/\tau_e})(1 - e^{-xT/\tau_e})$$

or $1 = e^{-(1-x)T/\tau_e} + 4 - e^{-(1-x)T/\tau_e} - 4e^{-xT/\tau_e} + e^{-(1-x)T/\tau_e}\, e^{-xT/\tau_e}$

Hence
$$e^{-xT/\tau_e} = (3 + e^{-T/\tau_e})/4 \tag{4.35}$$

For chopper frequency of 16 kHz, $T = 0.0625$ ms or 62.5 $\mu s$. $\tau_e = 6.4$ ms. Hence

$$T/\tau_e = (0.0625)/6.4 = 9.766 \times 10^{-3}$$

$$e^T/\tau_e = e^{-0.009765625} = 0.990282$$

$$\Rightarrow \qquad e^{-xT/\tau_e} = 3.99014 = 0.9975$$

This yields $x = 0.2491$. Hence $t_{on} = 15.56$ μs ≈ 15.6 μs and $t_{off} = 46.94$ μs ≈ 46.9 μs.

### 4A.3.3 Bipolar Chopper

The bipolar chopper circuit is the same as the H-bridge circuit shown in Fig. 4.31, except that

(i) the series resistance $R_s$ is not required, and
(ii) the transistors are operated in chopper mode.

The fixed frequency chopper is preferred. We get higher torque in this mode that with unipolar chopper because of current swings in the motor winding from $+I_{ph}$ to $-I_{ph}$ and vice versa as shown in Fig. 4.34.

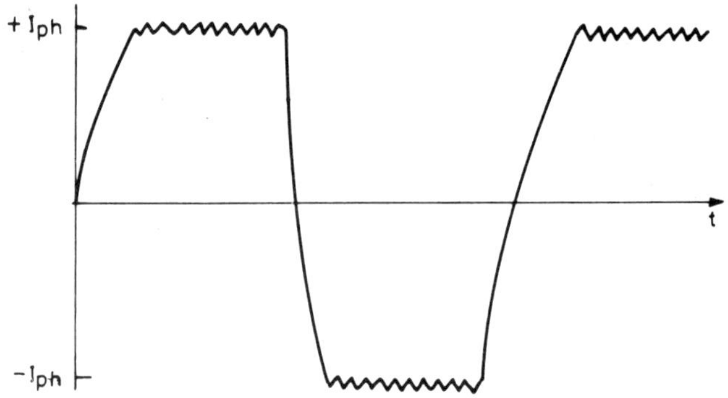


**Fig. 4.34** Bipolar Chopper Drive Waveforms

### 4A.3.4 Constant Current Drive

Constant current source would be the ideal drive for a stepper motor inasmuch as it would cause the current in the motor winding to assume the rated current value, $I_{ph}$, immediately on switching on. Such a constant current drive is shown in Fig. 4.35. It employes a difference op-amp in conjunction with current sensing resistor $R_{sh}$ to compare reference current with feedback current and to vary the operating point on the main power transistor characteristic in such a way as to cause the actual current to equal tie desired feedback current. High current ratings such as 10 A, can be obtained using power MOSFETS.

In the circuit shown in Fig. 4.35, the main power transistor is in the active region. A switch-mode constant current circuit, in which the duty cycle of main power transistor is adjusted according to the difference between desired and actual current, can be designed. Such a switch mode circuit would be much more efficient than the linear circuit shown in Fig. 4.35.

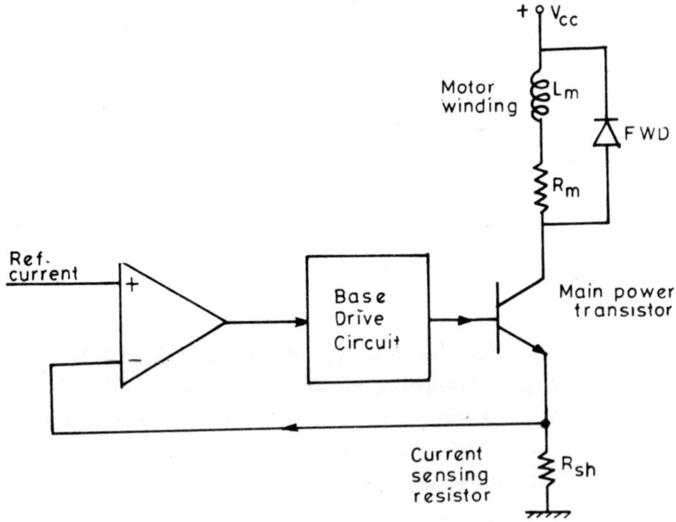


**Fig. 4.35** Circuit Diagram for Constant Current Drive

# CHAPTER - 5

# *Microprocessor Control of Stepper Motors*

This chapter aims at explaining how the stepper motor may be controlled using the microprocessor. Special IC chips for controlling stepper motors, including the so-called 'intelligent' controller, are also presented. Finally, a brief account of the ASIC for stepper motor control, being developed by Central Electronic Engineering Research Institute (CEERI), Pilani (India) is described.

There are basically two types of stepper motor controllers.

**(a) Translator.** Causes the motor to run at specified stepping rate $F_s$ (steps/sec.) in the desired direction. The motor continues to run at set speed $F_s$ until a 'stop' signal is applied. The motor is said to be operating in the free running mode during translation.

**(b) Preset Indexer.** Causes the stepper motor to move a specified number $N$ of steps at the required stepping rate $F_s$ (steps/sec.) in the desired direction. It includes automatic acceleration/deceleration feature in order to save time if $N$ is large enough. The so-called 'intelligent' controller is an extension of the preset indexer.

## 5.1 TASKS THAT CAN BE PERFORMED BY MICROPROCESSOR

We have already studied stepper motor drive circuits in Chapter 4. Let us see which of these can be implemented by the microprocessor software-wise.

### 5.1.1 Logic Sequence Generation

Is purely a logical operation inasmuch as logic sequence generator is a finite state logic machine that transits from its present state to the next state upon receipt of an input pulse.

The easiest way of performing logic sequence generation is to store the logic sequences given in Table 4.1 as look-up tables in an EPROM. For every input pulse received, the microprocessor goes to the look-up table and outputs the next step as a four bit word on one of the 8255 parallel ports. Flow-chart for this function is shown in Fig. 5.1. Notice that this function is timer interrupt driven.

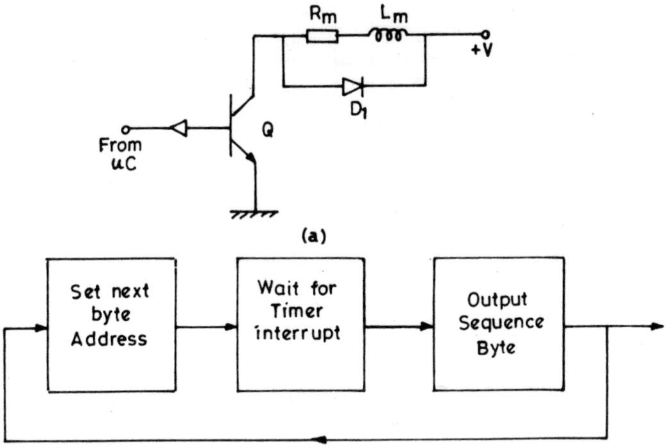


(b)
**Fig. 5.1** Logic Sequence Generation on Microprocessor

### 5.1.2 Direction Control

Is taken care of while setting the address of the next sequence byte. Depending on whether the direction bit is '0' (i.e. CCW rotation) or '1' (i.e. CW rotation), we go to either the succeeding step or preceding step in the concerned logic sequence.

As an example, suppose we are presently at step 3 of the logic sequence concerned, say the '2 phases on' sequence. Then, depending on the direction control bit, we proceed as follows:

Direction bit = 0 : 3 ⟶ 4 ⟶ 1 ⟶ 2 ⟶(CCW)
Control bit = 1 : 3 ⟶ 2 ⟶1 ⟶ 4 ⟶ (CW)

### 5.1.3 Variable Frequency Pulse Generator

Shown in Fig. 4.15, can be implemented by the constant speed algorithm shown in Fig. 5.2. It computes $T = 1/F_s$ and timer count $N_c$ corresponding to specified stepping rate $F_s$ (steps/sec). It loads $N_c$ into counter '0' of 8253/8354 timer chip. Counter '0' is programmed for 'rate generator' mode, so that it generates a timer interrupt when count therein reaches '0'.

### 5.1.4 Translator or Free Running

In this mode, the stepper motor goes on running at the sepcified stepping rate $F_s$ (steps/sec) in the desired direction until the 'Stop' button is pushed. Fig. 5.3 shows the translator algorithm. Note that this algorithm incorporates the variable frequency pulse generator algorithm of Fig. 5.2.

### 5.1.5 Indexing

The desired number $N$ of the steps to be covered is loaded into counter '1' of 8253/8254 timer chip. Output pulses generated by counter '0' are applied at

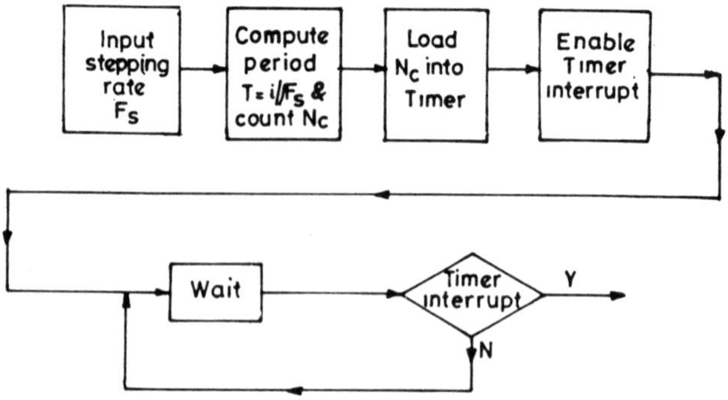


**Fig. 5.2** Variable Frequency Pulse Generator

input terminal of counter '1', so that the step count in counter '1' is decremented for each pulse from counter '0'. When the count in counter '1' becomes zero, we stop applying pulses to the motor. This algorithm is shown in Fig. 5.4.

### 5.1.6 Automatic Acceleration/Deceleration

Is warranted when $N$, the number of steps to be covered, is sufficiently large. We then start the stepper motor at a low rate of $F_1$ steps/sec (which is well below the pull-in rate, $F_{PI}$) and accelerate to high rate of $F_2$ steps/sec (which is such that $F_{PI} \leq F_2 \leq F_{PO}$, the pull-out speed). We cover most of the $N$ steps at high speed $F_2$. When we approach the end, we decelerate the motor from high rate, $F_2$ to low rate $F_1$ and then stop. In this way, $N$ steps are covered in minimum possible time without losing synchronism. The procedure is called velocity profiling and is shown in Fig. 5.5.

The input data required for this algorithm are: (1) initial rate $F_1$ final rate $F_2$ (steps/sec), and (2) either acceleration time $\Delta T$ or number of steps $\Delta N$ for accelerating, where

$$\Delta N = (F_1 + F_2)/2\,\Delta T \tag{5.1}$$

For linear acceleration,

$$\Delta F = (F_2 - F_1)/\Delta N \tag{5.2}$$

Suppose the motor is running at $F_i$ steps/sec. For linear acceleration, $F_{i+1} = F_i + \Delta F$. The corresponding times between pulses will be:

$$T_i = \frac{1}{F_i},\ T_{i+1} = \frac{1}{F_{i+1}},\ \Delta T_i = T_{i+1} - T_i = \frac{1}{F_i + \Delta F} - \frac{1}{F_i} \tag{5.3}$$

Thus $\Delta T_i$ and hence change in count $\delta N_i$ are not linear because of Eqn. (5.3). This makes the acceleration/deceleration complicated and tricky.

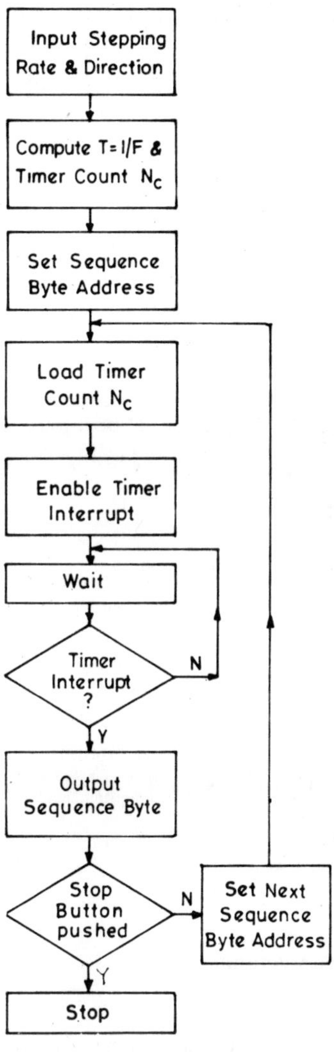


**Fig. 5.3** Translator Algorithm

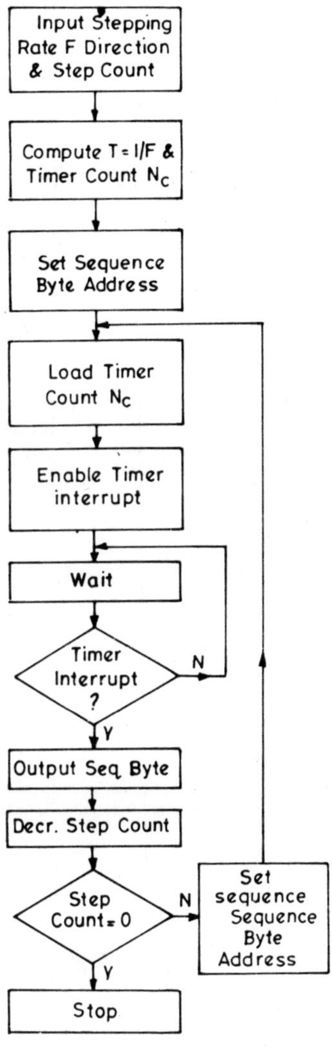


**Fig. 5.4** Preset Indexer Algorithm

## 5.2 MICROPROCESSOR BASED STEPPER MOTOR CONTROLLER

The commonly available, Intel 8085 A microprocessor based kit, such as Micro Friend – II kit manufactured by M/s. Dynalog Microsystems – Mumbai, can be used for controlling a stepper motor. In the system described below, Port *A* of 8255 PPI chip is configured as an output port, and lines PA0-PA3 are interfaced to the stepper windings as shown in Fig. 5.6. LD0-LD3 are LEDs meant for indication of winding energization. Driver transistor BC157 and power transistor 2N3055

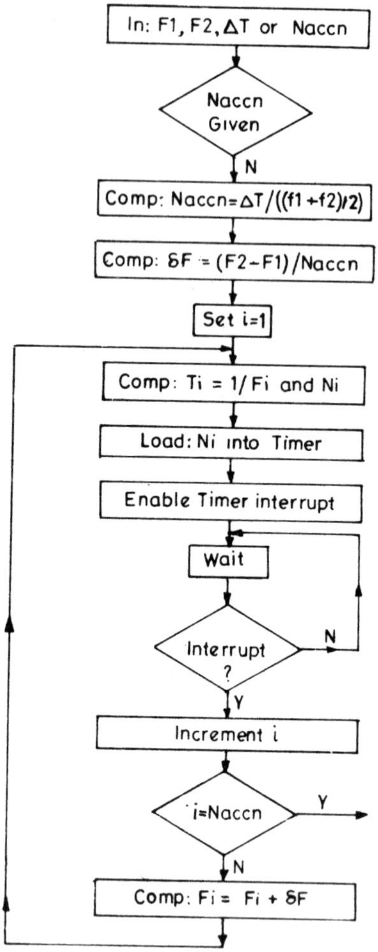


**Fig. 5.5** Acceleration Algorithm

constitute the power driver. Freewheeling diode BY126 is meant for current suppression.

Note that latches L0-L3 have been interposed between the PA0-PA3 lines and the power drivers. They are meant for isolation of the power driver circuit from the microprocessor control circuit. Such an isolation is a must in order to protect the microprocessor from faults like short circuits and open circuits as well as transients in the power driver circuit. Another and much better method of providing isolation would be to use opto-isolators as shown in Fig. 5.7.

The software for stepper motor control consists of the following major routines :

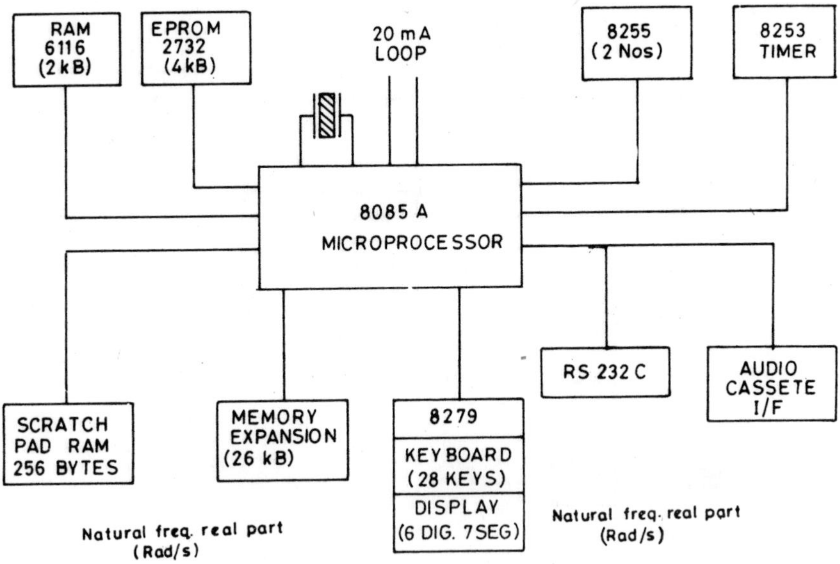


(a) Micro friend II : 8085A Microprocessor kit

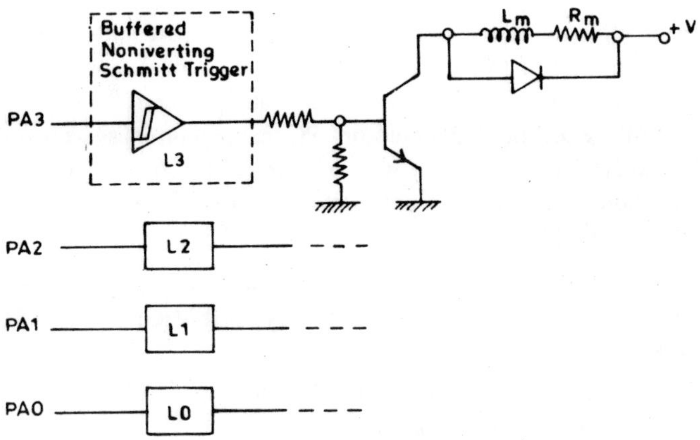


(b) Latch coupling

**Fig. 5.6** Stepper Motor Translator Algorithm

1. Initialization routine for setting up the system.
2. Rotate routine for running the motor.
3. ACCLN routine for automatic acceleration.
4. DECLN routine for automatic deceleration

Interested reader may contact the author for a listing of the above software.

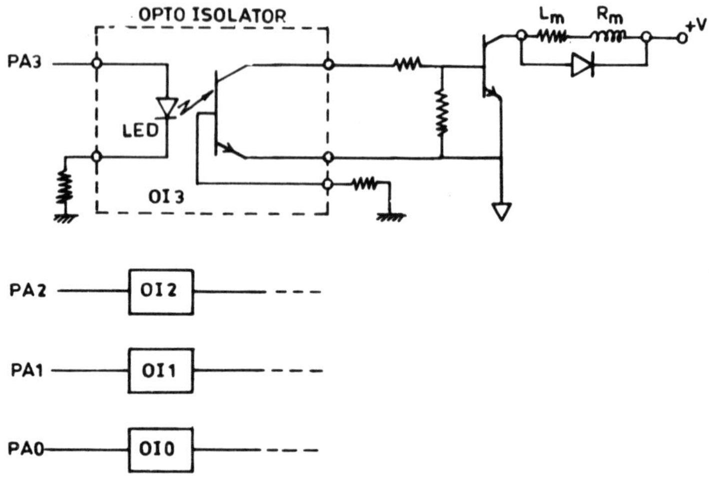


**Fig. 5.7** Opto Isolator Coupling

## 5.3 PC BASED STEPPER MOTOR CONTROLLER

Rapid technological advances in the last decade have resulted in popularization and proliferation of PC/AT's. It is, therefore, logical that PC's be used for stepper motor control. In fact, the much greater power of the PC can be utilized for controlling several stepper motors. PC manufacturers as well as PC add-on-cards makers have come out with add-on-cards capable of controlling 3-6 stepper motors. Such cards are convenient to use in 3-6 axis NC milling machines and lathes as well as 3-6 degrees of freedom robots.

As an example, the specifications for a commercially available PC add-on-card, PCL-211-E, manufactured by M/s. Dynalog Micro Systems Mumbai, are given below:

- Simultaneous control of 3 stepper motors
- Optoisolated motor control lines
- Complete control over steps, speed and direction, programmable initial speed
- Speeds from 1-4095 rpm (i.e. 3⅓ – 13650 steps/sec)
- 11 levels of acceleration/deceleration control
- Steps counts from 1-32767 steps
- Step position read-back facility
- Crystal controlled timing for high accuracy
- Wait state generation for communication with high speed PC/AT's

- On-board dedicated microcontrollers for independent control of each motor
- 8 digital input and 8 digital output lines.

## 5.4 COMMERCIAL STEPPER MOTOR CONTROLLER CHIPS/ BOARDS

In this action, we describe certain commercially available microprocessor based, stepper motor controllers.

### 5.4.1 "SRI-SYN" Electronic Step Motor Logic Controllers [3]

They are manufactured by M/s. Srijan Control Drives, Pune. They are meant to control upto 2 stepper motors. Their features are as follows:

*Model: Sri-Con-2260*

This is the low cost, low end model for the student and amateur. It has the following features:

1. Power ON/OFF Switch with Indicator
2. START/STOP Pushbuttons with 2 LED Indicators
3. Four Thumb wheel Switches for speed setting (steps/sec)
4. PUSH to MANUAL Pushbutton: the Motor Runs at a low speed as long as this Pushbutton is kept pressed
5. JOG/SLEW Pushbutton with 2 LED Indicators
6. JOG Pushbutton: the Motor Moves One Step per depression
7. HALF/FULL STEP Pushbuttons with 2 LED Indicators
8. STEP COUNT Setting with 8 Thumbwheels
9. INDEX/CONTINUOUS Pushbuttons with 2 LED Indicators
10. PANEL/REMOTE Pushbuttons with 2 LED Indicators.

*Step Count Setting*

8 Thumb wheels Index/CONTINUOUS Pushbuttons with 2 LED indicators. Panel/Remote Pushbuttons with 2 LED indicators.

*Model TS-881*

This is advanced and flexible model of controller, which is capable of controlling not only a pair of stepper motors but also a variety of digital devices. It processes the following characteristics:

1. Capable of controlling 2 Stepper Motors
2. 8 Opto-isolated Inputs for Interfacing Limit Switches, Encoder Inputs, A/D Converter Input, etc.
3. 8 Opto-isolated Outputs for controlling 8 Relays, Solenoids, Actuators, D/A converter, or 2 Stepper Motors
4. Battery backed RAM storing 12 Cycles of 64 Blocks Each

5. OPEN/CLOSED Loop Controls
6. 6-Digit Current Position Readout
7. INPUT/OUTPUT Status Indication
8. Manual Control
9. Remote Control through RS 232C Link.

### 5.4.2 Cybernetic Micro Systems Intelligent Stepper Motor Controller Chips

Cybernetic were one of the first to introduce stepper motor controller chips into the market [4]. They are CMOS 40-pin chips with features shown in Table 5.1. Their pin-out is shown in Fig. 5.8. Details of their interfacing to the stepper motor are shown in Fig. 5.8 (c).

### 5.4.3 SGS Thomsom Stepper Motor Controller Chip [5]

Their L297 and L298 combination of stepper motor controller and power drivers are widely used, and have become an industry standard. The features of L297/L297A, shown in Fig. 5.9, are as follows:

- Full/Half step Selection
- Normal/Wave Energization
- CW/CCW Direction Control
- Programmable Load Current
- Home (Open collector output indicating 'Home' state with A1, A2, B1, B2 = 0101)
- Reset Input (Restores Controller to 'Home' position)
- Load Current Sensing
- RC Oscillator/External Clock Inputs
- Pulse Double (L297A Only)

This Chip is used (in conjunction with monolithic bridge driver L298 shown in Fig. 5.10.

### 5.4.4 Galil Motion Control Co. Intelligent Motion Controller Chips [6]

These chips are meant to program simple moves from a local key-board using simple, high-level, user-friendly commands. Single Move Controller (DMC – 100): Can program a velocity profile shown in Fig. 5.11 as follows:

| Instruction | Comments |
|---|---|
| PR 4,000 | Distance = 4,000 encoder counts |
| SP 20,000 | Speed = 20,000 counts/sec |
| AC 200,000 | Acceleration = 200,000 counts/sec |

The encoder gives 2,000 counts/revolution.

**Table 5.1** Cybernetic Intelligent Stepper Motor Controller Chips

| *Type* | *CY512* | *CY525* | *CY545* |
|---|---|---|---|
| Max. Usable Stepping Rate (SPS) | 5,000 | 10,000 | 27,000 |
| Max. No. of Steps | 64K | 64K | 1.6M |
| No. of instruction in repertoire | 25 | 26 | 28 |
| Programme storage (bytes) | 48K | 60K | 64K |
| Acceleration | Exp. | Lin. | Lin. |
| Pulse and Direction Output | Y | Y | Y |
| Full Step | Y | Y | Y |
| Half Step | Y | 0 | 0 |
| Micro Step | N | N | 0 |
| Single Step (Jog Mode) | 0 | 0 | Y |
| Continuous Stepping | 0 | Y | Y |
| Constant Rate Stepping | Y | Y | Y |
| Ramped Stepping | Y | Y | Y |
| Low Power Standby | N | N | Y |
| Motor On/Off Output | N | N | Y |
| Limit Detection | 0 | 0 | Y |
| Serial Interface | N | N | Y |
| Parallel Interface | Y | Y | Y |
| Binary/ASCII Data | Y | Y | Y |
| Internal Stored Program | Y | Y | Y |
| Direct Command Mode | Y | Y | Y |
| Thumb Wheel Input/External Display Support | N | N | Y |
| Stand-Alone Operation | 0 | N | Y |
| Programmable Start Rate | 0 | Y | Y |
| Programmable Slew Rate | Y | Y | Y |
| Programmable Accel/Decel Slope | 0 | Y | Y |
| Programmable No. of Steps | Y | Y | Y |
| Home Seek Command | N | N | Y |
| Emergency Stop/Abort | Y | Y | Y |
| Decelerating Stop/Abort | Y | Y | Y |
| Close Loop Rate Control | Y | 0 | N |
| Motion Complete Indication | Y | Y | Y |
| Slow Indication | Y | Y | Y |
| Program Complete Indication | Y | Y | Y |
| On-the-Fly Rate/Position Change | N | Y | Y |
| Absolute/Relative Stepping | Y | Y | Y |

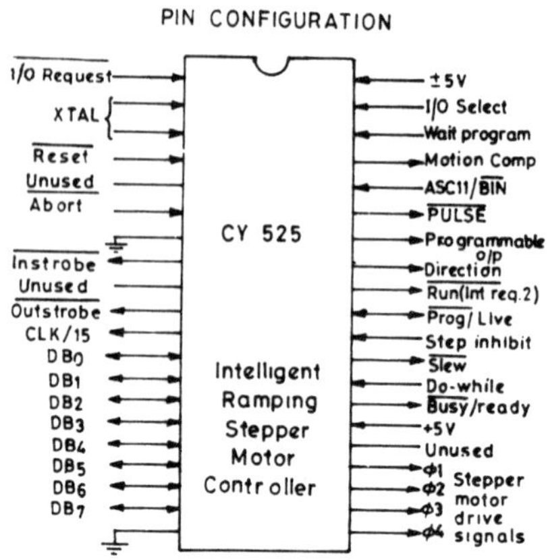


(a)

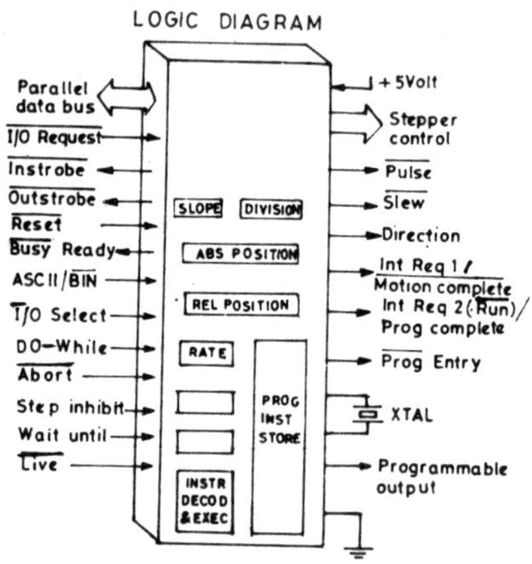


(b)

**Fig. 5.8** Cybernetic Stepper Motor Controller Chips

*Multiple Move Controller (DMC-201)*

A multiple move such as shown in Fig. 5.12 can be programmed easily as illustrated below:

| *Instruction* | *Comments* |
|---|---|
| PR 5000 | Distance = 5000 counts |
| SP 20000 | Speed = 20000 counts/sec |
| AC 200 000 | Acceleration = 200 000 counts/sec$^2$ |
| BG | Begin motion |
| AD 3800 | After moving 3800 counts |
| SP 5000 | Change speed to 5000 counts/sec |

Contd..

Contd...

| *Instruction* | *Comments* |
|---|---|
| AM | After completing the move |
| SB 01 | Set Output Bit |
| WT 50 | Wait for 50 msec |
| SB 00 | Reset Output Bit |
| PR 5000 | Distance = 5000 counts in Reverse |
| SP 200 000 | Speed = 200 000 counts/sec |
| BG | Begin motion |
| EN | End program |

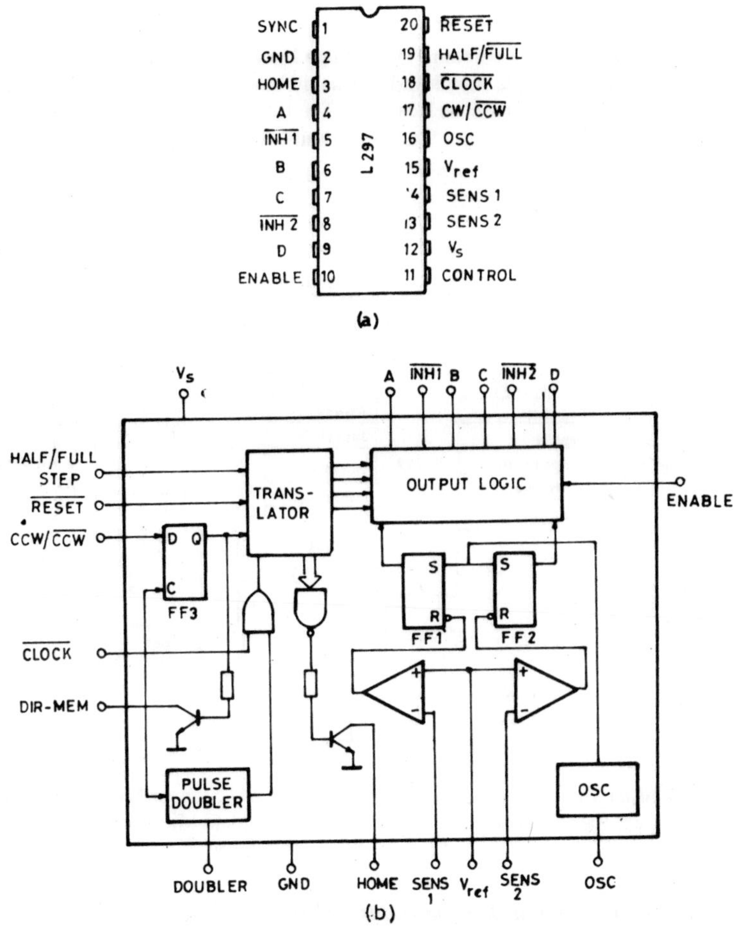


**Fig. 5.9** SGS - Thomson Stepper Motor Controller Chip L297

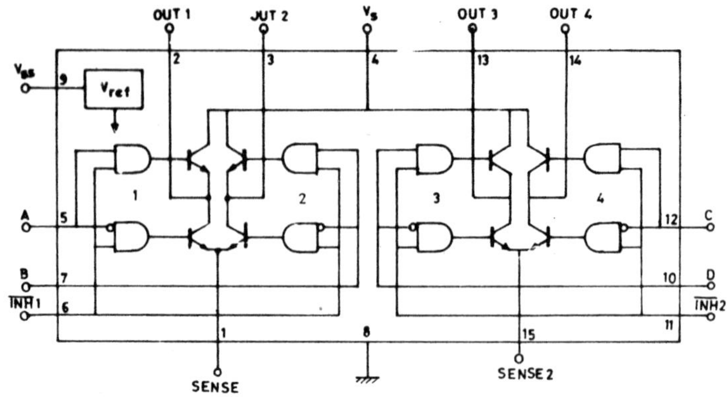


**Fig. 5.10(a)** The L298 contains Two Bridge Dirver (Four Push Pull Stages) Each Controlled by Two Logic Inputs and an Enable Input. External Emitter Connections are provided for Current Sense Resistors. The L293E has External Connections for all Four Emitters

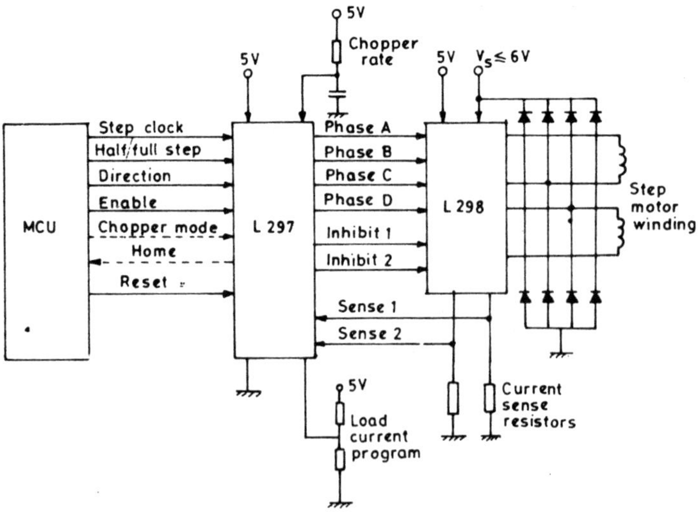


**Fig. 5.10(b)** In this Typical Configuration and L297 Stepper Motor Controller and L298 Dual Bridge Driver combine to form a Complete Microprocessor to Bipolar Step per Motor Interface

*Multi-Axis Coordination Chip (DMC-230)*

This chip is shown in Fig. 5.13. It controls two stepper motors as used in *X-Y* plotter or *X-Y* table. It has the capability of automatically generating St. lines,

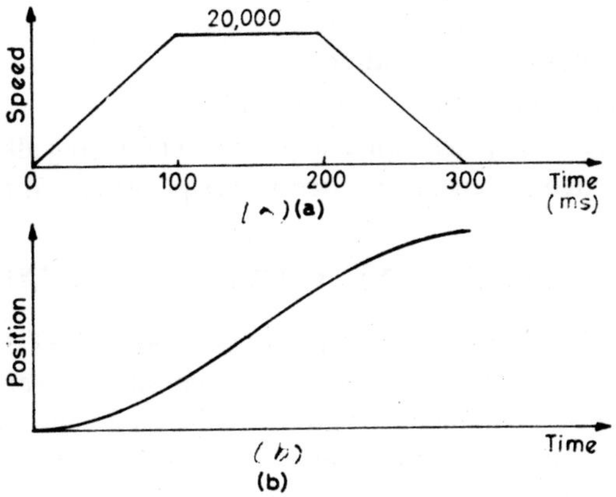


**Fig. 5.11** The Desired Velocity Profile (a) and the Corresponding Position Profile (b) for Galil Single Move Controller DMC-100

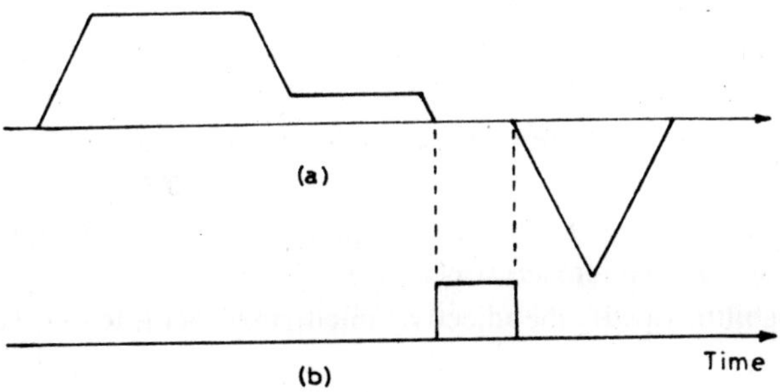


**Fig. 5.12** The Required Motion Sequence (a) and the Output Signal (b) for Galil Multiple Move Controller DMC-201

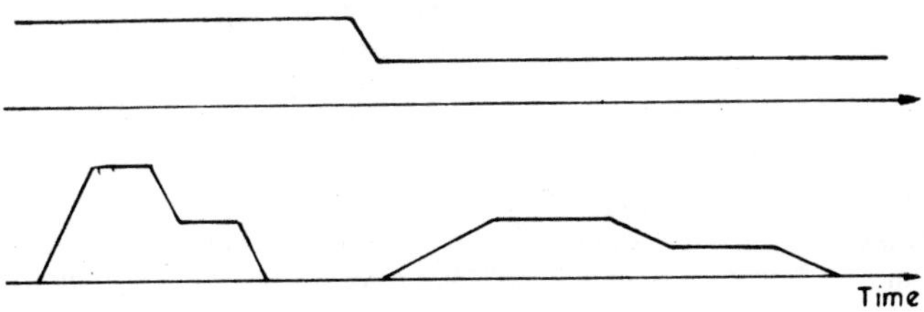


**Fig. 5.13** The Effect of the Meter Frequency (a) on the Motor Velocity (b). The Velocity is Proportional to the Master Frequency of Galil Multi Axis Coordinator DMC-230

circular arcs, parts of ellipse, parabola, hyperbola, etc. from given key information such as

(i) St. Lines: Coordinates of end-points, etc.

(ii) Circular arcs: End points, center and radius, etc.

This frees the host computer from computing and inputing all the points on the curve to be plotted or generated. Circular interpolation is also provided.

## 5.5 LOW COST 'INTELLIGENT' STEPPER MOTOR CONTROLLER

This section describes the versatile controller developed at IIT-Mumbai [ ]. It is based on Intel 8031, 8-bit, single chip microcontroller. The employment of 8031 reduces the chip count in the controller to the minimum and thus makes the controller low cost. The controller has the following capabilities:

1. Full step (2 phase on)/Half Step mode
2. Free running/Indexed mode
3. Jog
4. Home
5. Automatic acceleration/deceleration
6. CCW/CW direction control
7. Storage of upto 16 cycles of operation, each cycle consisting of indexing at constant speed or with automatic acceleration/deceleration.
8. Local programing through local hand-held keyboard and LED display
9. Remote programming through a serial link to PC/XT or AT.
10. Microstepping capability: Microstepping ratio: 4, 8 and 16; microstepping rate: 9600 microsteps/sec.

These capabilities justify the adjective 'intelligent' for the low cost controller developed.

Block diagram of this controller is shown in Fig. 5.14. The details of interfacing to the power driver are the same as in Fig. 5.1 (a). Software listings and details of hardware can be obtained by the interested reader from the author.

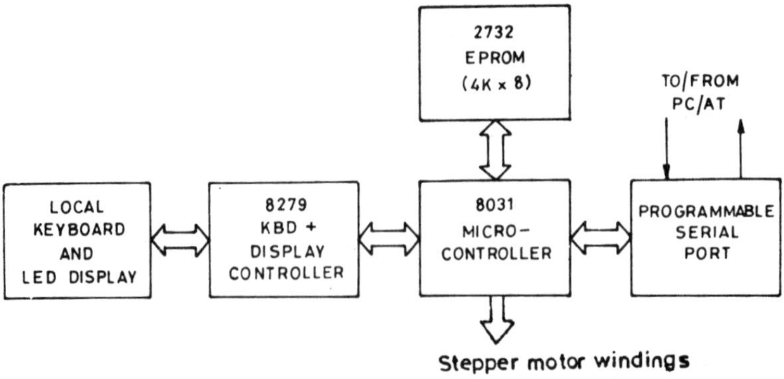


**Fig. 5.14** Block Diagram of Intelligent Controller

## 5.6 CEERI STEPPER MOTOR CONTROLLER CHIP

A versatile stepper motor controller chip is being designed by VLSI Group in CEERI Pilani [7]. It can be programmed locally through a keyboard or remotely by host computer. It is capable of tele-control of step motor, located far away, through 4-20 mA loop, a novel technique developed in CEERI. A brief description of this chip is given below.

The block diagram of the CEERI stepper motor controller chip is shown in Fig. 5.15(a). This can be programmed

(a) Locally through parallel port from

(i) Keyboard and display. (ii) local microprocessor, or (iii) EPROM.

(b) Remotely from a host computer through serial link.

The chip can be programmed for any of the four modes of operation:

**(i) Jog Mode** The motor runs at a very low stepping rate as long as the 'Jog' pushbutton is pressed. It is used for initialization to 'Home' or 'Reference' positions.

**(ii) Free run mode.** The motor runs continuously at the specified stepping rate in the desired direction until a 'stop' command is given.

**(iii) Indexed mode.** The motor covers a prescribed number of steps at a specified stepping rate in the desired direction. 'On the fly' change in stepping rate is possible.

**(iv) Profile mode.** Provides for velocity profiling, with smooth acceleration/deceleration, as shown in Fig. 4.16.

These modes are programmed by using appropriate program keys shown in Table 5.2. The methodology of programming is explained in Fig. 5.15 (b). This

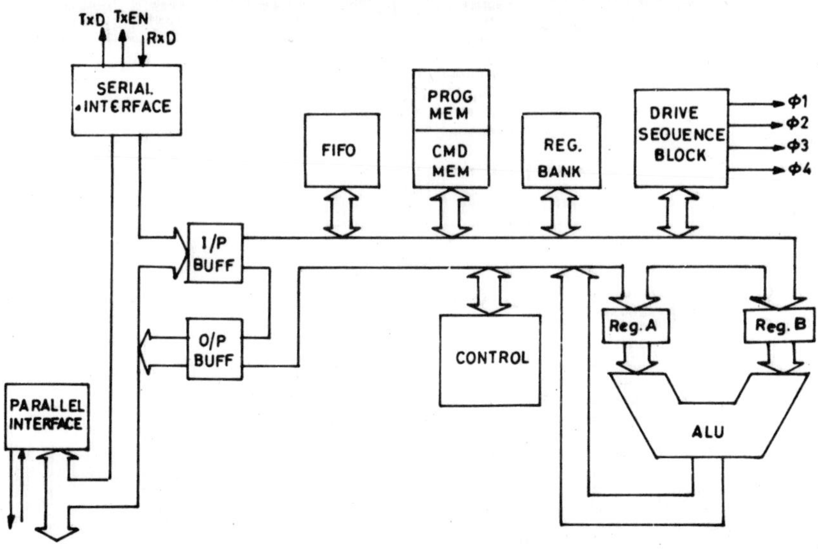


(a) Block Diagram

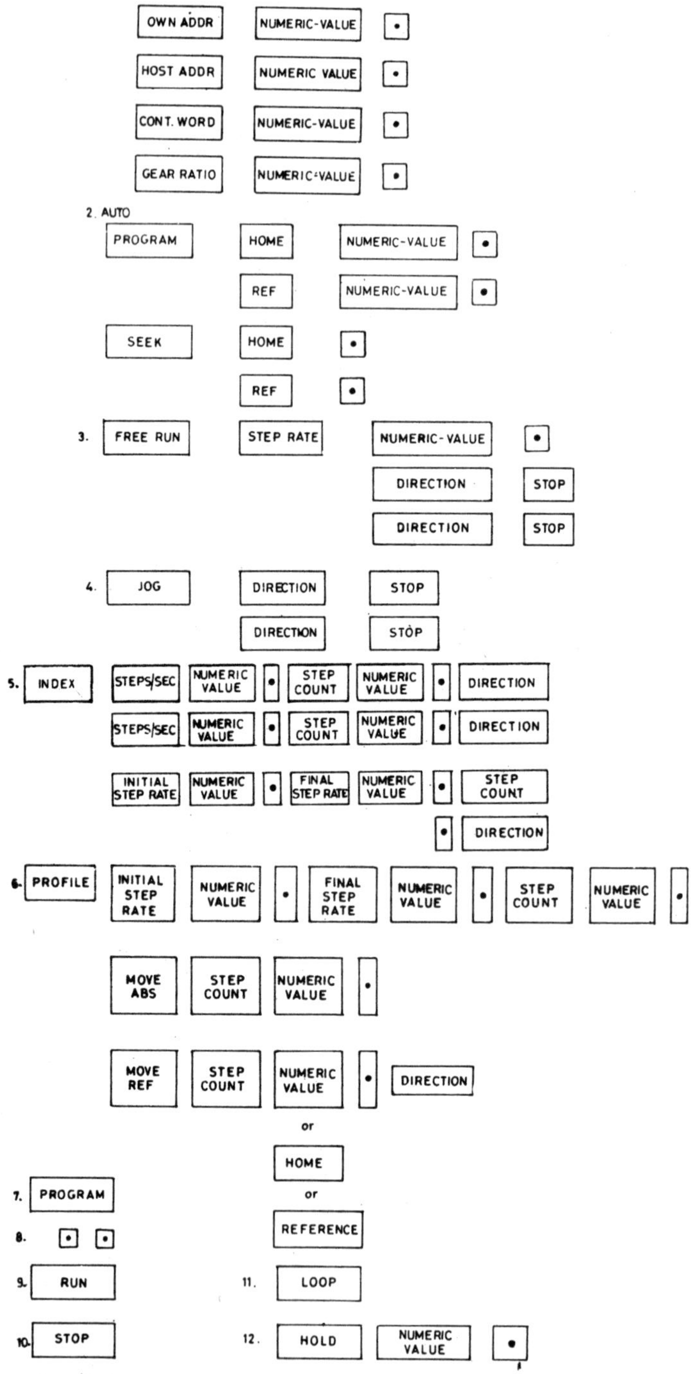


(b) Various Modes of Operation and How to Program them

**Fig. 5.15** ASIC for Stepper Motor Control Designed by CEERI (Pilani)

**Table 5.2** Keyboard for CEERI Stepper Motor Controller Chip

| *Program Keys* | *Parameter Keys* | *Execute Keys* |
|---|---|---|
| Control word | Step rate | CW |
| Gear ratio | Home | CCW |
| Progam | Ref. | STOP |
| Free run | Step cnt. | • |
| Profile | Max. Step rate | Run |
| Index | Loop | |
| Jog | Hold | |
| Seek | 0 | |
| Mov abs | 1 | |
| Mov ref. | 2 | |
| Own addr. | 3 | |
| Host addr. | 4 | |
| | 5 | |
| | 6 | |
| | 7 | |
| | 8 | |
| | 9 | |

is thus versatile and is suitable for application such as (i) process control, (ii) robotics, (iii) remote indication, (iv) numerical control of machine tools, computer peripheral control, etc.

This is the first time that such a versatile, user friendly, stepper motor controller chip is being developed in India. The author was consulted by the CEERI VLSI Group regarding features to be included so as to make the chip suitable for a wide class of users.

## 5.7 REMOTE CONTROL OF STEPPER MOTORS

This is another contribution to stepper motor control technology made by CEERI [8]. It would be interesting to know the background, so that we appreciate both the stepper motor control problem and its solution.

During the past decade, CEERI has pioneered the development of microprocessor based, multi-channel, data acquisition and control system (DACS) for sugar mills in general and the critical pan boiler portion in particular. In this DACS, process variables are sensed by transducers; electropneumatic control valves are used for controlling the process inputs, these control valves being actuated by stepper motors. Although the transducers and control valves are situated in or near the process, the control computer is located at a safe distance from the process. Hence the transducers transmit data to the control computer via 4-20 mA serial link. The question facing DACS designers was whether the same 4-20 mA loop could also be employed for actuating the stepper motors which actuate the control valves. The present development shows how this could be accomplished.

Figure 5.16 (a) shows the schematic diagram of system. The required form of analog or digital control signal, in the range of 4-20 mA, is generated by DACS and is transmitted over 4-20 mA loop to terminals *X* and *Y* of the remote end detector, which generates signals *D* and *S* for direction and stepping, depending on which of the four configurations is used. Signals *D* and *S* are applied to the stepper motor through local logic sequence generator and power driver.

One of the four configurations developed is shown in Fig. 5.16 (b). Here in the control signal sent by DACS over the 4-20 mA loop contains two pieces of information: (i) number of steps to be moved, and (ii) direction. The number of steps is proportional to absolute value of deviation of the current from the mean value of 12 mA (corresponding to 3 V) across the 250 ohms resistor). The direction of rotation depends on the sign of this deviation.

When triggered by sync. trigger pulse, monostable MS1 produces a pulse at *A* of a fixed width corresponding to the mean value of 12 mA or 3 V. Monostable MS2 is triggered simultaneously with MS1. It produces a pulse of variable duration at *D*. The pulse width *D* is proportional to the absolute deviation of actual current from nominal value of 12 mA, i.e. to the control signal. Exclusive 'OR'ing of *D* with *A* produces signal *C*. This signal *C* is 'AND'ed with local clock signal $f_0$ having the same frequency and phase as DACS clock frequency. The pulses so generated are applied to the local stepper motor controller.

Let $F_0$ (kHz) be the frequency, $\gamma$ be the monostable conversion factor (ms/mA), $n$ be the maximum number of bits of the *D*/*A* converter and $\Delta I$ be the control current range (mA). Then we have the relation

$$\gamma = (2^n - 1)/(\Delta I \,.\, f_0)$$

Thus for $f_0 = 1$ kHz, $\Delta I = 16$ mA, and $n = 8$ bit D/A converter, we get $\gamma = 15.9375$ ms/mA. Maximum number of steps in one sampling period is limited to 127 steps.

The main advantage of this circuit is that only one control signal is required to be transmitted by the DACS over the 4-20 mA loop. This simplicity of data transmission over the remote link is counter balanced by greater complexity of hardware at the remote end.

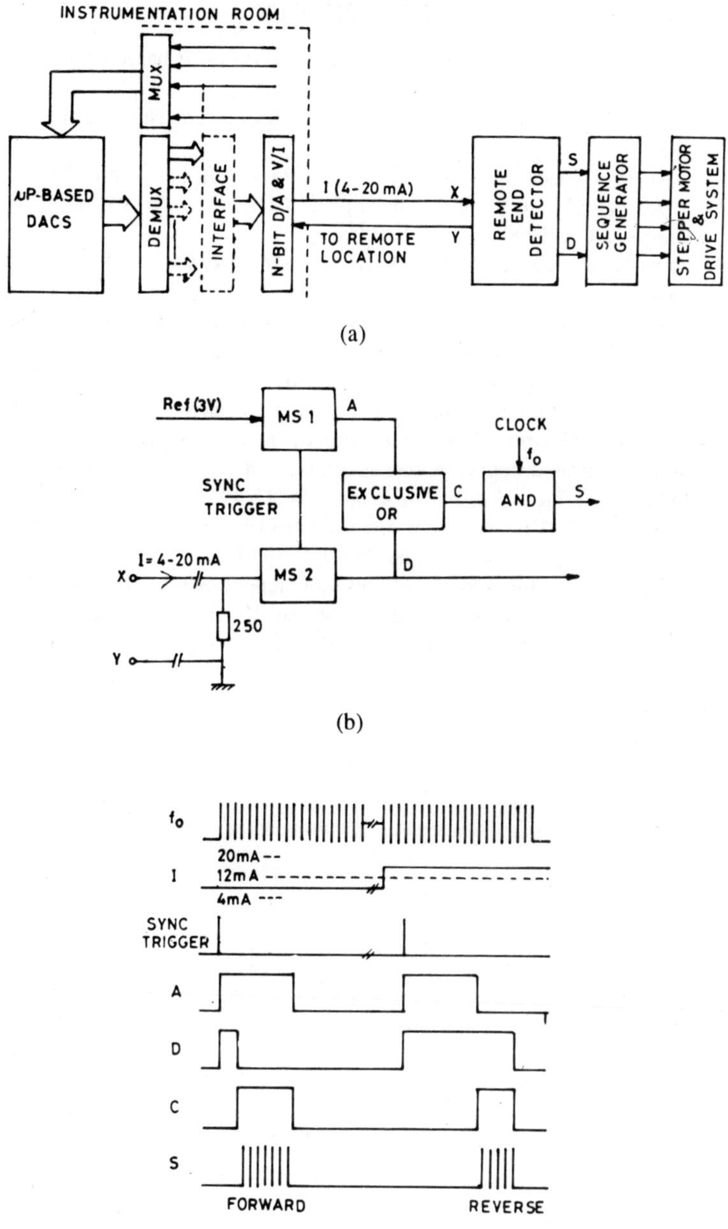


**Fig. 5.16** CEERI Remote Control of Step Motor via 4-20 mA Loop (a) Schematic Diagram of µP-based Multichannel DACS for Driving Stepper Motors as Actuators (b) Schematic diagram of the remote end detector (c) detector waveforms for forward and reverse motions

## REFERENCES

1. Kenjo, T., 'Stepping motors and their microprocessor based controls', Oxford University Press, Oxford, 1984.
2. Gopal, M. 'Digital control engineering', Wiley Eastern, New Delhi, Chapter 12, 1987.
3. 'SRI-SYN' Electronic step motor logic controller, Srijan Control Drives, Pune.
4. 'Cybernetic Micro System Control IC's', Cybernetic Micro Systems, Inc., San Gregoica, CA, 1990.
5. 'Data Book on Power Linear Actuators', (2/e), SGA - Thomson, pp. 219-234, 1984..
6. Tal, J. and Baron, W, 'Intelligent Motor Controllers', Proc. Annual Symposium on IMCSD, pp. 53-59, 1985..
7. Rao, K.V.S.H, Ms. Kausal, A., Sriniwas, M. Rao, Ch.V.N.S.N. Chandrashekhar. 'An ASIC for high performance stepper motor control', (Communicated), 1992.
8. Sing, H. and Sharma, S.M. 'Some novel $\mu P$-Based configurations for controlling remotely located stepper motors as actuators of control valves', IEEE Trans. on Indus Electronics, Vol. 38, No. 4, pp. 283-287, 1981.
9. Athani, V.V. 'Universal step motor controller indexer', Microprocessors and Microsystems, Vol. 4, No. 7, pp. 253-258, 1980.
10. Athani, V.V. 'Microprocessor control of stepper motors', Electronics for You, Vol. 17, Part I: March 1985, pp. 20-24; part II. April 1985, pp. 59-62, Part III: May 1985, pp. 45-47; Part IV: May 1986, pp. 60-61, 1980.

# CHAPTER - 6

# *Microstepping Control of Stepper Motors*

A new principle, called microstepping control, has been developed for control of stepper motors. This chapter is devoted to a study of the microstepping principle and its implementation.

## 6.1 INTRODUCTION

As we know, the stepper motor is an incremental actuator, which moves in steps of $\theta_s°$ in response to input pulses. Such incremental motion results in the following inherent limitations of the stepper motor.

**1. Limited resolution.** Inasmuch as $\theta_s°$ is the smallest angle through which the stepper motor can move, this has an effect on positioning accuracy of incremental servo systems employing stepper motors, because the stepper motor cannot position the load to an accuracy finer than $\theta_s°$. This limitation on positioning accuracy is felt in fine positioning systems such as *X-Y* plotters, NC systems, robotics, etc.

**2. Mid-frequency resonance.** A phenomenon in which the motor torque suddenly drops to a low value at certain input pulse frequencies, as shown in Fig. 3.6.

A new principle, known as microstepping control, has been developed with a view to overcoming the above limitations. It enables the stepper motor to move through a tiny microstep of size $\Delta\theta° << \theta_s°$, the full step angle, in response to input pulses. It is explained in the next section.

## 6.2 THE MICROSTEPPING PRINCIPLE

Assume that we are operating the stepper motor in "one phase on" sequence defined in Table 4.1. Assume also that only B2 winding is on and carrying current $I_{B2} = I_R$, the rated phase current. All other windings are off. In this state, the stator magnetic field is along the positive real axis as shown in Fig. 6.1(a). Naturally, the rotor will also be in $\theta = 0°$ position.

**Table 6.1** 8 Steps Per Step Sine/Cosine

| *MICROSTEP No.* | *% Phase A AMPS* | *% Phase B AMPS* |
|---|---|---|
| 0 | 0 | 100 |
| 1 | 19.51 | 98.08 |
| 2 | 38.27 | 92.39 |
| 3 | 55.56 | 83.15 |
| 4 | 70.71 | 70.71 |
| 5 | 83.15 | 55.56 |
| 6 | 92.39 | 38.27 |
| 7 | 98.08 | 19.51 |
| 8 | 100 | 0 |

When the next input pulse comes, B2 is switched off while A1 is switchea on. In this condition, $I_{A1} = I_R$, with all other phase currents = 0. As a result, the stator magnetic field rotates through 90° (elec) in CCW direction as shown in Fig. 6.1 (a). The rotor follows suit by rotating through 90° (elec) or $\theta_s°$ (mech) in the process of aligning itself with stator magnetic field.

Thus with the conventional controller (FSC), the stator magnetic rotates through 90° (elec) when a new input pulse is received, causing the rotor to rotate through a full step, $\theta_s°$ (mech).

However, in microstepping control, we want the stator magnetic filed to rotate through a small angle $\theta << 90°$ in response to an input pulse. How this can be achieved is illustrated in Fig. 6.1(b). We modulate current through B2 and A1 windings in such a way that

$$I_{B2} = I_R \cos\theta \tag{6.1a}$$

while

$$I_{A1} = I_R \sin\theta \tag{6.1b}$$

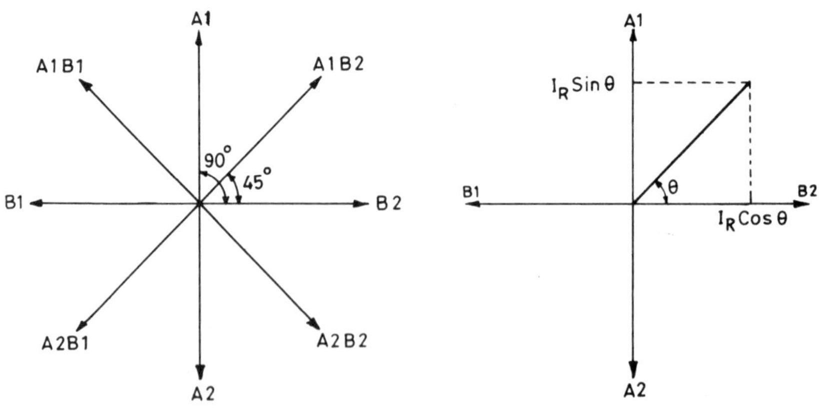


(a) Conventional (b) Microstepping

**Fig. 6.1** Principle of Microstepping

Then the resulting stator magnetic field will be at an angle θ° (elec) w.r.t. the positive real axis. Consequently, the rotor will also rotate through an angle θ° (elec) which << 90° (elec), corresponding to mechanical rotation through angle Δθ° which is << $\theta_s°$ , the full step angle.

This method of modulating currents through stator windings so as to obtain rotation of stator magnetic field through a small angle θ° (elec) to obtain microstepping action is known as the microstepping principle enunciated first by Fredrikssen [1]. Table 6.1 gives the ratios: $I_{B2}/I_R$ and $I_{A1}/I_R$, to cause rotation through $\theta = (1/8)\,\theta_s$ per input pulse. Table 6.2 shows the currents the stator windings to obtain microstepping action in all four quadrants.

**Table 6.2** Sequence in which Sine/Cosine Generators are to be Applied to step Motor Windings for Microstepping Direction Control in all Four Quadrants

| *Direction of rotation* | *Quadrant for this direction* | *Quadrant as per standard convention* | *Motor winding* | | | |
|---|---|---|---|---|---|---|
| | | | *A1* | *A2* | *B1* | *B2* |
| CCW | I | I | sine | | | cos |
| | II | II | sine | | cos | |
| | III | III | | sine | cos | |
| | IV | IV | | sine | | cos |
| CW | I | IV | | sine | | cos |
| | II | III | | sine | cos | |
| | III | II | sine | | cos | |
| | IV | I | sine | | | cos |

Note that, although currents $I_R \cos\theta$ and $I_R \sin\theta$ are flowing through individual stator windings, their resultant is $I_R$. The resulting stator magnetic field has the same magnitude as in Fig. 6.1. Consequently the stepper motor develops the same torque as developed under 'one-phase on' sequence. There is no reduction in motor torque on account of microstepping.

If we wish to have the same torque as in 'two phase' on mode, the magnitudes of the currents through the motor windings should be such that

$$I_A^2 + I_B^2 = 2 \tag{6.2}$$

## 6.3 ADVANTAGES OF MICROSTEPPING

The main advantages of microstepping control are:

(a) Improvement in resolution by the factor MSR (microstepping) ratio

$$\text{MSR} = \theta_s/\Delta\theta \tag{6.3}$$

inasmuch as the smallest angle through which the motor rotates per input pulse is

$$\Delta \theta = (1/\text{MSR}) . \theta_s \tag{6.4}$$

Usual values of MSR are 5, 10, 125, and in powers of 2 upto 128.

(b) Rapid motion at a microstepping rate ($MF_s$) which MSR times the full stepping rate ($F_s$).

Thus $M_{FS} = \text{MSR} . F_s$ (microsteps/sec) (6.5)

(c) DC motor like performance : under microstepping control, the stepper motor moves rapidly at microstepping rate $M_{FS}$ (step/sec) in tiny microsteps of size $\Delta \theta°$. The resulting motion is so smooth that it is practically indistinguishable from continuous motion of the DC motor. In this way, the dividing line between continuous motion of the DC motor and incremental motion of the stepper motor under microstepping control in getting obliterated.

(d) Elimination of mid-frequency resonance: again, on account of smooth and rapid motion under micro-stepping control, mid-frequency resonances are not excited.

## 6.4 HISTORY OF MICROSTEPPING CONTROL

As mentioned above, microstepping principle was introduced by Fredrickssen in 1975 [1]. He enunciated the basic microstepping laws (6.1) and (6.2). He also gave the basic configuration of MSC shown in Fig. 6.2. Pritchard [2-5] has done pioneering work in the development of practical MSCs. He first developed the *Anastepping driver* [3] which was analog MSC. He then came out with *Metis drive* [4] which was a hybrid analog plus digital unit. He finally developed *ATHENA-11 drive* [5] which was a computer controlled MSC. In the mean while, *Layer* [6] reported development of digital sine/cosine generator.

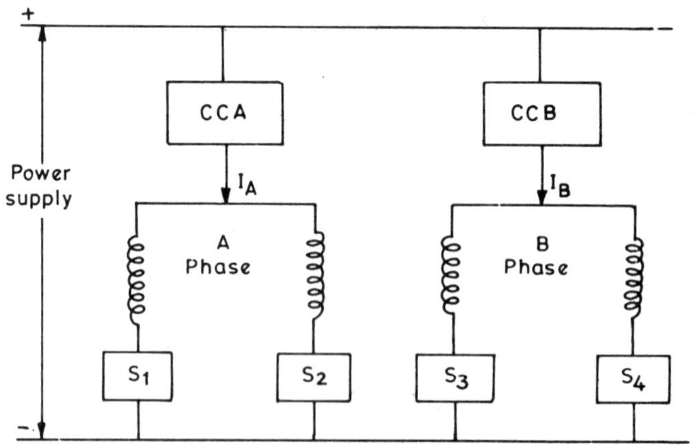


CC = Current Controller S = Switch

**Fig. 6.2** The Microstep Principle

The first commercial model of MSC to be introduced in the market was '*Modulynx*' controller by The Superior Electric Co. in 1983 [7], followed by the current '*Micro*' series controller in 1987 [8]. Sigma instrument brought their 38000 '*Sigmax*' microstepping system to the market in 1986 [9]. Other manufacturers such as Aerotech [10] and Portescap Company of Switzerland [11] followed suit with their models of MSCs.

Meanwhile, advances in the theory of MSC were reported in literature. For instance, Leenhouts [12-14] showed that the simple sine/cosine law for modulating phase currents, stated by Fredrksen, does not result in equidistant microsteps. Leenhouts analyzed factors such as harmonics, nonlinearities, etc. affecting the size of microsteps. He gave computer program for estimating their effects and to compute modified sine/cosine values which would ensure equidistant microsteps [13]. Determination of parameters required for the programs has been discussed by Leenhouts [14], Rahman and Poo [15].

Research on MSCs was initiated in IIT-Bombay in 1986. It has led to the development of the basic MSC in 1987 [19] followed advanced MSC [20]. Finally, a high performance MSC has been developed in 1988 [21], incorporating advanced features discussed above for ensuring equidistance microsteps.

## 6.5 DESIGN OF BASIC MICROSTEPPING CONTROLLER

We now describe a simple MSC meant for demonstrating the principle of microstepping and the advantages thereof. This system is thus meant for the student and the hobbyist, rather than the professional.

### 6.5.1 Systems Design

Since it is meant for the student to learn the fundamentals of microstepping the specifications of the basic MSC are quite modest:

Microstepping ratio : 4, 8, 16

Microstepping rate : 5.6 kHz

Rated voltage and current : 12 V, 2.5 A/phase.

The system is based on the popular 8085 A based microprocessor system. The block diagram of the system is shown in Fig. 6.3. Its hardware consists of 8085 A based microprocessor kit, DACs, multiplexers and power drivers. It is described on next page.

### 6.5.2 Microprocessor Kit

Micro Friend II microprocessor kit, manufactured by M/s Dynalog Micro System, Pune (India) has been employed in our basic MSC. It consists of 8085A CPU operating at 3 MHz, 4 K × 8 monitor ROM, 2 K × 8 RAM, two 8255A parallel I/O chips, a 8253 timer chip, 24 key keyboard and 6-digit 7-segment LED display as shown in Fig. 6.4.

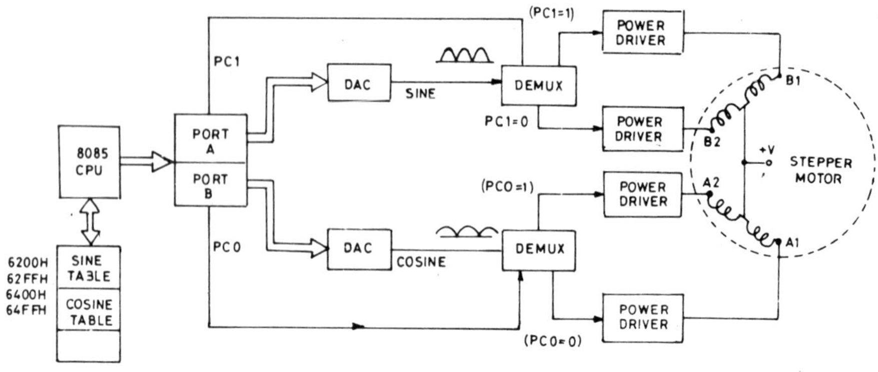


**Fig. 6.3** Block Diagram for Basic form of Microstepping Controller

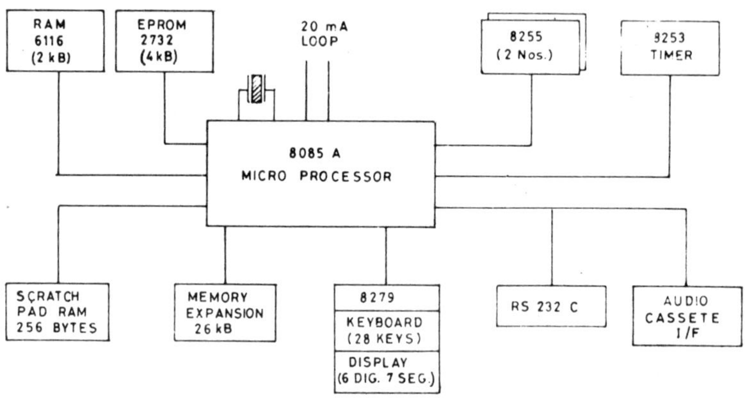


**Fig. 6.4** Block Diagram for Micro-Friend II Kit

### 6.5.3 Sine/Cosine Generator

Currents in the *A* and *B* windings of the stepper have to be modulated as per sine/cosine law of Eqn. (6.1). This is accomplished by storing 64 point sine and cosine values in the 2732 EPROM chip as a look-up table. They are output on the 8255A ports A and B. Port C is made use of for control purposes.

### 6.5.4 DAC and Multiplexers

Sine/Cosine values, received from the look-up table on PA and PB lines, are in the form of numerical code. They must be converted into analog voltages for application to stepper motor windings. This task is performed by two DACs, 1408. These are 8-bit microprocessor compatible DAC's. One DAC is used for controlling A1-A2 windings, while the second DAC controls B1-B2 windings.

The task of directing the DACs to the proper windings is performed by the demultiplexers shown in Fig. 6.3.

### 6.5.5 Power Drivers

A typical power driver employed for driving rated current through the stepper motor winding is shown in Fig. 6.5. It consists of a Darlington pair, made up of transistors 2N3970 and 2N3055. It is capable of driving 2.5 A current through the stepper motor winding. Current sensing resistor R1 gives current feedback to LM101. As a result, the output current in the motor winding exactly reproduces the input voltage. In this way, the power driver is essentially a voltage-to-current (V/I) converter.

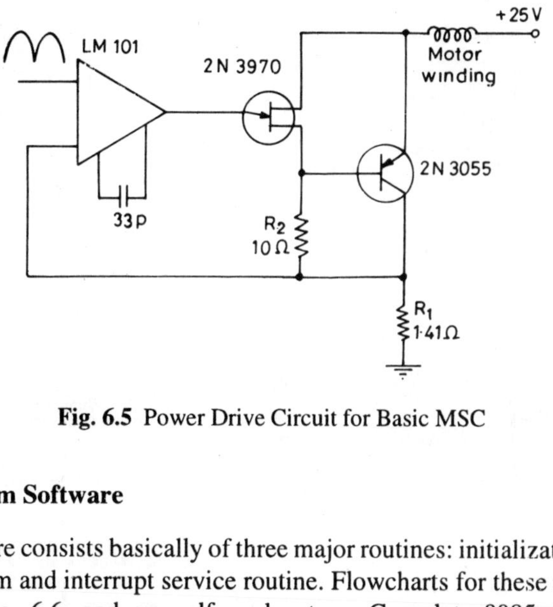


**Fig. 6.5** Power Drive Circuit for Basic MSC

### 6.5.6 System Software

MSC software consists basically of three major routines: initialization routine, main program and interrupt service routine. Flowcharts for these routines are shown in Fig. 6.6, and are self explanatory. Complete 8085 A assembly language software listing can be obtained from the author. Starting addresses for routines for generating stepping routes ranging from 50 to 350 full steps/sec are given in Table 6.3.

### 6.5.7 Experimental Results

The basic MSC has been fabricated in the form two PCBs. It has been tested on Step-Syn stepper motor, model STM 901, manufactured by M/s Srijan Control Drives, Pune (India). The torque vs. microstepping rate curve obtained is shown in Fig. 6.7. For convenience, the stepping rate is shown in full steps/sec rather than microsteps/sec. It is seen that the motor runs upto 350 full steps/sec rate with microstepping ratio of 8.

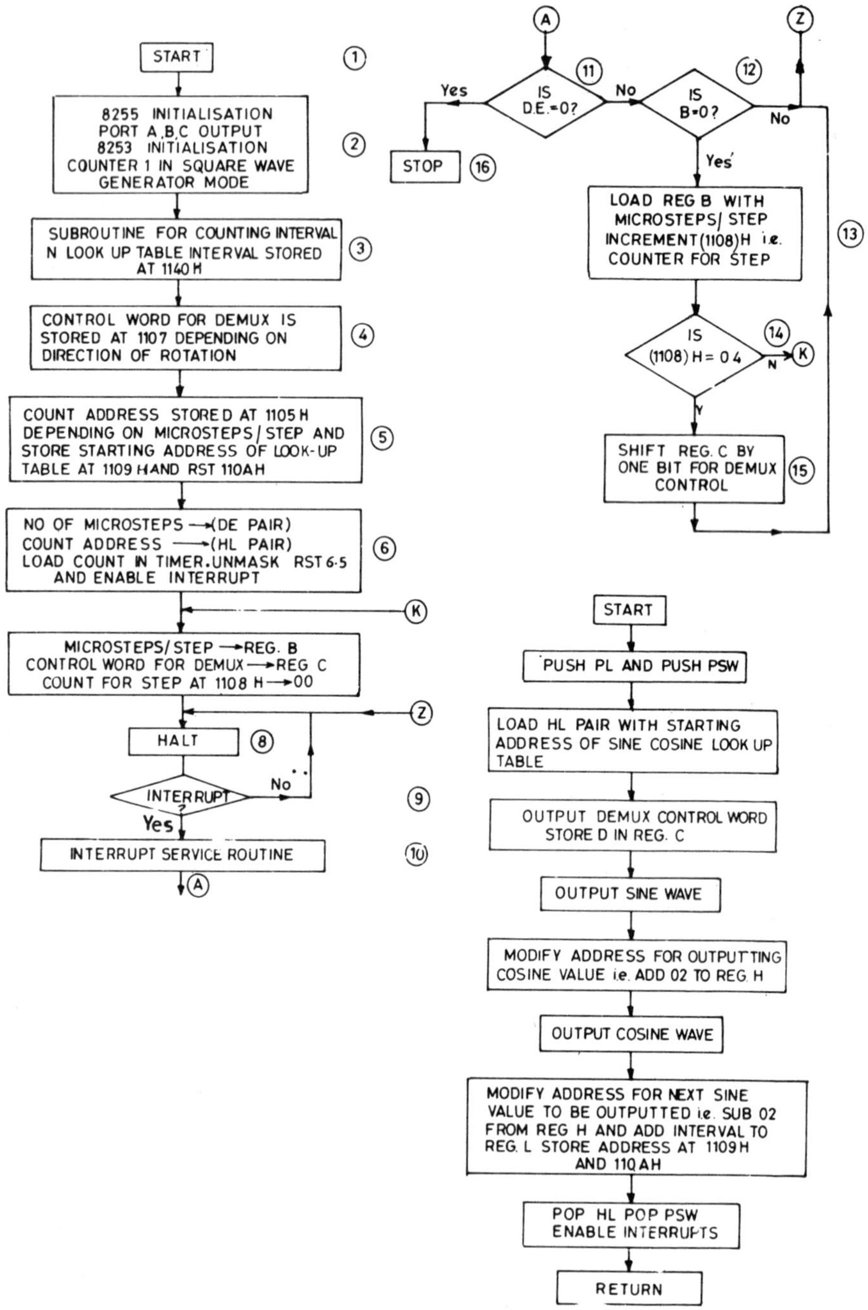


**Fig. 6.6** Software for Basic MSC

**Table 6.3** Starting Addresses for Various Stepping Rates for Basic MSC

| *Stepping rate (steps/sec)* | *Starting address of count table* |
|---|---|
| 50 | 6300H |
| 75 | 630AH |
| 100 | 6314H |
| 200 | 631EH |
| 225 | 6328H |
| 250 | 6332H |
| 300 | 6336H |
| 325 | 6346H |
| 350 | 6350H |

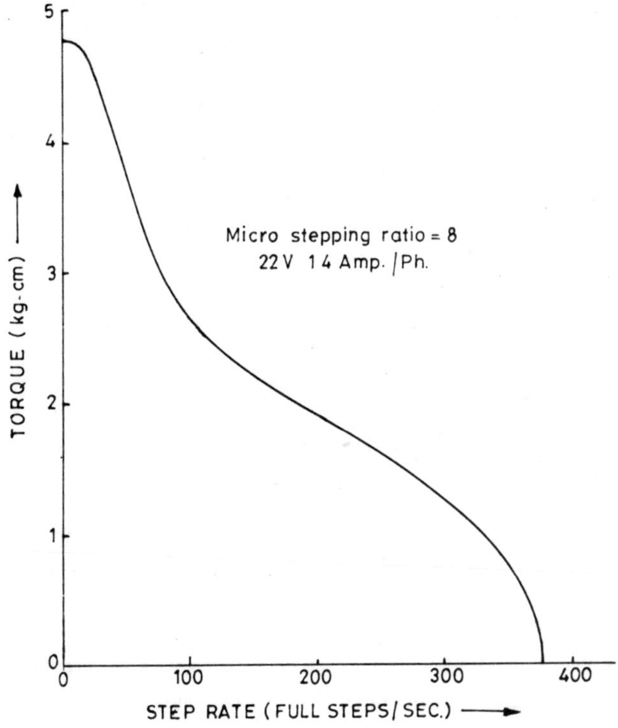


**Fig. 6.7** Pull Out Curve

## 6.6 HIGH PERFORMANCE MICROSTEPPING CONTROLLER (HPMSC)

We now describe the HPMSC developed at IIT-Bombay. This MSC is meant for the professional inasmuch as its performance compares very well with the best of the MSCs available in the market. It also incorporates advanced features meant to ensure equidistance microsteps.

### 6.6.1 System Design

Figure 6.8 shows the block diagram of our high performance MSC (i.e. HPMSC). It consists of the following main blocks: pulse generator, digital sine/cosine generator, power drivers and control unit.

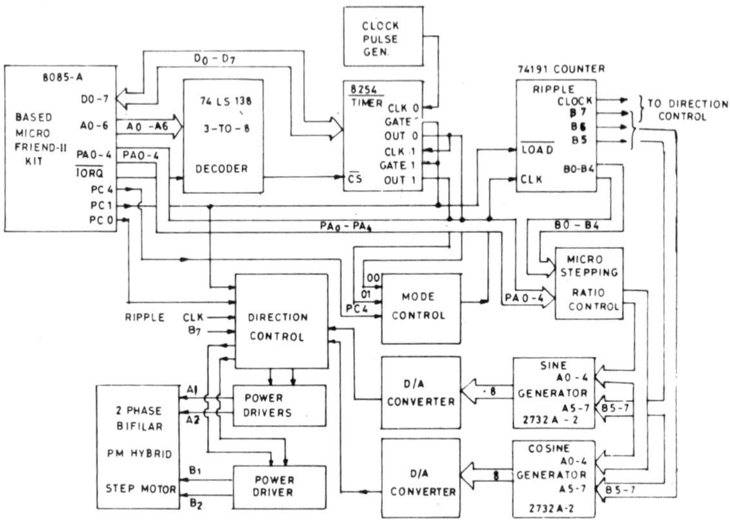


**Fig. 6.8** Block Diagram of High Performance Microstepping Controller (HPMSC)

The high switching rates of 3 MHz, encountered in HPMSC, are beyond the capability of 8 bit and even 16 bit microprocessors. Consequently, HPMSC has been implemented with the help of high speed digital ICs. The question that comes to mind is: What is the lowly 8085 based microcomputer, shown in Fig. 6.8 doing? The answer is: it meant for initial setting of microstepping ratio (MSR), microstepping rate ($MF_s$), microstepcount ($N_{ms}$) and direction of rotation. Once these settings have been made, HPMSC operates entirely off the hardware shown in Fig. 6.9.

With this introduction to its architecture, we are now ready for a discussion of the important blocks of the HPMSC.

### 6.6.2 Pulse Generator

As seen from Fig. 6.9, the pulse generator is built around 8254 timer chip, clock pulses to which are derived from 6.144 MHz crystal. Counter '0' is meant for generating pulses at the specified microstepping rate, while counter '1' contains

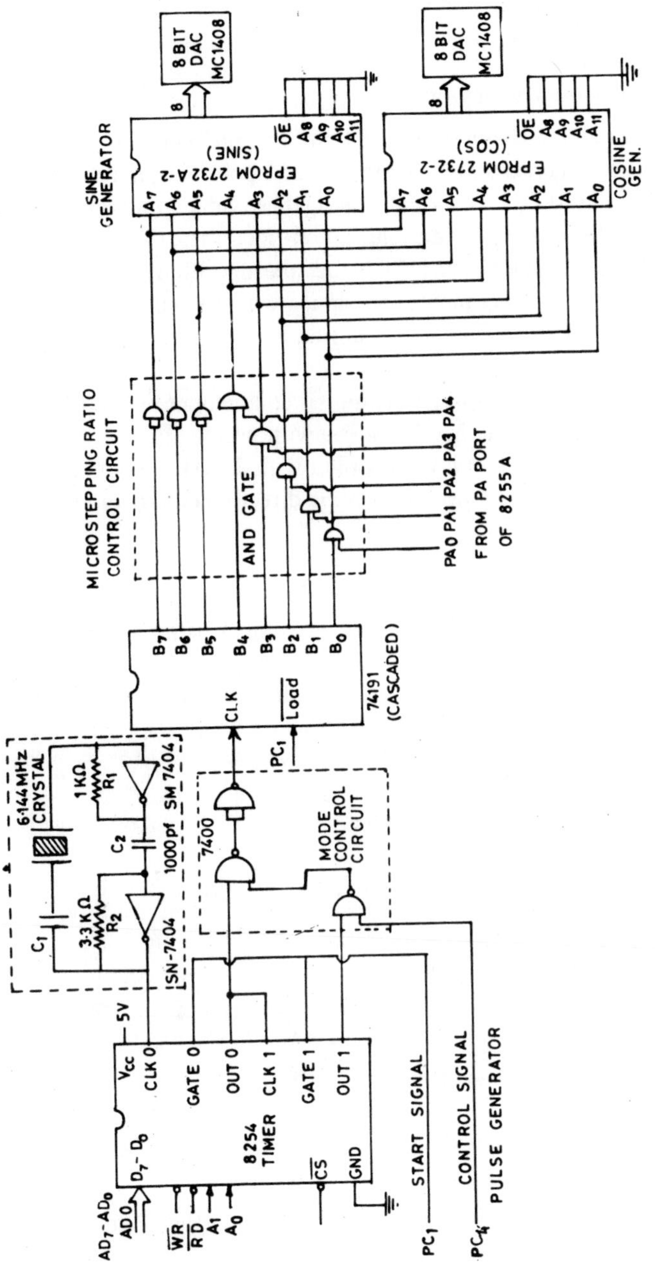


Fig. 6.9 HPMSC System Hardware

the microstep count $N_{ms}$. In the free running mode, pulses are continuously output from counter '0' output. On the other hand, in the indexed mode, only $N_{ms}$ pulses are output by counter '1'. Output of the pulse generator goes to sine/cosine generator via microstepping rate control circuit.

### 6.6.3 Sine/Cosine Generator

A pair of 2732A-2, having access time of 200 nanosecs, constitute the sine/cosine generator, as shown in Fig. 6.9. 256-point sine and cosine tables are stored in these EPROMs. While calculating these values, due consideration has been given to the effects of harmonics, non-linearities, detente torque, variations of stiffness constants, etc. [17]. In fact, the algorithms given by Leenhouts [18] have been used to compute the values which would ensure equidistant microsteps. The motor parameters required by the algorithm have been computed as outlined in [19, 20].

DACs are required to convert the digital code output by the EPROMs into voltages. Ultrafast DACs, MC1408-7N, with a conversion time of only 70 nanosecs, are used with a view to coping with 3 MHz switching frequency. DAC output is fed to the power drivers via direction control circuit.

### 6.6.4 Power Drivers

Fig. 6.10 shows typical power driver circuit. It consists of power MOSFET, IRF Z42, driven by NE5532. Current sensing resistor $R$ provides current feedback. Consequently, the power driver behaves as V/I converter. It causes current in the concerned step motor winding to faithfully reproduce the sine/cosine voltage variations its input end.

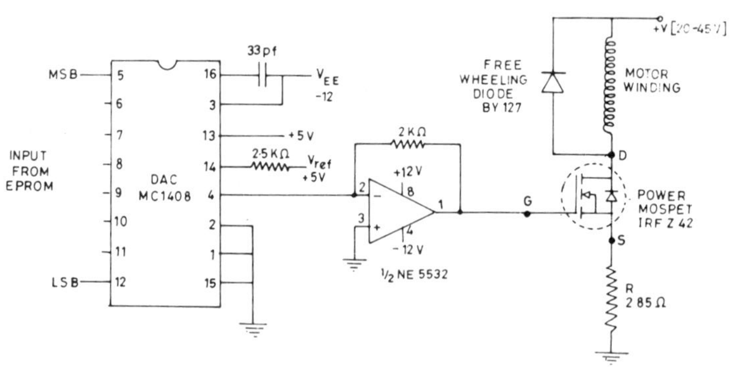


**Fig. 6.10** D/A Converter Inverter and Power Driver of High Performance MSC

### 6.6.5 Control Circuit

Four controls are provided in HPMSC. They are briefly discussed below.

*6.6.5.1 Microstepping Rate Control*

Is obtained by loading a count corresponding to time period, $T_{ms} = 1/MF_s$, where $MF_s$ is microstepping rate in Hz. This count is loaded into counter '0' via data bus A0-A7 of the microcomputer.

*6.6.5.2 Mode Control Circuit*

Consists of three NAND gates in conjunction with PC4 line from the microcomputer as shown in Fig. 6.9, when PC4 = 0, pulses from output '0' are passed on to 74191 irrespective of the count held in counter '1'. This is the *free running mode*, in which the step motor microsteps continuously. The motor can be stopped by disabling the counter gates by making PC1 = 0.

On the other hand, let us assume that a counter $N_{ms}$ is loaded into counter '1' and PC4 = 1. Then only $N_{ms}$ pulses from the output of counter '1' will be applied to 74191. This constitutes the *indexed mode*. Count $N_{ms}$ loaded into counter '1' is called the microstep count.

*6.6.5.3 Microstepping Ratio Control Circuit*

Shown in Fig. 6.9 consists of counter in conjunction with five AND gates. The desired microstepping ratio is set by loading a suitable bit pattern on lines PA0-PA4 of the PA port. Suppose PA0 = 0. Then pulses coming on lines 'B0' of 74191 are blocked by AND gate '0'. Consequently, alternate addresses input to sine/cosine generator are skipped, and hence MSR = 64 is realized. Other MSRs are similarly obtained. The bit patterns required to be loaded on the lines in order to obtain various MSRs are listed in Table 6.4.

**Table 6.4** Microstepping Ratios, Control Inputs and Max. Microstep Count for High Performance MSC (HPMSC)

| *Microstepping ratio* | *Control input (HEX NOS.)* | *Max. micro steps* |
|---|---|---|
| 128 | FF | 65,536 |
| 64 | FE | 32,768 |
| 32 | FC | 16,384 |
| 16 | F8 | 8,192 |
| 8 | F0 | 4,096 |
| 4 | E0 | 2,048 |

*6.6.5.4 Direction Control Circuit*

The principle of direction control is illustrated in Table 2.0 = 0° (elec) corresponds to IB2 = $I_m$ and IA1 = 0, where $I_m$ = rated current. For a rotation through + 0° (elec) in CCW direction, IB2 = $I_m \cos\theta$ while IA1 = $I = I_m \sin\theta$. This shows that cosine generator output ought to be applied to B2 winding while sine generator output s applied to A1 winding, as long as θ is in the first quadrant. Table 6.2 shows the winding to which sine and cosine generator outputs should be applied four all for quadrants.

On the other hand if we want rotation through θ° (elec) in CW direction, we have IB2 = $I_m \cos\theta$ and IA2 = $I_m \sin\theta$. Table 6.2 shows to which winding sine and cosine generator output ought to be applied to cause CW rotation in all four quadrants.

Note that θ° (elec) rotation in CW direction corresponds to a rotation of 360° – θ° rotation in CCW direction. As a result, I quadrant for CW rotation is IV quadrant for CCW direction, and so on.

Implementation of direction control is illustrated in Fig. 6.11. PC0 from the microcomputer is the direction control line. PC0 = 0 causes CCW rotation, whereas PC = 1 corresponds to CW motion. Reversal of direction causes inversion of control signal for cosine wave. It causes reversal of the sequence of addresses in EPROMs wherefrom sine and cosine values are output to appropriate windings. To illustrate this concept, suppose we are at address '$n$' in EPROMs. Then, in order to continue rotation in CCW direction, we go to addresses '$n + 1, n + 2, \ldots$'. On the other hand if we wish to reverse the direction of rotation, we output contents of addresses $n - 1, n - 2, \ldots$. Reversal of direction is thus smooth and trouble free.

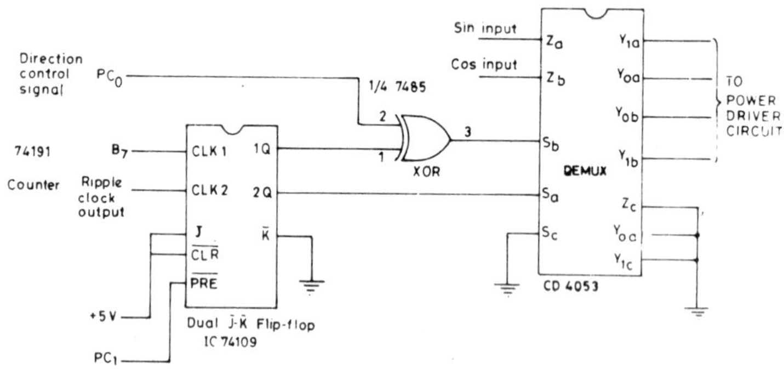


**Fig. 6.11** Direction of Rotation Control Circuit of HPMSC

*6.6.5.6 System Software*

As stated above, the 8085-based microcomputer is meant for initial setting only. Consequently, system software is limited to initialization only, and is shown in Fig. 6.12 which is self explanatory. Once intialization is over, the system operates off the hardware.

### 6.6.6 Fabrication and Testing

*6.6.6.1 Fabrication*

The HPMSC system has been fabricated in the form of two PCBs:

**(i) Logic card:** Containing pulse generator, sine/cosine generators, DACs, and control circuits.

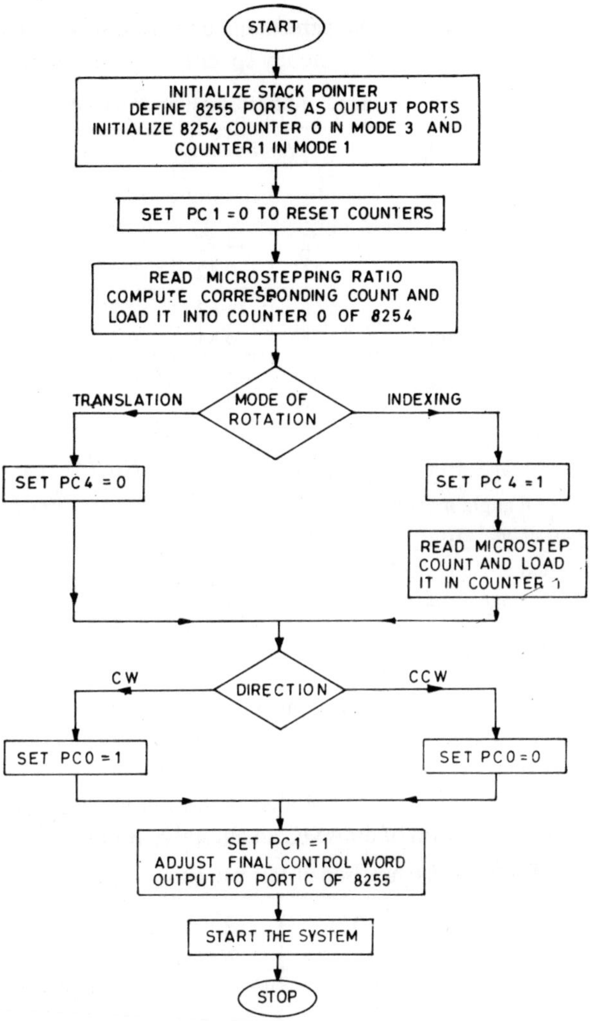


**Fig. 6.12** Flow Chart of Control Scheme of HPMSC

**(ii) Power card:** Contains power MOSFETs, NE5532, freewheeling diodes and current sensing resistors.

### *6.6.6.2 Accuracy Test*

Various tests have been carried out on the HPMSC. Two of them need special mention. The first test is *accuarcy test,* in which a 10-turn servo potentiometer is connected to step motor shaft. HPMSC is programmed for various rotations through both CCW and CW directions. The servopotentiometer output is measured with the help of a 5-1/2 digit DVM. Actual rotation so measured is compared with set values, and error between them is computed. Table 6.5 gives the results obtained. Note that the percentage error of 0.022-3.78% are within the step angle accuracy of ± 5% accuracy specified by the manufacturer.

**Table 6.5** Accuracy of Microstepping Controller

| *Micro-stepping ratio* | *Observations* | *Nominal angle to be moved (degrees)* | | | | |
|---|---|---|---|---|---|---|
| | | *9* | *45* | *90* | *180* | *360* |
| 128 | Actual angle moved<br>Percentage error | 8.72<br>3.11 | 44.72<br>0.62 | 89.12<br>0.98 | 179.12<br>0.49 | 359.87<br>0.04 |
| 64 | Actual angle moved<br>Percentage error | 8.66<br>3.78 | 44.62<br>0.84 | 89.39<br>0.68 | 180.44<br>– 0.24 | 361.62<br>– 0.45 |
| 32 | Actual angle moved<br>Percentage error | 9.08<br>– 0.89 | 43.93<br>2.38 | 88.89<br>0.12 | 180.28<br>– 0.16 | 360.69<br>– 0.19 |
| 16 | Actual angle moved<br>Percentage error | 9.10<br>– 1.11 | 45.36<br>– 0.80 | 90.07<br>– 0.078 | 180.17<br>– 0.094 | 360.23<br>– 0.064 |
| 8 | Actual angle moved<br>Percentage error | 9.10<br>– 1.11 | 45.27<br>– 0.60 | 88.08<br>1.02 | 179.49<br>0.28 | 359.52<br>0.13 |
| 4 | Actual angle moved<br>Percentage error | 8.70<br>3.33 | 44.69<br>0.69 | 88.98<br>0.022 | 179.85<br>0.083 | 359.51<br>0.14 |

## 6.7 CONCLUSION

A high performance microstepping controller, HPMSC, has been successfully developed. Comparison of its performance with available MSCs is shown in Table 6.6. It is seen that out HPMSC compares favorably with commercially available MSCs. Its simplicity, combined with high performance, makes its implementation in the form of an ASIC an attractive proposition.

**Table 6.6** Comparison of Microstepping Controllers

| *Sr. No.* | *Manufacturer* | *Model No.* | *Microprocessing* | | *Rated V and I per phase* |
|---|---|---|---|---|---|
| | | | *Ratio* | *Rate* | |
| 1. | Superior Electric Co. | 3180-P1/125 | 125, 10, 5, 2 | 1.25 kHz | 6.5 V, 3 A |
| 2. | Superior Electric Co. | IMD 128 | 128, 100, 10, 5 | 640 kHz | 5 V, 2 A |
| 3. | Sigma Instruments | Sigmax 3800 | 20, 10 | 200 kHz | 7.5 A |
| | | 3075 A | 20, 10, 5, 2 | 200 kHz | |
| 4. | Aerotech. | Dynacron 4000 | 250 | 1 MHz | 48 V, 3-6 A |
| | | 6006 | up to 250 | 1 MHz | 60 V, 6 A |
| | | 8005 | up to 250 | 1 MHz | 80 V, 10 A |
| 5. | Escape (Switzerland) | ESC-100 | 64, 32, 16, 8, 4 | 500 kHz | 5 V, 5 A |
| 6. | I.I.T. Bombay | Basic MSC | 16, 8, 4, 2 | 5.6 kHz | 12 V, 2.5 A |
| | | Advanced MSC | 128, 64, 32, 16 | 1.28 kHz | 12 V, 2.5 A |
| | | High Performance MSC (HPMSC) | 128, 64, 32, 16, 8, 4 | 3 MHz | 16-45 V 1.4A |

## REFERENCES


1. T.R. Fredriksen, "Microstepping – A New Concept for Rotary Step Motors", Proc. 4th Annual Symp. on IMCSD, pp. HH1-HH6, 1975.
2. E.K. Pritchard, "Ministepping Motor Drives", Proc. 5th Symp. on IMCSD, pp. Q1-Q11, 1976.
3. E.K. Pritchard, "Analog Operation to Stepper Motors", Proc. 6th Symp. on IMCSD, pp. 283-295, 1977.
4. E.K. Pritchard, "Concepts and Characteristics of Ministepping", Proc. 9th Symp. On IMCSD, pp. 229-242, 1980.
5. E.K. Pritchard, "ATHENA-11: A Computer Motion Control system using Ministepping Stepping Motor Drives", Proc. 10th Symp. on IMCSD, pp. 243-254, 1981.
6. H.P. Layer, "Digital Sine/Cosine Ministepping Motor Drive", Proc. oth Symp. on IMCSD, pp. 176-185, 1977.
7. "Modulynx Motor Control", The Superior Electric Co., Bristol, CT, Catalog No. SE-L-8321, 1983.
8. "Slosyn Micro Series Step Motor Drives and Programmable Motion Controls", The Superior Electric Co., Bristol, CT, Catalog No.SE-L-6871, 1987.
9. "38000 Sigmax Microstepping Systems", Sigma Instruments Inc, Braintree, MA, Catalog No. MC 252-9186 R, 1986.
10. "Positioning Systems and Laser Accessories Handbook", Aerotech Inc., Pittsburgh, PA, Catalog No. K-US-675-986, 1986.
11. "Escap Motion Systems", Protescap US Inc., Happauge, NY., 1986.
12. A.C. Leenhouts, "Compensation Techniques in Microstepping". Proc. 15th Symp. on IMCSD, pp. 175-180, 1986.
13. A.C. Leenhouts, "The Art and Practice of Microstepping", Intertec Communications Inc., Ventura, CA., 1986.
14. A.C. Leenhounts, "Measuring Step Motor Parameters for Microstepping", Proc. 16th Symp. on IMCSD, pp. 183-187, 1987.
15. M.F. Rahman, and A.N. Rao, "Application Oriented Test Procedure for Designing Microstepping Step Motor Controllers", IEEE Trans. on Indus. Electron., Vol. IE-35, no. 4, pp. 542-546, 1988.
16. S.R. Rampurkar, "Design of Microstepping Controller for Stepper Motor", M.Tech. Thesis, I.I.T. Bombay, 1987.
17. N.N. Kolte, "Microprocessor Based Controller for Stepper Motors", M. Tech. Thesis, I.I.T. Bombay, 1988.
18. B.C. Kuo, "Microstepping for Step Motors", Incremental Motion Control Systems Society, Champaign, IL (USA), 1990.
19. V.V. Athani, "Micro Stepping Control". Electronics for You, vol. 22, no. 8, pp. 64-66, 1990.
20. V.V. Athani, "Microstepping Controller for Stepper Motors", I.E.T.E. Tech. Rev., vol. 6, no. 3, pp. 157-162, 1989.
21. V.V. Athani, "High Performance Mircostepping Controller Operates at 3 MHz", Power Conversion and Intelligent Motion (PCIM) Magazine (USA), vol. 19, no. 4, pp. 17-25, 1993.

# CHAPTER - 7

# *Stepper Motor Applications*

The stepper motor is a digital actuator which requires input in the form of pulses and which responds by rotating in discrete angular steps. As a result, it is eminently suited for use in digital, numerical and computer control systems. Consequently, it finds wide application. Our aim in this chapter is to get acquainted with some of these applications.

Stepper motor applications may be divided into the following classes:

(a) Instrumentation (low torque applications)

(b) Computer peripherals and office equipment (medium torque, high performance, high volume applications)

(c) Numerical control of machines tools and robotics (high torque applications)

(d) Electromedical (high torque applications)

(e) Miscellaneous

We discuss some of these applications.

## 7.1 INSTRUMENTATION APPLICATIONS

These are essentially low torque applications in which the torque ranges from a few gm-cm to a maximum of 1 kg-cm. Typical examples of such applications are; quartz watches, remote camera shutter operations, clocks on railway platforms, mechanical D/A converter, etc.

### 7.1.1 Quartz Watches [1]

Figure 7.1 shows how a tiny stepper motor is utilized in a quartz watch. In a tvpical watch of this type, a stable oscillation at $2^{15}$ Hz is produced by a crystal oscillator. This high frequency is brought down to 1 Hz with the help of frequency dividers. This signal is amplified and applied to the stator winding of a tiny stepper motor to drive it at half a rev/sec. The rotor of this motor carries a REC permanent magnet of about 1.5 mm dia. Since this motor rotates always in forward direction, a single phase salient pole motor is adequate, the whole assembly consisting of the crystal oscillator, frequency divider, stepper motor and its controller is compact enough to be housed inside the watch.

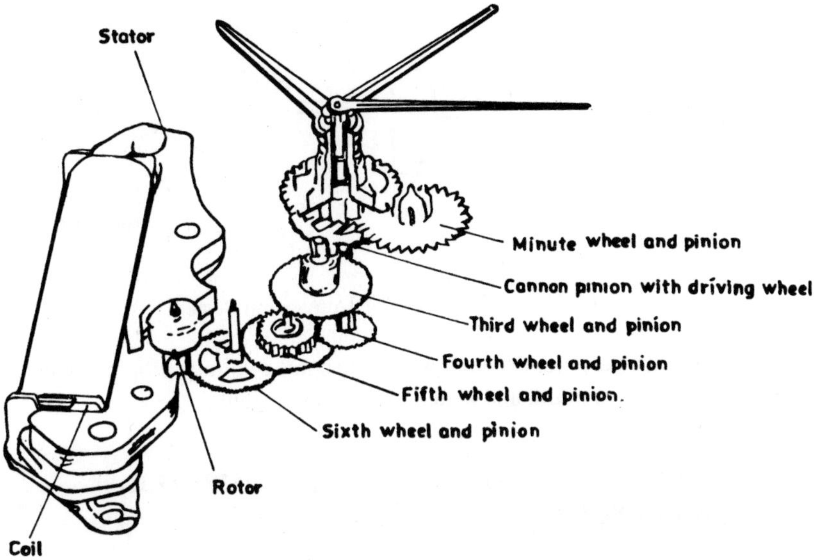


**Fig. 7.1** Principle of the Watch Employing a Single Phase Stepping Motor. (By Courtesy of Citizen Watch Co., Ltd.)

Tiny stepper motors for this application were first manufactured by M/s Portescap of Switzerland. They are now being manufactured by a few firms in Japan also.

### 7.1.2 Synchronized Clocks

Instead of using regular electric or mechanical or electronic clocks on railway platforms, in factories and large office buildings, it is much cheaper to employ synchronized clocks. There is one accurate crystal controlled clock in, say, the watch and ward office, whereas all others are slave clocks employing stepper motors. The master transmits one or two pulses per sec. On receipt of these pulses, the stepper motor advances by one step/pulse. This causes the minute and hour hands to advance through suitable gearing. In this way, an economic solution is achieved.

### 7.1.3 Camera Shutter Operation

Remote control is required in TV and movie cameras which are operated by remote control. Tiny two phase stepper motor of a few gm-cm torque rating are located inside the camera itself. Remote control signal is conveyed by an armoured connecting cable.

### 7.1.4 Mechanical Converter (D/A)

A stepper motor is connected to a potentiometer or synchro as shown in Fig. 7.2. The signal to be converted has to be in the form of pulses applied to the motor controller. The motor responds to the pulses by rotation through step angle $\theta_s$.

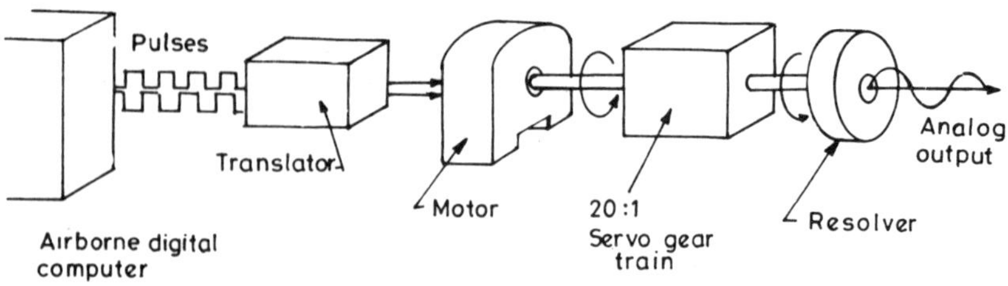


**Fig. 7.2** Digital-to-analog Conversion System

The output from the potentiometer will be an analog voltage proportional to the number of pulses applied, and hence to the digital signal.

## 7.2 STEPPER MOTOR APPLICATION IN COMPUTER PERIPHERALS

This important class of application of stepper motors is characterized by the phrase 'high performance high volume'. The motors employed in this application have medium torque rating (1 to 2 kg-cm). However, they must be capable of developing high speed upto several thousand steps/sec. Special designs of stepper motors have been brought out by manufacturers to cater to this market. In addition to performance, cost is also an important criterion since these motors are utilized by thousands.

### 7.2.1 Dot Matrix and Line Printers

A typical line printer is shown in Fig. 7.3 in which the stepper motor is used in paper advance mechanism. An AC motor is used for actuating the print hammers.

### 7.2.2 Floppy Disk Drive [3]

Fig. 7.4 shows this application. The stepper motor positions the read/write magnet on the specified sector of the disk. The motor is coupled to a lead screw which is integral with the motor. The head carriage moves forward or backwards, and can be positioned to an accuracy of ± 0.001″.

The head step time is 10 ms plus 10 ms settling time.

### 7.2.3 Digital X-Y Plotter

Two stepper motors are utilized in this application : one for carriage drive and the other for pen assembly drive. The pen motor is often carried on the carriage. The pen motor must therefore be as light as possible. Precision ball screws are employed for ensuring accuracy and elimination of backlash. Positioning accuracies of ± 0.1 mm and plotting speeds of 100 points/sec are required.

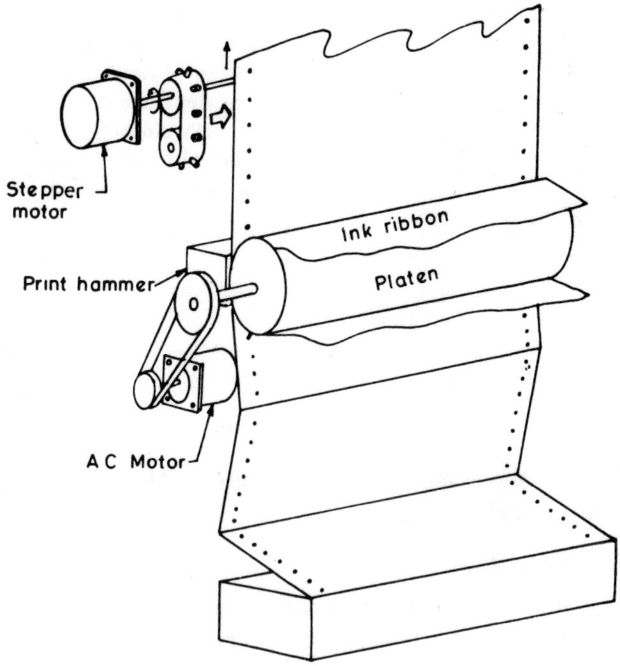


**Fig. 7.3** Line Printer

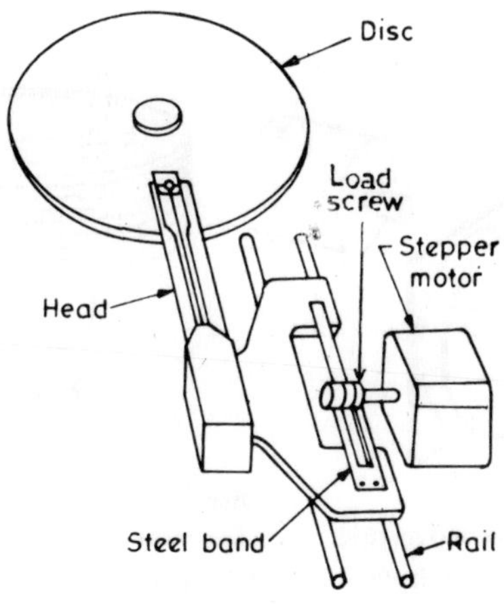


**Fig. 7.4** Floppy Disc Drive

### 7.2.4 Magnetic Tape Transport [3]

A typical magnetic tape transport system is shown in Fig. 7.5 (a). The internal drive mechanism appears in Fig. 7.5 (b). The magnetic tape runs smoothly between disks A and B at a typical speed 33 inches/sec. Frequent starts and

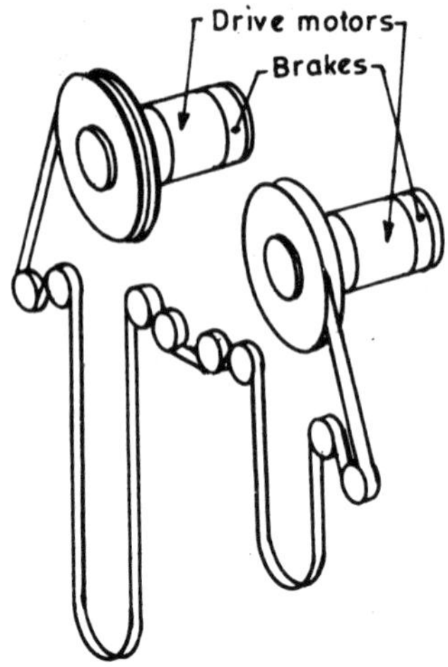


**Tape Transport**
Simple friction brakes working at a fraction of rated volts provide smooth consistent tape deceleration and long life. No cinching of faulting is encountered and periodic brake adjustments are not required

**Fig. 7.5** Magnetic Tape Transport

stops are encountered in this drive which is provided by two identical stepper motors as shown in Fig. 7.5 (b).

### 7.2.5 Paper Tape Drive [3]

This drive is used for reading or punching paper tape. A stepper motor is coupled directly to the tape drive as shown in Fig. 7.6. A reading speed of 500 characters/sec and a punching speed of 100 characters/sec are needed.

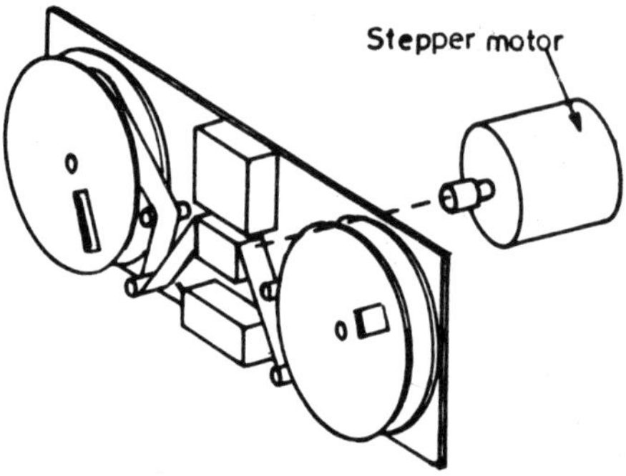


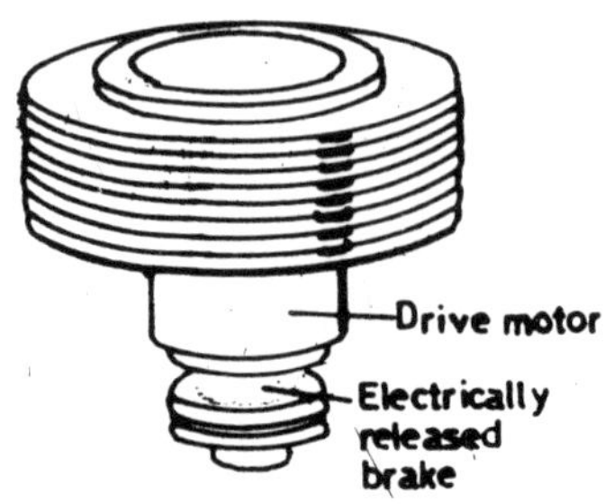


**Paper Tape Drive**
500 Characters/sec are achieved on this paper tape drive with a direct drive step motor Positional overshoot on settling is below 2°

**Disc Pack Drive**
15 second controlled and noiseless stopping is provided on this 3600 rpm disc drive. The brake is engaged by power shut off (tailsafe)

**Fig. 7.6** Paper Tape Drive

## 7.3 OFFICE EQUIPMENT

Application in this area also belong to high performance, high volume category. They include the electronic typewriter, facsimile machine, telex, xerox and several other machines of this type. We describe a couple of them as typical examples.

### 7.3.1 Electronic Typewriter [Serial Printer]

The machine utilizes two stepper motors and 2 DC or stepper motors as shown in Fig. 7.7. One stepper motor is used for paper feed, while the other is used for ribbon feed. Two other motors which are meant for carriage transport and for positioning the daisy wheel are either DC or high speed stepper motors. The printing speeds are 30 to 100 characters/sec.

**Fig. 7.7** Electronic Typewriter

### 7.3.2 Facsimile Machine

This machine operates as transmitter as well as receiver. The transmitter scans the picture to be transmitted, converts it into digital form and transmits it over telephone lines. The receiver receives the signals in digital form, decodes it and reconstructs the picture.

In both these operations, *X-Y* scanning is essential. It is performed by two stepper motors as shown in Fig. 7.8.

## 7.4 MACHINE TOOL APPLICATIONS

Numerical control (NC), and its subsequent advances, viz CNC (computer NC) and DNC (direct NC), of machine tools forms an important application area for stepper motors. High torques, in the range, 10-100 kg-cm, are required for controlling machine tools. Some typical applications are described below.

### 7.4.1 NC System for Milling Machine

Milling machines are employed when three or more axes machining is needed. A three axis milling machine is shown in Fig. 7.9. Here the *x*, *y*, *z* motions are controlled independently by three stepper motors. Provision for fast return is required for *x*- and *y*-axes motors. This implies that provision for velocity profiling incorporating automatic acceleration and deceleration has to be made in its controller.

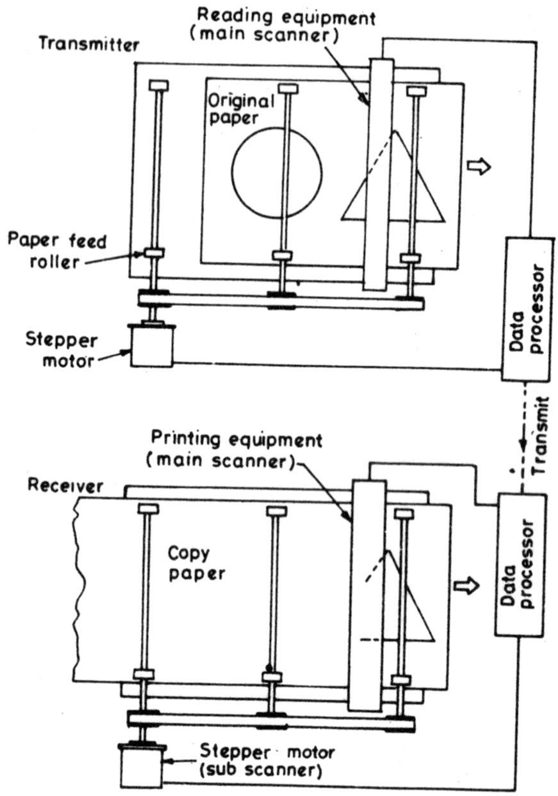


**Fig. 7.8** Facsimile Machine

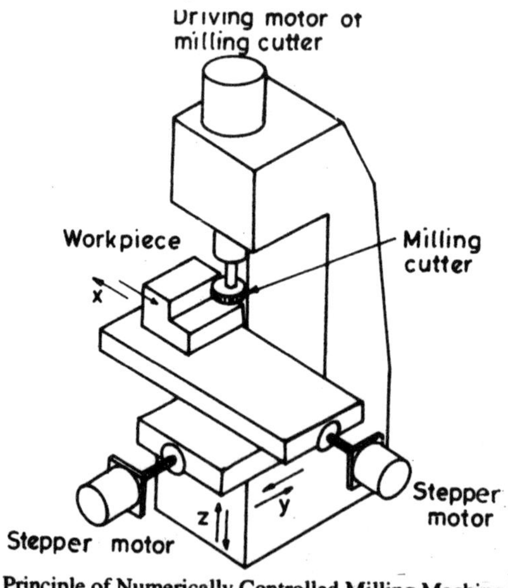


**Fig. 7.9** Principle of Numerically Controlled Milling Machine Using Three Stepping Motors

### 7.4.2 Index Table

Index table is used in automatic assembly and machining operations. The indexing shown in Fig. 7.10 can accommodate 4 operations at 4 work stations. After operations at one work station are completed, the job has to be moved to the next work station. This is achieved by moving the index table through 90°. Stepper motor is ideal for such fixed angular rotations. In this application, the stepper motor is coupled to a worm gear and the fly wheel on which is mounted the index table.

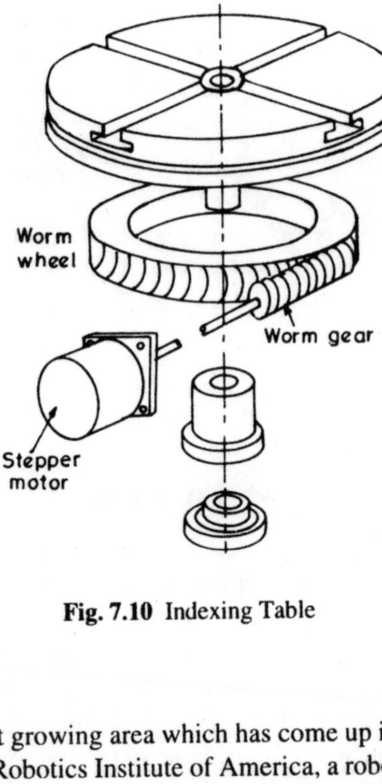


**Fig. 7.10** Indexing Table

## 7.5 ROBOTICS

This is a new and fast growing area which has come up in the last decade and a half. According to Robotics Institute of America, a robot is reprogrammable manipulator which is meant to carry parts, machines, materials, etc. through programmed movements. Stepper motor is quite popular as an actuator for activating joints of the robot. As an example, a six degrees of freedom robot was developed and exhibited in the Silver Jubilee Exhibition of I.I.T. Bombay in 1983 and described in [5].

## 7.6 ELECTROMEDICAL APPLICATIONS

X-ray machines, radiation therapy units, CAT-Scanners ultrasound scanners, etc. require precise positioning. Step motors have been used in these applications. For example, the X-ray machine has to be positioned on the part of the patient's body which is to be X-rayed. Similarly, the radiation head of radiation therapy unit has to be positioned such that only cancer cells will be exposed to radiation and destroyed, and not healthy cells in nearby areas. This requires precision *X-Y* positioning for which a pair of stepper motor are used as seen from Fig. 7.11. Lastly, the scanner in the CAT-Scanner has to be moved in precise increments to scan the head or any other part of the body. Stepper motors are ideal for such an application.

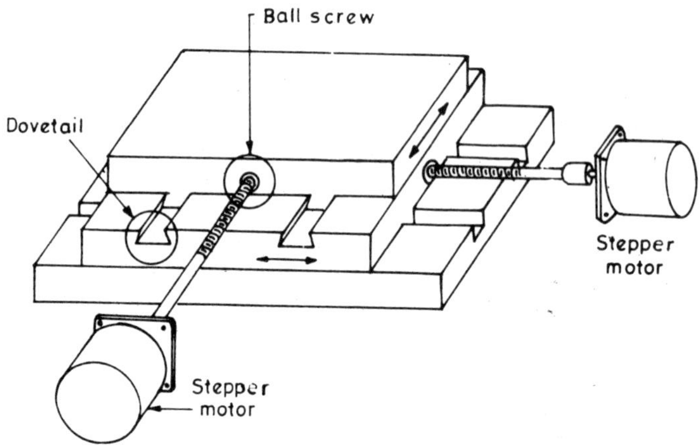


**Fig. 7.11** X-Y Table

## 7.7 MISCELLANEOUS APPLICATIONS

These include nuclear reactors, aerospace, and industrial applications. In nuclear reactors, stepper motor operated robots are used for carrying out repair and maintenance work in 'hot' areas. The author had designed an on-line refuelling machine driven by high torque stepper motors for replacing spent-up fuel rods by fresh fuel rods when the reactor is operating at its full capacity. Stepper motors have also found application in positioning reactor control rods to regulate the reactor power level.

Stepper motors have also gone into space; for example, it is reported that Mariner and Voyager spacecrafts employed stepper motors for tele-operating TV camera, ultra violet spectrometer, etc. Tele-operation of deploying solar panels and suntracking are reported to have been performed by stepper motors. The author has designed low step angle, high torque stepper motors for this application [6]. Another interesting applications shown in Fig. 7.12. It concerns the control of a constant flow hydraulic pump.

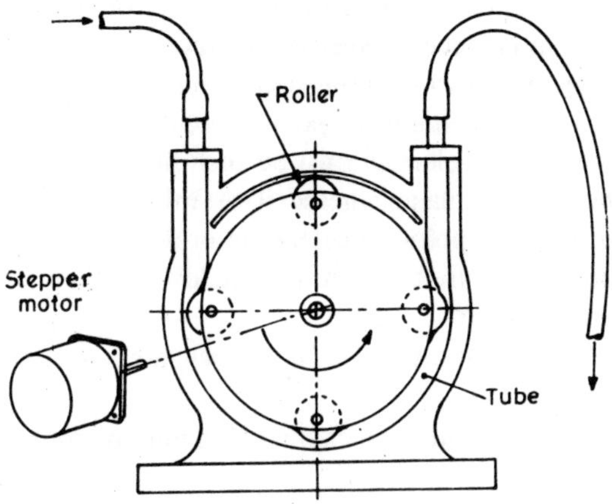


**Fig. 7.12** Constant Flow Pumps

## 7.8 STEPPER MOTOR SELECTION

Having studied a variety of stepper motor applications, we now turn our attention to the problem of how to select a stepper motor for a given application. This is the problem faced most commonly by users, especially in developing countries such as India. The problem is aggravated by factors such as

(i) Stepper motors are hardly discussed in textbooks and handbooks on electrical machines and drives. del Toro [7] and Veinott [8] do discuss stepper motors in their books. However, the discussion is too elementary to go into stepper motor selection criteria.

(ii) Reference material on stepper motor selection is available only in specialty symposium/conference records [9-14] and manufacturers' catalogues [15-24], which are not easily available to practising engineers as well as students.

Consequently, the user is handicapped, and is in need of guidance. This and the following sections are meant to provide such guidance [25].

## 7.9 BASIC CONSIDERATIONS IN STEPPER MOTOR SELECTION

The first and foremost point which the stepper motor user must bear in mind is that *80–90 percent of stepper motor applications are open loop incremental motion control systems* (IMCSs), inasmuch as they offer the following advantages:

(a) they are simple in structure and inexpensive,
(b) being open loop systems, they pose no stability problems,
(c) even then they are capable of yielding positioning accuracies comparable to closed loop DC and AC Servo Systems, and
(d) they can be directly interfaced to a computer.

All these advantages are based on the concept of *synchronism*, i.e. a strict one-to-one correspondence between the number of input pulses applied and the number of steps through which the stepper motor has actually moved. Thus, *Synchronism is the cardinal principle of stepper motor selection.* This means that the stepper motor selected must be such that it neither misses steps nor overshoots the mark, no matter whether it is starting or stopping, single stepping or slewing or micro-stepping, accelerating or decelerating, etc. If the stepper motor happens to lose synchronism, you are lost; you have no feedback device to tell you where you are.

The second basic consideration in stepper motor selection is that it must provide specified

(a) *Positioning accuracy* ($\delta$), expressed in mm/microns, or deg./minutes of arc

(b) *Speed of operation* ($V$), specified in mm/sec. or deg./sec. or rad/sec,

(c) *Acceleration* ($\alpha$), expressed as the time $\Delta T$ or number of steps $\Delta N$ in which to attain the operating speed $V$, starting from rest.

The steps in selection of stepper motor are as follows:

1. Compute (i) step angle $\theta_S$ from $\delta$; (ii) stepping rate $F_S$ (steps/sec) from $V$; (iii) acceleration $\alpha$ (rad/sec$^2$) from $V/\Delta T$; (iv) total moment of inertia $J_T$ reflected on the motor shaft; (v) total torque $T_M$ required to be developed by the motor.
2. Select a range of stepper motors having step angle $\theta_S$.
3. Refer to torque-vs-stepping rate curves of the motors selected in Step 2. Select a stepper motor which is capable of delivering torque, $T \geq T_M$ computed in Step 1(v) at a stepping rate $F \geq F_S$ (steps/sec) computed in Step 1(ii).
4. Determine whether the stepper motor selected can provide the necessary acceleration ($\alpha$).
   If so, confirm motor selected; else select the next higher rating of the motor.

This procedure for stepper motor selection is illustrated in Fig. 7.13.

## 7.10 SELECTION OF STEPPERS USED IN TYPICAL DRIVES

Four typical drives are used in IMCS's to couple the motor to the load : (i) direct drive (ii) string and pulley drive, (iii) rack and pinion drive, and (iv) lead screw drive. They are illustrated in Fig. 7.14.

These drives are considered in detail below. The calculation of (a) total moment of inertia $J_T$ reflected to the motor shaft, (b) required stepping rate $F_S$ and acceleration $\alpha$ and (c) accelerating, friction, load and total torque, are given in detail. Numerical examples are given to illustrate not only the above calculation but also the selection of stepper motor for the drive.

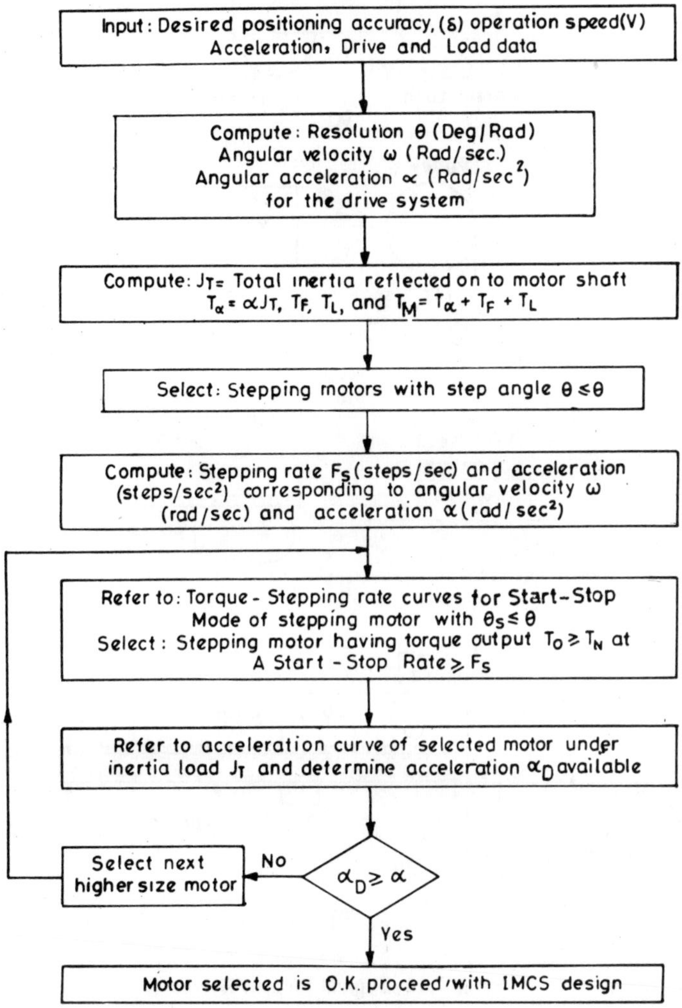


**Fig. 7.13** Stepping Motor Selection for Open Loop Incremental Motion Control System

### 7.10.1 Direct Drive

This is the simplest possible drive in which the stepper motor is directly connected to the load as shown in Fig. 7.14 (a).

**Problem.** Determine the motor required to achieve a positioning accuracy $\delta$ (deg) and to reach a speed of response of $N$ (rpm) from rest in specified time $\Delta t$ (sec).

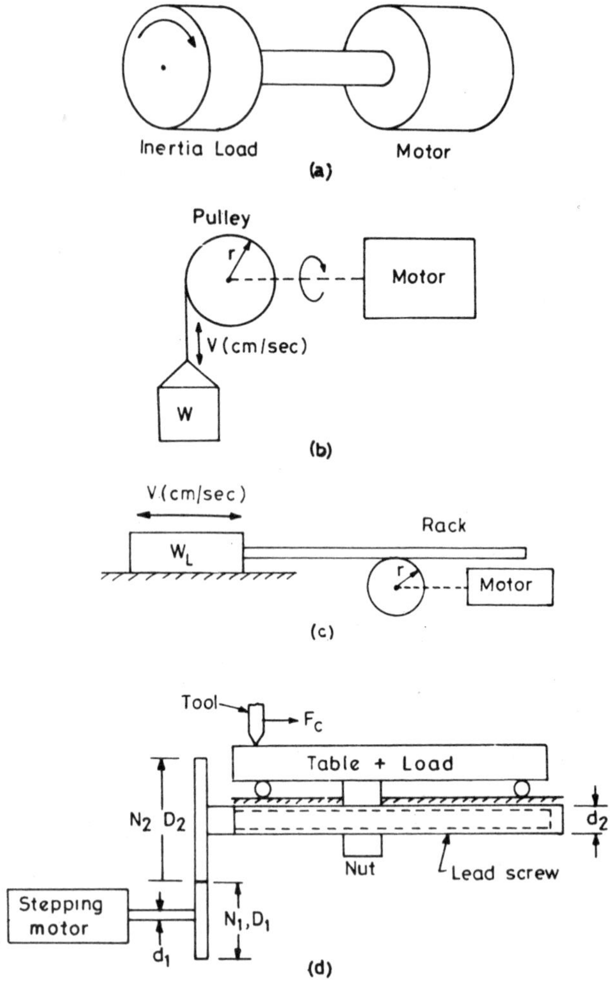


**Fig. 7.14** Typical Stepper Drives

**Data Required.** Load inertia $J_L$ (kg-cm$^2$), motor inertia $J_M$ (kg-cm$^2$) positioning accuracy $\delta$ (deg), operating speed $N$ (rpm) and time $\Delta t$ (sec) to attain speed $N$.

**Solution.** In order to achieve the specified positioning accuracy $\delta$, we must select a stepper motor having a step size $\theta_S$ (deg) $\leq \delta$. Common values of $\theta_S$ are 1.8, 3.6, 6, 7.5, 9, 15 and 30 deg.

The stepping rate corresponding to operating speed $N$ (rpm) is given by

$$F_S = NZ/60 = 60\ N/\theta_S \text{ (steps/sec)} \tag{7.1}$$

where $Z$ = no. of steps/revolution = $360°/\theta_S$

The total inertia reflected to the motor shaft is given by

$$J_T = (J_L + J_M)/g \text{ (kg-cm-sec}^2\text{)} \tag{7.2}$$

Hence the motor torque becomes

$$T_M = J_T \,.\, \alpha = \frac{(J_L + J_M)}{g} \cdot 2\,\pi \frac{F_S}{Z} \cdot \frac{1}{\Delta t} \tag{7.3}$$

We thus have to select a motor which (i) has a step size $\theta_S$ ana (ii) develops a torque $T_M$ given by (7.3) at a pull-in stepping rate $F_S$ of (7.1).

**Example 7.1.** Select a stepper motor which will drive directly a load of 26.9 $Kg_f$-$cm^2$ upto 200 steps/sec. The time to attain this period 0.5 sec. positioning accuracy desired is 1.8 deg.

**Solution.** Assuming $J_M = J_L$, we get from (7.1) the motor torque as

$$T_M = \frac{(2)\,(26.9)}{980.665} \cdot \frac{2\pi\,(500)}{(200)\,(0.5)} = 1.72 \text{ kg-cm} \tag{7.4}$$

From the torque-vs-stepping rate curve for Sri-Syn STM 601 motor + bipolar drive, shown in Fig. 7.15, we observe that it is capable of developing 1.9 kg-cm torque at 200 to 500 steps/sec. Hence Sri-Syn STM 601 is suitable for this application.

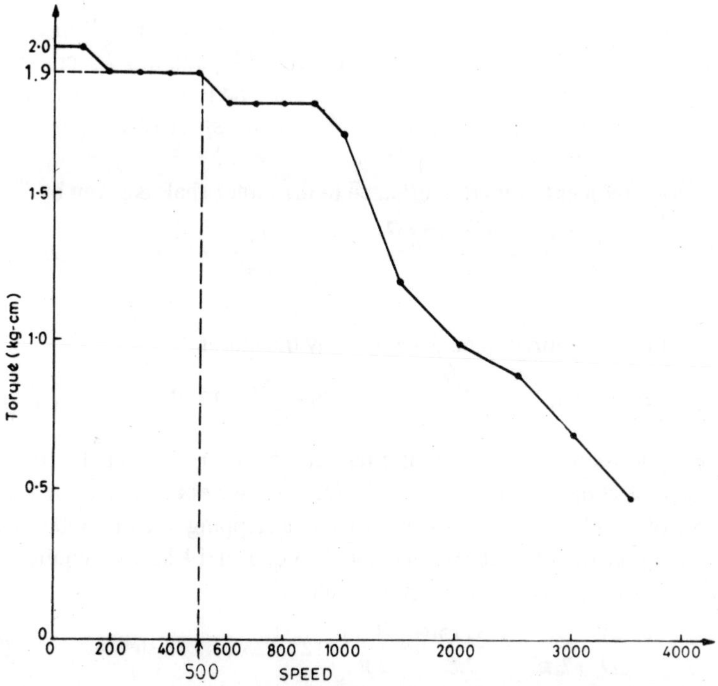


**Fig. 7.15** Torque-Speed Curve for Sri-Syn STM 601 Motor, with Bipolar Chopper, SCR Controlled, 60 V DC, 1 A/Phase

### 7.10.2 String and Pulley Drive

This drive is used when the stepper motor has to raise a load. This drive is illustrated in Fig. 7.14 (b).

**Problem.** Compute the motor torque required to raise a given load at the specified speed of $V$ (m/sec.).

**Data Required.** $W_L$, $W_P$ = wts. of load and pulley (kg), $D$ = dia. of pulley (cm), $V$ = speed of operation (cm/sec), $J_M$ = motor inertia (kg-cm$^2$), $\Delta t$ = time to attain speed $V$ (sec)

**Solution.** The total inertia reflected to motor shaft is given by

$J_T$ load inertia + pulley inertia + motor inertia

$$= \frac{W_L}{g} \cdot \frac{D^2}{4} + \frac{W_P}{g} \cdot \frac{D^2}{8} + \frac{J_M}{g} \text{ (kg-cm-sec}^2\text{)} \tag{7.5}$$

The total motor torque required to attain an operating speed of $V$ rad/sec in time $\Delta t$ is given by

$$T_M = J_T \frac{2V}{D\,\Delta t} + \frac{W_L \cdot D}{2} \text{ (kg-cm)} \tag{7.6}$$

The positioning accuracy for a step size $\theta_S$ (deg.) or $Z$ (steps/rev) is given by

$$\delta = \frac{\pi D}{Z} \text{ (cm)} = \frac{10\,\pi D}{Z} \text{ (mm)}$$

**Example 7.2.** A load of 2.75 kg is to be raised at a speed of 150 cm/sec using a string and pulley drive. The pulley weighs 0.5 kg and has 7.5 cm dia. The stepper motor inertia is estimated as 2.5 kg-cm$^2$ and has a step size of 1.8 deg. Compute the motor torque if the load is to attain the speed of 150 cm/sec in 0.5 sec.

The total moment of inertia reflected to the motor shaft is given by (7.5) as

$$J_T = \left[ \frac{(2.75)\,(7.5)^2}{4} + \frac{(0.5)\,(7.5)^2}{8} + 2.5 \right] \frac{1}{980.665} = 0.04557 \text{ kg-cm-sec}^2 \tag{7.8}$$

Total torque required to be developed by the motor

$$T_M = \left[ (0.04556)\,\frac{(2)\,(150)}{7.5} \cdot \frac{1}{0.5} \right] + 2.75\,\frac{(7.5)}{2} = 13.958 \approx 14 \text{ kg-cm} \tag{7.9}$$

Referring to the torque-vs-stepping rate curve for Sri-Syn STM 1101 motor with bipolar chopper drive, shown in Fig. 7.16, we observe that the motor is capable of developing 17.5 kg-cm torque at a stepping rate of 1300 steps/sec. This is higher than the above calculated torque of 14 kg-cm required to be developed by the motor at the stepping rate

$$F_S = \frac{2V}{D} \cdot \frac{Z}{2\pi} = \frac{(2)\,(150)}{7.5} \cdot \frac{200}{2\pi} = 1273.23 = 1273 \text{ step/sec} \tag{7.10}$$

We therefore select Sri-Syn STM-1101 motor with bipolar chopper drive in this case.

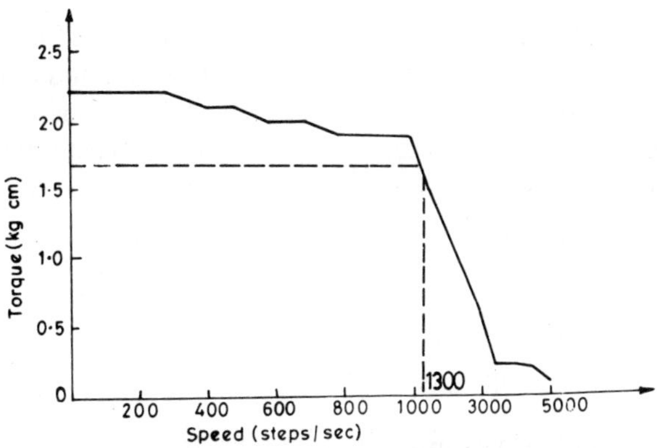


**Fig. 7.16** Torque – Speed Curve for Sri-Syn STM 1101 Motor with Bipolar Chopper, SCR Controlled, At 80 VAC, 4A/Phase

The positioning accuracy achievable with 1.8 deg. step size is

$$\delta = 10\left(\frac{\pi D}{Z}\right) = 1.18 \text{ mm} \tag{7.11}$$

If this accuracy is not sufficient, we have to use a suitable gear train.

### 7.10.3 Rack and Pinion Drive

This drive shown in Fig. 7.14 (c) is selected when the load is to be moved linearly in a horizontal plane.

**Problem.** Compute the motor torque required to move a given load at a speed of $V$ cm/sec. in a horizontal plane, and hence select a suitable stepper motor.

**Data Required.** $W_L$, $W_P$ = *wt.* of load and pinion (kg), $D$ = pinion dia (cm), $V$ = operating speed (cm/sec), $\Delta t$ = time to attain speed $V$ (sec), $\mu$ = coefficient of friction $J_M$ = motor inertia (kg-cm$^2$), $\theta_S$ = motor step size (deg.)

**Solution.** Total inertia reflected to motor shaft is given by

$J_T$ = (load + pinion + motor) inertia

$$J_T = \frac{W_L}{g}\cdot\frac{D^2}{4} + \frac{W_P}{g}\cdot\frac{D^2}{8} + \frac{J_M}{g} \text{ (kg-cm-sec}^2\text{)} \tag{7.12}$$

The total torque required to attain operating speed $V$ (cm/sec) in time $\Delta t$ is given by

$T_M$ = (acceleration + friction) torque

$$= J_T\cdot\frac{2V}{D\,.\,\Delta t} + \frac{\mu\, W_L\,.\,D}{2} \text{ (kg-cm)} \tag{7.13}$$

The positioning accuracy

$$\delta = \frac{10\,\pi\,D}{Z}\ \text{(mm)} \tag{7.14}$$

**Example 7.3.** A load of 5 kg is to be moved at a speed of 250 cm/sec. A rack and pinion drive is used in which the pinion has 10 cm dia. and weighs 300 gm. The estimated motor inertia is 6 kg-cm$^2$. The friction coefficient is 0.02. Compute the motor torque and select a suitable motor. What is the positioning accuracy achievable with motor step size of 1.8 deg ?

**Solution.** Total moment of inertia reflected on to motor shaft is

$$J_T = \frac{\frac{5\,(10^2)}{4} + 0.3\left(\frac{10^2}{8}\right) + 6}{980.665}\ \text{(kg-cm-sec}^2\text{)}$$

$$= 0.1374\ \text{(kg-cm-sec}^2\text{)} \tag{7.15}$$

$$T_M = \frac{(0.1374)\,(2)\,(250)}{(10)\,(0.5)} + \frac{(0.02)\,(5)\,(10)}{2} = 14.24\ \text{(kg-cm)} \tag{7.16}$$

The stepping rate corresponding to 250 cm/sec is

$$F_S = \frac{VZ}{\pi\,D} = \frac{(250)\,(200)}{\pi\,(10)} = 1592\ \text{steps/sec} \approx 1600\ \text{steps/sec.} \tag{7.17}$$

Torque-vs-stepping rate curve of Fig. 7.17 for Sri-Syn STM 1102 motor with bipolar chopper drive shows that it is capable of developing about 18.5 kg-cm

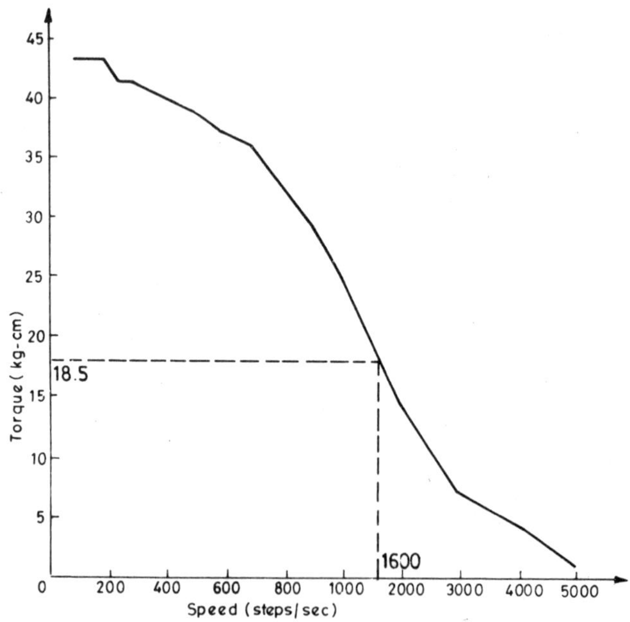


**Fig. 7.17** Torque – Speed Curve for Sri-Syn STM 1102 Motor with Bipolar Chopper Drive, SCR Control, 80 V AC, 4A/Phase

torque at 1600 steps/sec. Hence Sri-Syn STM 1102 motor with bipolar chopper drive may be selected for this application.

### 7.10.4 Lead Screw Drive

This drive is preferred in NC and CNC systems for milling machines, turret lathes and planing machines, etc. This drive is shown in Fig. 7.14 (b).

**Problem.** Compute the gear ratio, total inertia reflected to motor shaft and the motor torque needed to obtain a specified accuracy, cutting speed and rapid traverse speed.

**Data Required.** $\delta$ = positioning accuracy (cm/step), $\theta_S$ = step size (deg), $V_c$ and $V_r$ = cutting and rapid return speed (cm/sec), $J_m$ = motor inertia (kg-cm$^2$), $a_1 = N_1/N_2$ = gear ratio, $D_1$ and $D_2$ = diameters of driving and driven gear wheels, $h$ = lead screw pitch (cm/rev), $a_2 = h/2\pi$ = lead screw pitch (cm/rad), $t$ = thickness of gear wheels (cm), $\rho$ = density of gear material (kg/cm$^3$), $W_T$ and $W_L$ = weights of table and load (kg), $F_c$ and $F_g$ = cutting and clamping forces (kg), $L_1$ and $L_2$ = length of driving and driven shafts (cm), $\mu$ = coefficient of friction, $\eta$ = lead screw efficiency (35-45 per cent for acme type and 85-95 per cent for ballnut screw type lead screw) $l$ = lead screw length (cm).

**Solution.** The step size of the motor to yield the specified positioning accuracy

$$\theta_S = \frac{360\,\delta}{2\pi\, a_1 a_2} \text{ (deg)} \tag{7.18}$$

The total moment of inertia reflected to the motor shaft $J_T$ = (table + load) + (driving wheel) + (driven wheel) + (lead screw) + (motor inertia)

$$= \frac{W_T + W_L}{g}\left[\frac{\delta}{\left(\frac{\pi}{180}\cdot\theta_S\right)}\right]^2 + \frac{\pi D_2^4\, t\,\rho}{32\,g}\cdot a_1^2 + \frac{\pi D_1^4\, t\,\rho}{32\,g} + \frac{\pi d^4\, l\,\rho}{32\,g}\, a_1^2 + \frac{J_M}{g} \quad \text{(kg-cm-sec}^2\text{)} \tag{7.19}$$

Total motor torque during cutting period

$T_{MC}$ = (accelerating + cutting + friction) torque

$$= J_T\cdot\frac{V_c}{60\,\delta}\cdot\frac{2\pi}{Z.\Delta t} + \frac{F_c.Z.\delta}{2\pi\,\eta} + \frac{\mu\,(W_T + W_L + F_g).Z.\delta}{2\pi\,\eta} \text{ (kg-cm)} \tag{7.20}$$

Total motor torque during rapid traverse

$T_{MR}$ = (accelerating + frictional) torque

$$= \frac{J_T.V_r}{60\,\delta}\cdot\frac{2\pi}{Z.\Delta t} + \frac{\mu\,(W_T + W_L + F_g)\,Z.\delta}{2\pi\,\eta} \text{ (kg-cm)} \tag{7.21}$$

**Example 4.** Data for a stepper motor drive for a milling machine are as follows: $\delta$ = 0.001 cm/step; weight of table + load = 4000 kg. clamping force $F_g$ = 2000 kg., cutting force $F_C$ = 1200 kg., cutting speed of 2000 steps/sec. is to be reached in 100 msec; rapid return speed = 5000 steps/sec to be reached in 500 msec; leadscrew dia = 55 mm, length = 1100 mm, pitch = 8 mm/rev and efficiency = 90 per cent; gear train: driving wheel dia = 3.9 cm, thickness = 15 mm, teeth $N_1 = 24$, driven wheel dia = 15.6 cm, and teeth $N_2 = 96$.

Compute the motor torque and hence select a suitable motor.

Motor step size to yield specified accuracy is given by

$$\theta_S = \frac{(360)\,(0.001)}{2\pi\left(\frac{24}{96}\right)\left(\frac{0.8}{2\pi}\right)} = 1.8 \text{ (deg)} \tag{7.22}$$

Total moment inertia on motor shaft

$$J_T = \left[4000\left[\frac{(180)\,(0.001)}{\pi\,(1.8)}\right]^2 + \frac{\pi\,(3.9)^4\,(1.5)\,(0.0078)}{32}\right.$$

$$+ \frac{\pi\,(15.6)^4\,(1.5)\,(0.0078)\,(0.25)^2}{32}$$

$$\left. + \frac{\pi\,(0.55)^4\,(110)\,(0.0078)\,(0.25)^2}{32} + 61.5\right]\frac{1}{980.665}$$

$$= 0.07636 \text{ kg-cm-sec}^2 \tag{7.23}$$

Motor torque during rapid return

$$T_{MR} = \frac{(0.07636)\,(2\pi)\,(5000)}{60\,(200)\,(0.5)}$$

$$+ \frac{(0.02)\,(4000 + 2000)\,(200)\,(0.001)}{2\pi\,(0.9)} = 28.23 \text{ kg-cm} \tag{7.24}$$

Motor torque during cutting is given by

$$T_{MC} = \frac{(0.07636)\,(2\pi)\,(2000)}{(60)\,(0.001)\,(200)\,(0.1)} + \frac{(1200)\,(200)\,(0.001)}{(2\pi)\,(0.9)}$$

$$+ \frac{(0.02)\,(4000 + 2000)\,(200)\,(0.001)}{2\pi\,(0.9)} = 94.668 \approx 95 \text{ kg-cm} \tag{7.25}$$

Thus the stepper motor selected must (i) have step size of 1.8 deg. (ii) develop a torque of 95 kg-cm at 2000 steps/sec. and a torque of 28.5 kg-cm at 5000 steps/sec. Steeper motors of such high torque rating are not made in India. Hence we select the well-known Slosyn stepper motor type M172-FD308 which develops 100 kg-cm torque at 2000 steps/sec and 28.8 kg-cm torque at 5000 steps/sec. as shown in Fig. 7.18.

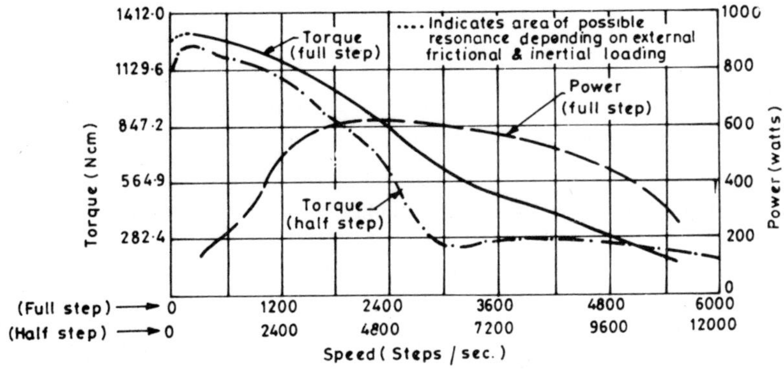


**Fig. 7.18** M 172 FD 308 Motor

## 7.11 SELECTION OF STEPPER MOTOR ON THE BASIS OF POWER RATE

We studied 'figures of merit' for stepper motors in Section 3.4. One of them was 'power rate' [26] defined as

$$\dot{P}_m = \frac{dP_m}{dt} = \frac{d}{dt}(T \,.\, \omega) = T \cdot \frac{d\omega}{dt} = T \,.\, \alpha = \frac{T^2}{J} \text{ (kW/sec)} \qquad (7.26)$$

where $P_m$ = power developed by the motor (kw), $T$ = rated torque (N-m), $\omega$ = motor speed (rad/sec.) $\alpha$ = motor acceleration (rad/sec$^2$), $J$ = moment of inertia of the motor (kg-m$^2$).

The power rate may alternatively be expressed as

$$\dot{P}_m = \frac{T^2}{J} = \frac{(K_t \,.\, I)^2}{J} = \frac{K_t^2 I^2 R}{JR} = \frac{I^2 R}{JR/K_t^2} = \frac{I^2 R}{\tau_m} \qquad (7.27)$$

where $K_t$ motor torque constant (N-m/A), $I$ = motor current (A) $R$ = resistance of motor winding, $\tau_m$ = motor time constant (sec). = $JR/K_t^2$.

The power rate is thus a comprehensive figure of merit inasmuch as it takes into account (i) magnetic circuit design ($K_t$), (ii) electric circuit design ($I^2R$), (iii) mechanical design ($J$), and speed of response ($\tau_m$). It indicates the ability of the motor to accept electric power input and to provide usable mechanical output power. The larger the power rate, the better is the ability of motor to accelerate the load.

We had pointed out in Section 3.4 that the power rate may be used a criterion selection of stepper motor [27]. This section explains how this can be done.

### 7.11.1 Basic Relationships

Consider the case in which the load is connected to the motor through a drive such as (i) rack and pinion, (ii) pulley and string or belt or chain drive, (iii) lead screw, etc.

Then the load power rate is given by

$$\dot{P}_L = (J_L \cdot \alpha_L + T_L)\, \alpha_L/\eta \tag{7.28}$$

where $J_L$ = load inertia (kg-m$^2$), $\alpha_L$ = load acceleration (rad/sec$^2$), $T_L$ = constant load torque (e.g., friction torque, torque due to cutting force, etc.), $\eta$ = efficiency of the drive.

The motor power rate is related to load power rate is given by

$$\dot{P}_m = (R + 1/R)^2 \cdot \dot{P}_L \tag{7.29}$$

where $R = R_g/R_{go}$, $R_g$ = actual gear ratio, $R_{go}$ = optimum gear ratio which matches motor inertia $J_m$ to reflected load inertia $J_L$.

The optimum gear ratio $R_{go}$ is given by

$$R_{go} = [(J_L\, \alpha_L + T_L)/(\alpha_L \cdot J_m)]^{1/2} \tag{7.30}$$

For a given $P_L$, $P_m$ is a minimum when $R = 1$. The minimum motor power rate $\dot{P}_m$ (min) has been derived by Newton [28] as

$$\dot{P}_m\,(\text{min}) = 4\, \dot{P}_L \tag{7.31}$$

Finally the peak power of the motor has been shown by Newton [28] to be:

$$\dot{P}_m = [(1 + R^2)\, a + (\tau_m/T_m)\, (R + 1/R)^2]\, T_m \cdot \dot{P}_L \tag{7.32}$$

where $\sigma$ = acceleration interval as a fraction of motion time. $T_m$ , $\tau_m$= electromechanical constant of the motor.

### 7.11.2 Motor Selection Procedure

With this background, we may now proceed to motor selection on the basis of power rate. The steps to be followed are :

(a) Compute the load power rate, $\dot{P}_L$ using (7.28)

(b) Calculate power of the motor = load power + power to drive rotor where load power = $P_L \cdot T_m$
where $T_m$ = motion time

(c) Obtain the minimum motor power rate using Eq. (7.31)

(d) Select the motor on the basis of $P_m$ and $\dot{P}_m$

(e) Compute $R_{go}$ and set $R_g = R_{go}$ so that motor and load inertias are matched.

(f) Check whether peak velocity and peak torque required are within the capability of the motor selected.

This selection procedure is shown in Fig. 7.19.

### 7.11.3 Illustrative Example*

Consider the printer carriage drive shown in Fig. 7.7. Data pertaining to the drive are:

Load $W = 12$ Oz $= 3.336$ N
Constant load friction force, $F = 10$ Oz $= 2.78$ N
Load velocity, $V_L = 60$ in./s $= 1.524$ m/s
Time to reach load velocity $= 50$ ms $= T_{acc}$.

**Problem.** Select a suitable motor and determine the optimum gear ratio.

**Solution.** Peak load acceleration, $a = V_L/t_{acc}$ (7.33)

Therefore $a = 1.524/0.05 = 30.48$ m/s$^2$ (7.34)

Load mass, $M = W/g = 3.336/9.80616 = 0.3402$ kg (7.35)

**Step 1 :** Load power rate, $\dot{P}_L = (Ma + F)\, a$

$$= (0.3402 \times 30.48 + 2.78) \times 30.48 = 0.401 \text{ kW/s} \quad (7.36)$$

**Step 2 :** Required load power, $P_L = \dot{P}_L \times T_{acc}$

$$= 0.4 \times 0.05 \times 10^3 = 20 \text{ W} \quad (7.37)$$

Motor power, $P_m = 2P_L = 40$ W if $R = 1$

$R = 1$ implies that the gear ratio is so selected as to match load inertia to motor inertia.

**Step 3 :** Motor power rate, $\dot{P}_m = 4\dot{P}_L = 4 \times 0.4 = 1.6$ kW/s (7.38)

**Step 4 :** Select a stepper motor having $\dot{P}_m = 1.6$ kW/s and motor power

$$P_m = 40 \text{ W} \quad (7.39)$$

**Step 5 :** Gear ratio $R_g = R_{go}$ so that $R = R_g/R_{go} = 1$,

where $R_{go} = \sqrt{(J_L\, \alpha_L + T_L)/(J_m\, \alpha_L)} = (1/\alpha_L)\sqrt{\dot{P}_L/J_m}$

$$= \frac{1}{30.48}\sqrt{\frac{0.4 \times 10^{3}}{2.182 \times 10^{-5}}} = 140.47 \text{ rad/m} \quad (7.40)$$

This requires a pulley radius $= 1/140.47 = 0.00712$ m

$$= 7.12 \text{ mm} \quad (7.41)$$

**Step 6 :** Peak velocity $\omega_{max} = V_L \cdot R_{go} = 1.524 \times 140.47$

$$= 214.0763 \text{ rad/sec} \quad (7.42)$$

---

* Source : Arnold and Floresta, Ref. No. 26

This corresponds to 2046 rpm = 6820 steps/s. If such a high stepping rate is not feasible, we have to select a smaller gear ratio $R_g$. This will make $R > 1$ and hence $\dot{P}_m > 4\dot{P}_L$

$$T_{max} = (J_m \alpha_L R_g) + (J_L \alpha_L + T_L)/R_g = 7.367 \text{ N-m} \tag{7.43}$$

The motor selected has $T_{max} = 8.896$ N-m.

Finally, power required to drive its own inertia,

$$P_{mot} = (J_m . \alpha_L . R_g) (\omega . R_g) \tag{7.44}$$

$$= 20 \text{ W as assumed above.}$$

This completes the motor selection.

## SUMMARY

Load acceleration, $\alpha_L = 30.48/\text{sec}^2$
Acceleration time, $t_{acc} = 0.05$ sec
Load velocity, $V_L$ = 1.542 m/sec
Gear ratio $R_g$ = 140.47 rad/m
Peak motor torques, $T_{PK}$ = 7.367 N-m
Peak motor speed, $\omega_{PK}$ = 214 rad/s
= 2046 rpm
Peak motor power, $P_m$ = 40 W
Peak power rate, $\dot{P}_m$ = 1.6 kW/s

## 7.12 CONCLUSION

This chapter has dealt with practical questions regarding stepper motor, viz. (i) What are the typical applications of stepper motors, and (ii) how to select a suitable stepper motor for an application. In answer to the first question, we have surveyed multifarious applications of stepper motors. In reply to the second question, we have studied two methods of stepper motor selection: (i) based on torque vs. stepping rate characteristics and (ii) based on power rate.

## REFERENCES

1. Kenjo, T. (1987). "Stepping motors and their microprocessor controls", Oxford University Press, Chap. 8.
2. Kuo, B.C. (1974). "Theory and applications of the step motor". West Publishing Co., St. Paul. Chap. 1.
3. — "Warner Electric's guide to selecting and controlling step motors", Warner Electric Clutch & Brake Co., Beloit, WI, Form No. P-172.
4. Athani, V.V. (1979). Final report on the project, "refuelling mechanism for R5 reactor", Submitted to B.R.N.S., DAE.

5. Dodeja, R.K., Amarnath, C., and Athani, V.V. (1983). "Microprocessor controlled 2R-P-3R industrial robot", Proc. 1st Intl. Conf. on Computer Applns. in Prodn. Engg., Vol. 3, pp. 707-715.
6. Athani, V.V. (1992). Final report on the project, "design of low angle, high torque PMH stepper motors for IRS satellites", Submitted to Vikram Sarabhai Space Center, Trivandrum (India).
7. Kordik, K.S. and Senica, K.M., "Step motor selection", Proc. 3rd Annual Symp. on IMCSD, 1974, pp. J1-J26.
8. Veinott, C.G. and Martin, J.E. "Fractional and Subfractional HP electric motors" (4th Edn), McGraw Hill, New York, 1986.
9. Bianculli, A.J. "Stepper motors: applications and selection", IEEE Spectrum, Vol. 7, No. 12, Dec. 1970, pp. 25-29.
10. Kordik, K.S., "Step motor selection", in Kuo, B.C., "Step motors and control systems", SRL Pub. Co., Champaign, IL, 1979, pp. 204-214.
11. Dahmen, J., "Stepper motors, Part I: selecting and specifying", Electromech. design, System designer's handbook', 1973/74, pp. 227-233.
12. De Sa e Silva, "What size stepper?" Machine Design, Dec. 14, 1972, pp. 136-143.
13. Jocz, A., "Selecting high performance incremental motion devices", Proc. 2nd Annul Symp. on IMCSD, 1973, pp. A1-A17.
14. Halbeck, R. and Stevens, H.G., "Recent applications of PM stepper motor systems", Proc. Int. Conf. on Stepping Motors and Systems, University of Leeds, U.K., pp. 217-230.
15. "Design engineer's guide to stepper motors", No. SE-L 8753, Superior Electric Co. Inc., Bristol. CT, USA, 1975.
16. SLOSYN DC Stepping Motors, Catalog No. SE-L-8836, The Superior Electric Co., Bristol, CT, USA 1979.
17. 'SLOSYN stepping motor controllers", Catalog No. SE-L127811, The Superior Electric Co., Bristol, CT, USA 1979.
18. "Stepping Motors", Moore, Read and Co. Ltd., Andover, UK, June 1979.
19. "Stepper motor handbook", Form MR-116, Cheshire, Div., Cheshire, CT, USA 1979.
20. "Step servo motors", IMC, Western Div., Catalog No. WS 109, R, 19
21. "SRISYN AC Synchronous and DC Stepper motors", Srijan Control Drives, Pune 411009.
22. "Fujitsu pulse motors", No.B-51094E, Comm. and Electron, Div. Tokyo, Japan.
23. "Technical data on stepping motors", No. 89W 2K 17925M, Oriental Motor Co. Ltd., Tokyo, Japan.
24. "Guide to selecting a controlling step motors", Form P-1172 Rev 1/80, Warner Electric Brake and Clutch Co., Beloit, WI, USA, 1979.
25. Athani, V.V. "Selection & Sizing of Stepper Motors, IEEMA J., Vol. 12, No. 11, pp. 13-27, 1992.
26. Arnold, F. and Floresta, J.G. "Power rate: the most Important figure of merit to incremental motion design", Proc. 13th Annual Symp. on IMCSD, pp. 11-18, 1984.
27. Arnold, F. "Designing Incremental motion systems with power rate", 14th Annual Symp. on IMCSD, pp. 37-50, 1985.
28. Newton, G.C. "Selecting the optimum electric servomotor for incremental positioning applications", Proc. 10th annual Symp. on IMCSD, 1981.

# CHAPTER - 8

# *Modelling of Stepper Motors*

In this chapter we develop models for stepper motors to explain various aspects of stepper motor behaviour: (i) permeance model for magnetic circuit analysis, (ii) transfer function model for single step response analysis, and (iii) state space models for dynamic operation and mid-frequency resonance analysis. Since single step response of a stepper motor is highly oscillatory in nature, we take up a study of various methods of damping out these oscillations.

## 8.1 PERMEANCE MODEL OF A STEP MOTOR

The stepper motor is simple in construction and operation. However, its electromagnetic field analysis is fraught with difficulties, on account of (i) double slotting, (ii) presence of permanent magnet on the rotor, (iii) saturation of magnetic circuit, etc. Naturally, magnetic circuit analysis of stepper motors has been extensively discussed in literature [1-4]. We present below the permeance model developed by Chai [15-18]. This model explains various phenomena in stepper motors; yet it is easy to understand. It also provides an insight into the factors influencing the design of stepper motors.

## 8.2 MOTOR DESCRIPTION

Fig. 8.1 shows a cutaway view of a 1.8-degree, four-phase PMH step motor, which is the most widely used stepper motor at present. An axially magnetized cylindrical permanent magnet, bounded by a pair of soft-iron rotor disks, is mounted on a shaft. With the polarity of the magnet shown, the flux from the magnet leaves the left-side rotor disc radially outward to the stator, traverses the stator axially, enters the rightside rotor disc, and then returns to the magnet, as shown in Fig. 8.2.

The rotor has 50 teeth. Teeth on the left and right rotor disks are offset by one-half tooth pitch to provide an additive torque generation on the shaft. This will become clear as we examine the magnetic circuit.

Teeth on both the stator poles and the rotor have the same pitch. For proper motor operation, the pole pitch must be related to the tooth pitch by

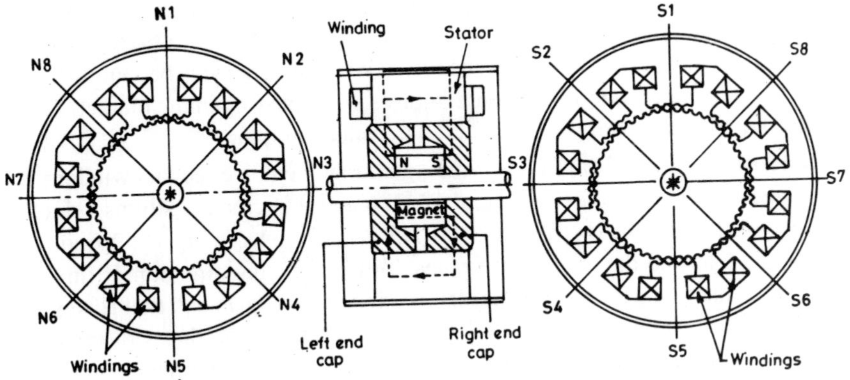


**Fig. 8.1** Cutaway View of a 1.8-Degree PM Step Motor

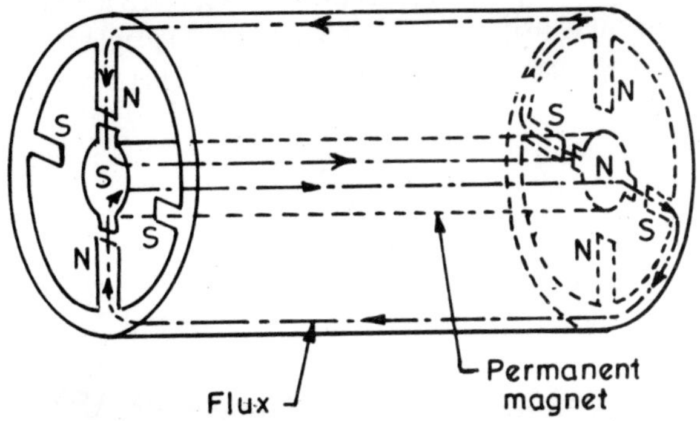


**Fig. 8.2** Typical Flux Paths in a Hybrid PM Step Motor

$$\text{Pole pitch} = \left(m \pm \frac{1}{n}\right) \times \text{tooth pitch} \tag{8.1}$$

where $m$ is a positive integer suitably chosen from design considerations, and $n$ is a number of full steps required for covering one tooth pitch. For the motor shown in Fig. 8.1, the tooth pitch is 7.2 mechanical degrees (1.8 degree per full step); $n$ is 4 since it takes four full steps to move one tooth pitch; and $m$ is 6. With these values and the positive sign, the pole pitch of 45 degrees is obtained, resulting in a balanced pole arrangement with the teeth of the opposite poles having the same angular displacement relationship with respect to the rotor teeth. A value of $m$ other than 6 can be used also; however, the resulting structure will not be balanced, giving an undesirable radial force on the motor bearings.

For four-phase PM motors two types of winding arrangements are used. One is a monofilar winding scheme shown in Fig. 8.3 (a) and the other, a bifilar winding scheme shown in Fig. 8.3 (b). The rotor and teeth are omitted for clarity. Bifilar-wound motors use four drivers instead of the eight used in monofilar-wound motors. The use of four drivers was a significant "plus" for bifilar-wound motors in the past when electronic drivers were expensive. However, with the discrete driver cost decreasing and the emergence of low-cost integrated motor drivers, the bifilar winding scheme is becoming less attractive and more monofilar-wound motors are appearing in the market. The monofilar-wound motors are well suited for microstepping.

Referring to Fig. 8.3 (a) for the winding arrangement, we see that winding 1 is wound around the poles located at 12, 3, 6 and 9 O'clock positions, which correspond to N1 (S1), N3 (S3), N5 (S5), and N7 (S7) poles in Fig. 8.1. Winding 2 is wound around the other set of poles. To examine the direction of flux at each pole due to a winding current, let us excite winding 1 such that fluxes at 12 and 6 O'clock poles enter the rotor. This same current produces fluxes at 3 and 9 O'clock positions leaving the rotor. Fluxes due to the permanent magnet and the fluxes due to the winding current are additive at the poles N3, N7, S1, S5, and subtractive at the poles N1, N5, S3, S7. By offsetting two end disks of the rotor by one-half tooth pitch, teeth at the pole N3, N7, S1, S5 have the same relative displacement with the rotor teeth making them magnetically identical. The same is true with other sets of poles. As a result, a net torque is generated.

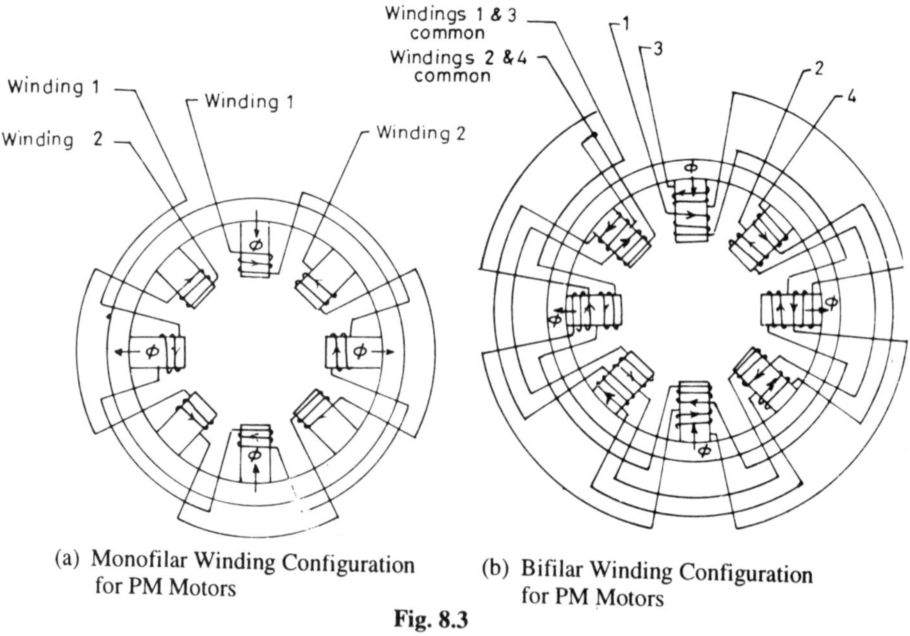


(a) Monofilar Winding Configuration for PM Motors

(b) Bifilar Winding Configuration for PM Motors

**Fig. 8.3**

Further examination of the winding and motor structure shows two sets of poles that are magnetically identical for each rotor disk. Each set has four poles whose teeth are respectively offset by one-fourth tooth pitch relative to the rotor teeth. Since there are two rotor disks in the rotor, we can draw a magnetic equivalent circuit consisting of four identical sets of subcircuits, as shown in

Fig. 8.4. What this implies is that a four-phase PM motor, such as the one shown in Fig. 8.1, has four small identical motors within it. Modelling of the motor then is reduced to modelling of one small motor, as shown in Fig. 8.5. Since the teeth on each pole have same relative displacement as the rotor teeth, we can further simplify the structure into one shown in Fig. 8.6. Fig. 8.7 corresponds to the magnetic equivalent circuit applicable to both Figs. 8.5 and 8.6. The only difference between the two is magnitude of permeance, which is discussed in the following sections.

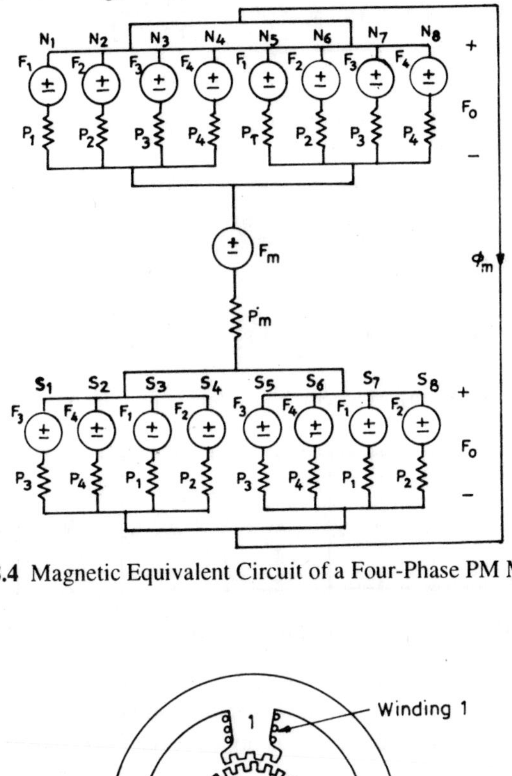

**Fig. 8.4** Magnetic Equivalent Circuit of a Four-Phase PM Motor

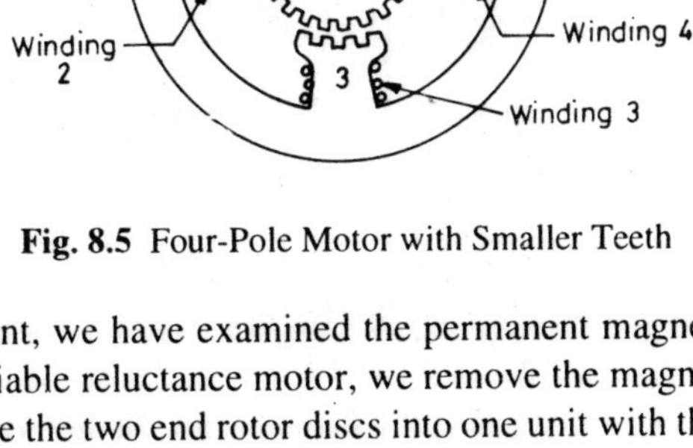


**Fig. 8.5** Four-Pole Motor with Smaller Teeth

Up to this point, we have examined the permanent magnet hybrid (PMH) motor. For a variable reluctance motor, we remove the magnet from the rotor in Fig. 8.1, merge the two end rotor discs into one unit with the teeth lined up,

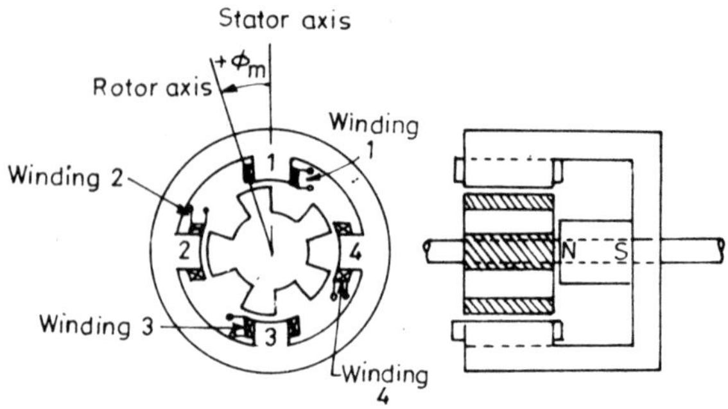


**Fig. 8.6** Five-Tooth Rotor, Four-Pole Stator Step Motor

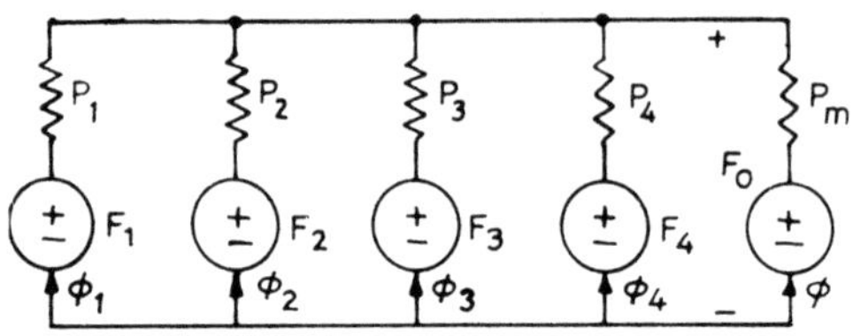


**Fig. 8.7(a)** Magnetic Equivalent Circuit for Motors

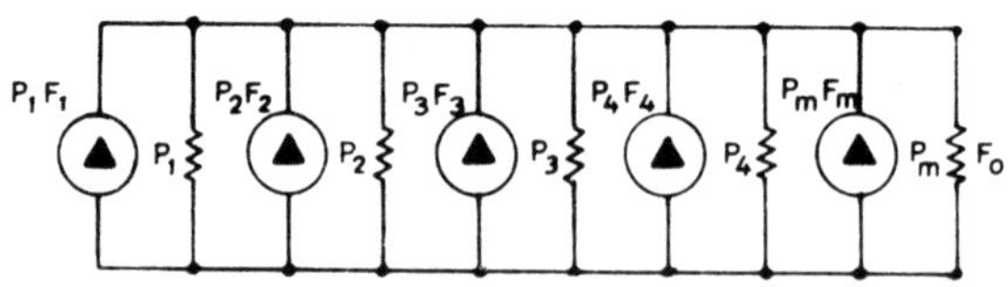


**Fig. 8.7(b)** Norton's Equivalent Circuit of Figure 5.5

and arranged windings as shown in Fig. 8.8. The result is a four-phase variable reluctance (VR) motor. The same reasoning can be carried out to develop a corresponding magnetic circuit as was done for the PMH motor. By taking just

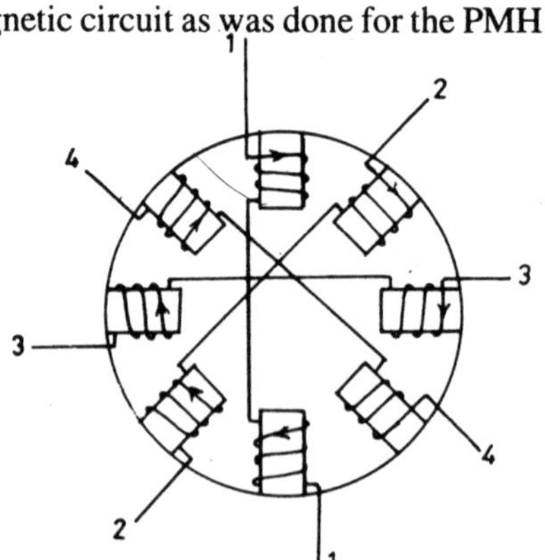

**Fig. 8.8** Winding Configuration for VR Motors

two sets of the sub-circuits in parallel in Fig. 8.4 and by open-circuiting (or removing) the branch representing the magnet, we have the magnetic circuit for the VR motor. The simplified motor structure shown in Fig. 8.6 and the corresponding magnetic circuit in Fig. 8.7 with the branch for the magnet removed can be used to investigate the behaviour of the VR motor.

## 8.3 MAGNETIC EQUIVALENT CIRCUIT

Let us examine the magnetic equivalent circuit shown in Fig. 8.7. Subscripts 1, 2, 3, 4 and $m$ denote respectively the poles 1, 2, 3, 4 and the permanent magnet in Fig. 8.6. The $\phi$'s are fluxes through the respective poles and the magnet, $F$'s represent magnetomotive forces supplied by winding currents and the magnet. $F_0$ is the mmf drop across the air gap and the mmf source (NI). Similarly, $P$'s represent respective air gap permeances. For quantitative analysis, we must include permeances (or reluctances) representing the stator sections, the rotor, and leakage reluctances around the winds for accurate numerical results. For the qualitative analysis that offers important physical insights into the motor operation, the inclusion of the stator, rotor and leakage reluctances makes the analysis unmanageable and obscures significant insights. Consequently, they are omitted from the circuit.

For the PMH motor, windings 1 and 3 (Fig. 8.6) are connected in series in such a way that $F_1 = -F_3$. The same is true for windings 2 and 4. For the bifilar winding arrangement (Fig. 8.3(b)), each winding represents two coils and the corresponding mmf contains two current terms. For example, winding 1 is represented by $F_1 = N(I_1 - I_1')$, where $N$ is a number of turns per winding around pole 1, and $I_1$ and $I_1$, represent currents in the bifilar winding set. For the VR motor each winding is independent, and $F_i = NI_i$ $(i = 1, 2, 3, 4)$.

The permanent magnet is represented by permeance $P_m$ mmf source $F_m$. The values can be obtained from

$$P_m = \frac{\mu_m A_m}{L_m} \tag{8.2a}$$

$$F_m = \frac{B_0 L_m}{\mu_m} \tag{8.2b}$$

where $\mu_m$, $A_m$, $L_m$, and $B_0$ are respectively incremental permeability, cross-sectional area, length and residual magnetic flux density of the magnet, as defined in Fig. 8.9.

This magnetic circuit forms the basis for the analysis.

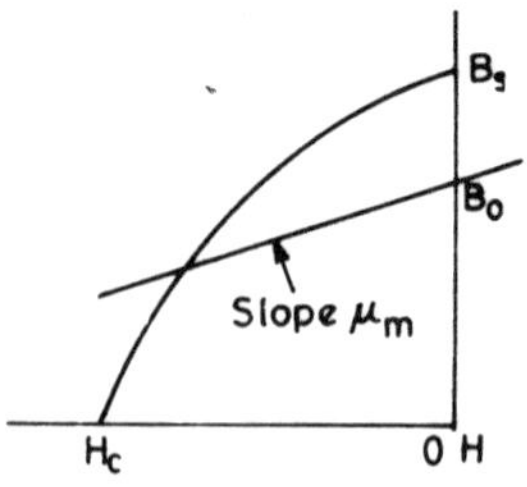


**Fig. 8.9** Demagnetization Curve of Permanent Magnet

## 8.4 PERMEANCE

The gap permeance is the fundamental parameter affecting torque, inductance, and speedance of the motor. It relates tooth dimensions of the motor to other parameters, and a design goal is to select tooth geometry in such a way that an optimum motor performance can be realized.

Fig. 8.10 shows a portion of the tooth profile at the air gap. We can think of the upper teeth as belonging to a stator pole and the lower ones to the rotor. Flux lines emanate from the upper teeth and enter the lower ones. The useful force (or torque) is produced by the flux emanating from the side of the teeth (portions 2, 3 and 4 in the figure).

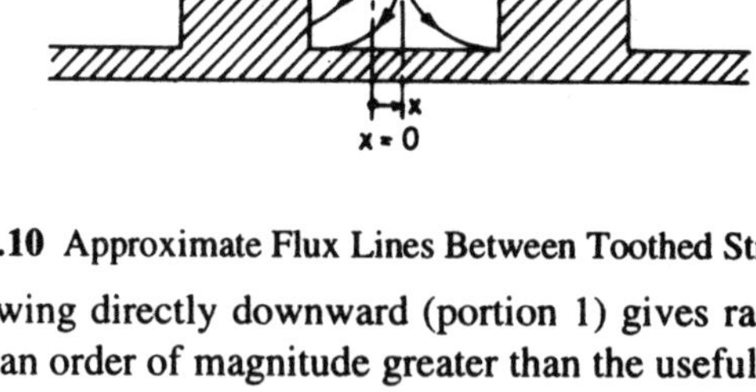


**Fig. 8.10** Approximate Flux Lines Between Toothed Structures

The flux flowing directly downward (portion 1) gives radial force on the rotor, which is an order of magnitude greater than the useful force, and it is a good design practice to balance this radial force by having an identical pole on the opposite side of the rotor, as in Fig. 8.1. Otherwise, a strong force will be exerted on the bearings, resulting in great bearing friction and shorter bearing life.

Since the rotor and stator teeth are in relative motion, airgap permeances are function of position and are periodic, with the period equal to the tooth pitch, $T_p = (W_t + W_v)$. Therefore, they can be expressed in a Fourier series form:

$$P_i = \rho_0 + \sum_{n=1}^{\infty} \rho_n \cos n\,\xi_i + \sum_{n=1}^{\infty} \rho'_n \sin n\,\xi_i \tag{8.3}$$

where
$$\xi_i = \theta_e - (i-1)\frac{\pi}{2}, \quad i = 1, 2, 3, 4 \tag{8.4a}$$

and
$$\theta_e = N\,\theta_{Rj} \tag{8.4b}$$

where $\theta_e$ refers to an electrical angle. For a motion of the one tooth pitch, $\theta_e = 360°$.

For a uniform bidirectional motion, the tooth must be symmetric, so that sine terms drop out. However, if a motor is designed for one-directional motion (say clockwise), performance may be improved by considering a nonsymmetric profile. In this case, sine terms will be present.

For the motor that we are examining, there are four gap permeances. Equation (8.2) can be expanded to give

$$\left.\begin{aligned} P_1 &= \rho_0 + \rho_1 \cos\theta_e + \rho_4 \cos 4\,\theta_e + \ldots \\ P_2 &= \rho_0 + \rho_1 \cos(\theta_e - 90°) + \rho_4 \cos 4\,(\theta_e - 90°) + \ldots \\ P_3 &= \rho_0 + \rho_1 \cos(\theta_e - 180°) + \rho_4 \cos 4\,(\theta_e - 180°) + \ldots \\ P_4 &= \rho_0 + \rho_1 \cos(\theta_e - 270°) + \rho_4 \cos 4\,(\theta_e - 270°) + \ldots \end{aligned}\right] \tag{8.5}$$

The permeances are offset by 90 electrical degrees. This is a characteristic of four-phase motors. For three-phase motors permeances are offset by 120 degrees.

As we will see subsequently, the first two terms in Eqn. (8.5) are the significant terms that affect motor performance. One other term that is important is the 4th harmonic because it gives rise to a detent (or cogging) torque for four-phase PMH motors. The other terms are of secondary importance.

or
$$\begin{aligned} P_1 &= \rho_0 + \rho_1 \cos\theta_e + \rho_4 \cos 4\,\theta_e \\ P_2 &= \rho_0 + \rho_1 \sin\theta_e + \rho_4 \cos 4\,\theta_e \\ P_3 &= \rho_0 - \rho_1 \cos\theta_e + \rho_4 \cos 4\,\theta \\ P_4 &= \rho_0 - \rho_1 \sin\theta_e + \rho_4 \cos 4\,\theta_e \end{aligned} \tag{8.6}$$

Then
$$\begin{aligned} \partial P_1/\partial\theta_e &= -\rho_1 \sin\theta_e - 4\,\rho_4 \sin 4\,\theta_e \\ \partial P_2/\partial\theta_e &= \rho_1 \cos\theta_e - 4\,\rho_4 \sin 4\,\theta_e \\ \partial P_3/\partial\theta_e &= \rho_1 \sin\theta_e - 4\rho_4 \sin 4\,\theta_e \\ \partial P_4/\partial\theta_e &= -\rho_1 \cos\theta_e - 4\,\rho_4 \sin 4\,\theta_e \end{aligned} \tag{8.7}$$

Further more,

$$\sum_{i=1}^{4} P_i = 4\,\rho_0 + 4\,\rho_4 \cos 4\,\theta_e \approx 4\,\rho_0 \tag{8.8a}$$

$$\sum_{i=1}^{4} \partial P_i/\partial\theta_e = -16\,\rho_4 \sin 4\,\theta_e \qquad (8.8b)$$

$$\sum_{i=1}^{4} P_i + P_m \approx 4\,\rho_0 \qquad (8.8c)$$

The above assumptions are justified since $\rho_4 << \rho_0$ and $P_m << P_0$.

Evaluation of the gap permeance involves solving the Laplace equation. Some effort has been made to evaluate the gap permeance by numerical techniques such as the moment method and the finite element method. Unfortunately, they do not give simple analytical results that can be generalized to various applications.

One way to obtain the permeance is to consider flux lines to consist of arcs and straight lines as suggested by Rotors. This method enables us to come out with simple equations to describe the gap permeance as a function of relative rotor-stator displacement. Since this method is approximate, special care is needed in applying it. Indiscriminate use can result in serious error. As pointed out by Harris, the error can be severe for a tooth pitch-to-gap ratio less than 20. However, the approximation is satisfactory and very useful for design work if the ratio is greater than 25. This means that for an air gap of 3 mil, the tooth pitch has to be greater than 75 mil.

The accuracy of the arc-straight line method can be improved by adding a correction term in the model, which can be obtained either through experiments or numerical results of field solutions.

## 8.5 FLUX LINKAGE AND ITS DERIVATIVE

The flux linkage of the $i^{th}$ winding is related to flux and inductances by

$$\lambda_i = N\,\phi_i = \sum_{n=1}^{4} [L_{in}\,I_n + L_{in'}\,I_{n'}] + \lambda_{im} \qquad (8.9)$$

where $L_{in}$ is an inductance between $i^{th}$ and $n^{th}$ windings; $L_{in'}$ is that between $i^{th}$ windings where $n^{th}$ and $n'^{th}$ windings are a bifiliar-wound set occupying the same $n^{th}$ pole; and $\lambda_{in}$ is the flux linkage on the $i^{th}$ winding due to the permanent magnet.

Since the flux is given by

$$\phi_i = P_i\,(F_i - F_0) \qquad (8.10)$$

the flux linkage can also be expressed in terms of permeances as

$$\lambda_i = NP_i\left[\left(1 - \frac{P_i}{P_t}\right)F_i - F_t\right] \qquad (8.11)$$

where

$$F_t = \sum_{j=1}^{4} \frac{P_j F_j}{P_t} + \frac{P_m F_m}{P_t}\; j \neq i \qquad (8.12a)$$

and $$P_t = \sum_{j=1}^{4} P_j + P_m \tag{8.12b}$$

For subsequent numerical examples, $P_t$ will be approximated as $4\,\rho_0$. This approximation is valid because all the harmonic terms drop out except those that are multiplies of the 4th harmonic, and the remaining terms including the permanent magnet, are small compared to $\rho_0$.

By equating terms containing the same current in Eqs. (8.9), (8.10), we obtained inductance in terms of permeances. Similarly, to obtain the functional relationship among inductances, permeances, and speedances, we differentiate the flux linkage in Eq. (8.9), giving

$$\frac{d\lambda_i}{dt} = \sum_{n=1}^{4}\left[L_{in}\frac{dI_n}{dt} + L_{in'}\frac{dI_{n'}}{dt}\right] + \sum_{n=1}^{4}\left[\frac{\partial L_{in}}{\partial\theta_e}I_n + \frac{\partial L_{in'}}{\partial\theta_e}I_{n'}\right]\cdot\frac{d\theta_e}{dt} + \frac{\partial\lambda_{im}}{\partial\theta_e}\cdot\frac{d\theta_e}{dt} \tag{8.13a}$$

where $$\lambda_{im} = -\frac{NP_m F_m P_i}{P_t} \tag{8.13b}$$

## 8.6 INDUCTANCES

From the equation for flux linkage, we find inductances in terms of permeances:

$$L_{ii} = -L_{ii'} = N^2 P_i\left[1 - \frac{P_i}{P_t}\right] \tag{8.14}$$

$$L_{ij} = -L_{ij'} = -\frac{N^2 P_i P_j}{P_t} \tag{8.15}$$

where $L_{ii}$ and $L_{ij}$ are self-and mutual-inductances, respectively.

Since the dominant terms for the permeances are the first two terms, we let

$$P_i \approx \rho_0 + \rho_1 \cos\xi_i \tag{8.16a}$$

$$P_t \approx 4\,\rho_0 \tag{8.16b}$$

Using these values and neglecting higher-order terms, we have

$$L_{ii} = L_0 + L_1 \cos\xi_i \tag{8.17a}$$

$$L_{ij} = -\frac{1}{3}L_0 - \frac{1}{2}L_1(\cos\xi_i + \cos\xi_j) \tag{8.17b}$$

where

$$L_0 = \frac{3}{4}N^2\rho_0 \tag{8.18a}$$

$$L_1 = \frac{1}{2}N^2\rho_1 \tag{8.18b}$$

## 8.7 BACK EMF CONSTANTS

Back emf constants is defined as a space derivative of inductance such as that

$$K_{ii} = \frac{\partial L_{ii}}{\partial \theta_e}, \; K_{ii'} = \frac{\partial L_{ii'}}{\partial \theta_e} \tag{8.19a}$$

$$K_{ij} = \frac{\partial L_{ij}}{\partial \theta_e}, \; K_{ij'} = \frac{\partial L_{ij'}}{\partial \theta_e} \tag{8.19b}$$

$$K_{im} = \frac{\partial \lambda_{im}}{\partial \theta_e} \tag{8.19c}$$

Note that

$$K_{ii} = -K_{ii'} \text{ and } K_{ij} = -K_{ij'} \tag{8.19d}$$

with

$$P_i = \rho_0 + \rho_1 \cos \xi_i \tag{8.20a}$$

$$P_t = 4\,\rho_0 \tag{8.20b}$$

and by equating the time derivatives of Eq. (8.11) and Eq. (8.13), we obtain

$$K_{ii} = -L_1 \left[ \sin \xi_i - \frac{\rho_1}{2\,\rho_0} \sin 2\,\xi_i \right] \tag{8.21a}$$

$$K_{ij} = \frac{L_1}{2} (\sin \xi_i + \sin \xi_j) + \frac{L_1\,\rho_1}{2\,\rho_0} \sin (\xi_i + \xi_j),\; i \neq j \tag{8.21b}$$

$$K_{im} = \frac{N\,\rho_1\,P_m\,F_m}{4\rho_0} \sin \xi_i \tag{8.21c}$$

## 8.8 STATIC TORQUE

The torque on the rotor is the sum of torques produced at each pole, and is given by

$$\begin{aligned} T &= -(1/2) \sum_{i=1}^{4} \phi_i^2 \, (\partial P_i/\partial \theta_m) \\ &= (1/2) \sum_{i=1}^{4} (\phi_i^2/P_i^2)\, (\partial P_1/\partial \theta_m) \\ &= (1/2) \sum_{i=1}^{4} (F_i^2 - F_0^2)/(\partial P_i/\partial \theta_m) \\ &= (N_R/2) \sum_{i=1}^{4} (F_i^2 - F_0^2)/(\partial P_i/\partial \theta_e) \end{aligned} \tag{8.22}$$

where $N_R$ = number of rotor teeth and $F_0$ = mmf drop between rotor and stator including the mmf source.
$F_0$ is given by

$$F_0 = \frac{\sum_{i=1}^{4} P_i F_i + P_m F_m}{\sum_{i=1}^{4} P_i + P_m} \qquad (8.23)$$

The winding mmf ($F_i$) is given by

$$F_i = N(I_i - I_{i'}) \qquad (8.24)$$

where $N$ is a number of turns of the $i^{\text{th}}$ pole and $I_i$ and $I_{i'}$ are currents in a bifilar winding set. For a monofilar-wound motor, $I_{i'}$ is zero.

Equation (8.23) can be easily obtained by converting Fig. 8.7 into its Norton's equivalent circuit and summing up all the fluxes through the gap permeances.

## 8.9 PERMANENT MAGNET MOTOR

Up till now we have developed the equations for torque, flux linkage, inductance, and speedance as functions of the gap permeances. We have not related them to a particular class of motors. Now we apply the foregoing results to a class of single-stack PMH motors and gain some useful insights.

For clarity, let us limit the analysis to the monfilar-wound motors. Our results can be easily extended to the bifilar-wound motors.

### 8.9.1 Inductance

Referring to Fig. 8.11, the flux linkage for the circuit with voltage $E_d$ includes the linkages for windings in poles 1 and 3, giving

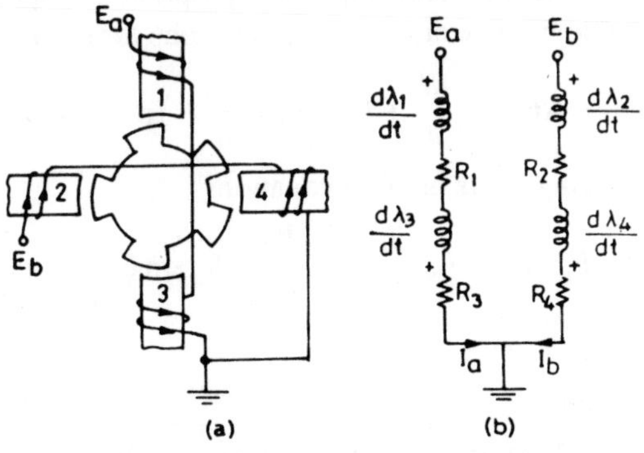


**Fig. 8.11** PM Motor Winding Arrangement and its Electrical Equivalent Circuit

$$\lambda_a = \lambda_1 - \lambda_3 = L_{aa}\, I_a + L_{ab}\, I_b + (\lambda_{1m} - \lambda_{3m}) \tag{8.25}$$

where

$$L_{aa} = L_{11} + L_{33} - 2\, L_{13} = \frac{8}{3} L_0 \tag{8.26a}$$

$$L_{ab} = L_{12} - L_{14} - L_{32} + L_{34} = 0 \tag{8.26b}$$

In an ideal motor, because of the winding connection used in PM motors, the mutual-inductance is zero, and the self-inductance is constant. The only non-zero mutual-inductance is the one between the bifilar-wound coils, which is same as the self-inductance. In contrast, variable reluctance (VR) motors have strong mutual coupling among the windings. In real-life situations, again due to manufacturing tolerances, the inductances deviate somewhat from the ideal ones. Because of the reluctances of the iron paths, the actual value is expected to be smaller.

### 8.9.2 Back EMF Constants

Since speedance is defined as space derivative of inductance (Eq. 8.21), and self- and mutual-speedance are constant and zero respectively,

$$K_{aa} = K_{ab} = 0 \tag{8.27a}$$

The only nonzero speedance term is

$$K_{am} = K_g \sin \theta_e \tag{8.27b}$$

where

$$K_g = \frac{N \rho_1 P_m F_m}{2 \rho_0} \tag{8.27c}$$

$K_g$ is normally called voltage constant, generator constant, or back-emf constant.

### 8.9.3 Voltage Equations

A solution of dynamic problems requires appropriate voltage equations. For the monofilar winding, there are two equations, one for each phase, giving

$$E_i = RI_i + L_{ii} \frac{dI_i}{dt} + K_g \sin \xi_i \frac{d\,\theta_e}{dt} \quad \text{for } i = a, b \tag{8.28}$$

For the bifilar winding, there are four equations

$$E_i = RI_i + L_{ii} \frac{dI_i}{dt} - L_{ii} \frac{dI_{i'}}{dt} + K_g \sin \xi_i \frac{d\,\theta_e}{dt} \tag{8.29}$$

for $i = a, b, a', b'$

### 8.9.4 Static Torque

As shown in Fig. 8.3 (a), the PM motors have windings connected in such way that

$$F_1 = -F_3 \text{ and } F_2 = -F_4 \tag{8.30}$$

*8.9.4.1 Single Phase Energization*

$F_1 = -F_3 = -NI$ and $F_2 = -F_4 = 0$. Hence

$$T = -K.I\left[\sin\theta_e - \frac{NI\,\rho_1}{F_m\,P_m}\sin 2\,\theta_e\right] + \nabla T \tag{8.31a}$$

where $\nabla T$ contains higher-order terms, and the torque constant $K_t$ is given by

$$K_t = \frac{NN_R}{2}(F_m\,P_m)\left(\frac{\rho_1}{\rho_0}\right)\text{Nm/amp} \tag{8.31b}$$

Note that $K_t$ is proportional to the flux due to the permanent magnet $(F_m\,P_m)$, $\frac{\rho_1}{\rho_0}$, the number of coil turns ($N$) and the number of teeth on the rotor ($N_R$).

The permanent magnet flux $\phi_m = F_m\,P_m$ may be expressed as

$$\phi_m = F_m\,P_m = \left[\frac{B_0\,l_m}{\mu_m}\right]\left[\frac{l_m\,A_m}{\mu_m}\right] = B_0\,A_m \tag{8.32}$$

where $B_0$ = operating point on the demagnetization curve and $\mu_m$ is the incremental permeability of the rotor permanent magnet. These are shown in the demagnetization curve of Fig. 8.9. $l_m$ and $A_m$ are the length and cross-sectional area of the rotor permanent magnet.

With this substitution, static torque equation (8.31) becomes

$$T = -\frac{N_R}{2}(NI)\,(B_0\,A_m)\left[\frac{\rho_0}{\rho_1}\right]\left[\sin\theta_e - \frac{NI\,\rho_1}{B_0 A_m}\sin 2\,\theta_e\right] + \nabla T \tag{8.33}$$

For the case when $NI\,\rho_1 << B_0\,A_m$, the second harmonic term becomes negligible and we have

$$T = -\frac{N_R}{2}(NI)\,(B_0\,A_m)\left[\frac{\rho_0}{\rho_1}\right]\sin\theta_e \tag{8.34}$$

This equation leads to the torque profile shown in Fig. 8.12. Stable equilibrium points are at $\theta_e = 0$ and 360 deg., whereas $\theta = 180$ deg. represents an unstable equilibrium point.

*8.9.4.2 Effect of Second Harmonic Term*

As the excitation amphere turns $NI$ are increased by increasing $I$, the second harmonic term in Eq. (8.31) also increases. It is no longer negligible. To study the effect of second harmonic term, we rewrite Eq. (8.33) in normalized form as

$$T_n = -(\sin\theta_e - K_a \sin 2\,\theta_e) \tag{8.35}$$

where

$$T_n = T/\left[-\frac{N_R\, NI\, B_0\, A_m\, \rho_o}{2\,\rho_1}\right] \tag{8.35b}$$

and

$$K_a = NI\,\rho_1/B_0\,A_m \tag{8.35c}$$

Fig. 8.12 shows torque profiles for various values of $K_a$. For $K_a < 0.5$, the stable and unstable equilibrium points are the same as those for $K_a = 0$. However, for $K_a > 0.5$, the stable equilibrium points move towards 90 deg. and 270 deg. respectively. The larger the value of $K_a$, the greater is the maximum torque. The maximum torque points approach 135 deg. and 225 deg.

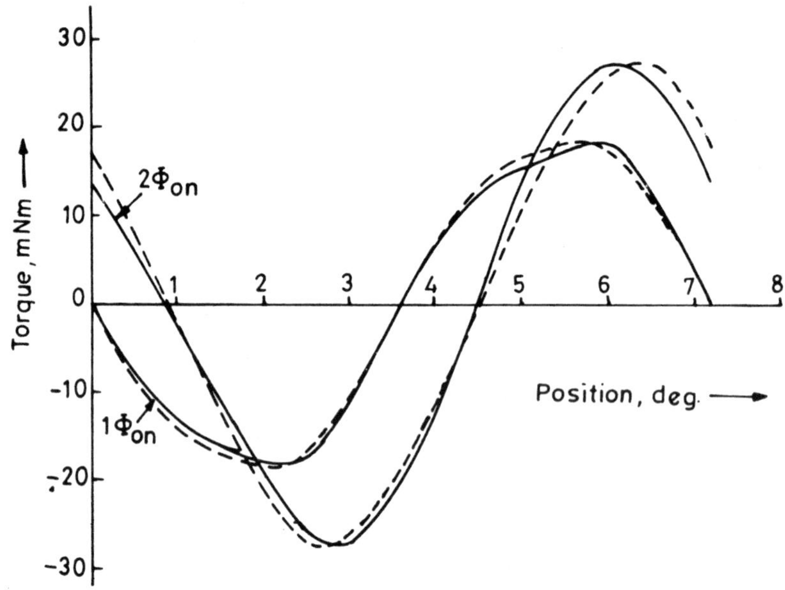


**Fig. 8.12** Torque Characteristics, 1 Phase and 2 Phases on ... Measured ... Calculated

*8.9.4.3 Two Phase Energization*

In order to increase the torque output, it is common practice to energize two sets of windings. This is equivalent to setting

$$F_1 = -F_3 = -F = -NI \tag{8.36a}$$

$$F_2 = -F_4 = -F = -NI \tag{8.36b}$$

Then $\sum_{i=1}^{4} P_i F_i = F(-P_1 + P_2 - P_3 + P_4) = -2\sqrt{2}\,F\,\xi_1 \sin(\theta_e + 45^\circ)$ (8.37a) and $$F_0 = \frac{1}{4\,\rho_0}\,[P_m\,F_m - 2\sqrt{2}\,F\,\rho_1 \cos(\theta + 45°)] \qquad (8.37b)$$

Hence the motor torque

$$T = -\sqrt{2}\,\frac{N_R}{2}\,(NI)\,(P_m\,F_m)\left(\frac{\rho_1}{\rho_0}\right)[\sin(\theta_e - 45°)]$$

$$-\frac{\sqrt{2}\,NI\,\rho_1}{F_m\,P_m}\sin 2\,(\theta_e - 45°)] + \nabla T \qquad (8.38)$$

where $\nabla T$ contains fourth and higher harmonic terms.

Comparing Eq. (8.33) with Eq. (8.38), we find that the effect of two phase energization is to increase the static torque by a factor of $\sqrt{2}$ and shifting the equilibrium point from $\theta_e = 0$ to $\theta_e = 45$ deg. Fig. 8.13 shows the torque profile with two-phase energization which brings out the above points.

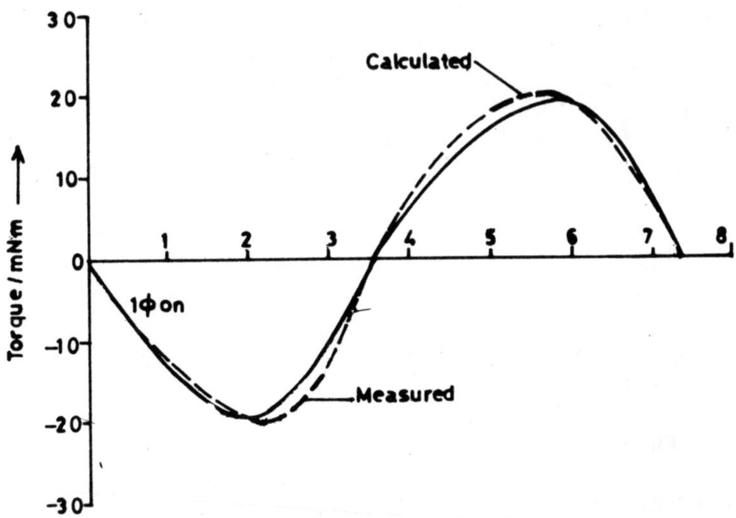


**Fig. 8.13** Torque Profiles with Two-Phase Energization

*8.9.4.4 Detent (Cogging) Torque*

It is interesting to note that even in the absence of an exciting current, i.e.,

$$F_i = 0, \quad i = 1, 2, 3, 4 \qquad (8.39)$$

there exists a torque component given by

$$T_{detent} = \frac{N_R}{2}\left(\frac{P_m\,F_m}{\rho_0}\right)^2 \rho_4 \sin 4\,\theta_e \qquad (8.40)$$

This toque is due to the 4th harmonic component of the gap permeance and has a four-cycle variation over one tooth pitch. Other multiples of the 4th harmonic exist, but their magnitudes are negligible. Also other harmonics (1st, 2nd, 3rd, 5th, ...) drop out because of the phase cancellation.

The detente torque is approximately 5-10 per cent of the holding torque. Fig. 8.14 shows the torque with one-phase energization and the detent torque. Note that the detent torque increases the stiffness around the stable equilibrium position. However, this same torque reduces the stiffness around the equilibrium position when two phases are on ($\theta_3 = 45°$).

In some applications, such as paper advance in printers, the motor with a positive detent is considered an attractive feature. But in microstepping applications, the detent torque is detrimental because it introduces a positional error. Much attention has been paid to the elimination of this torque. One obvious solution is to minimize the 4th harmonic component of the permeance by proper choice of the valley-to-tooth ratio.

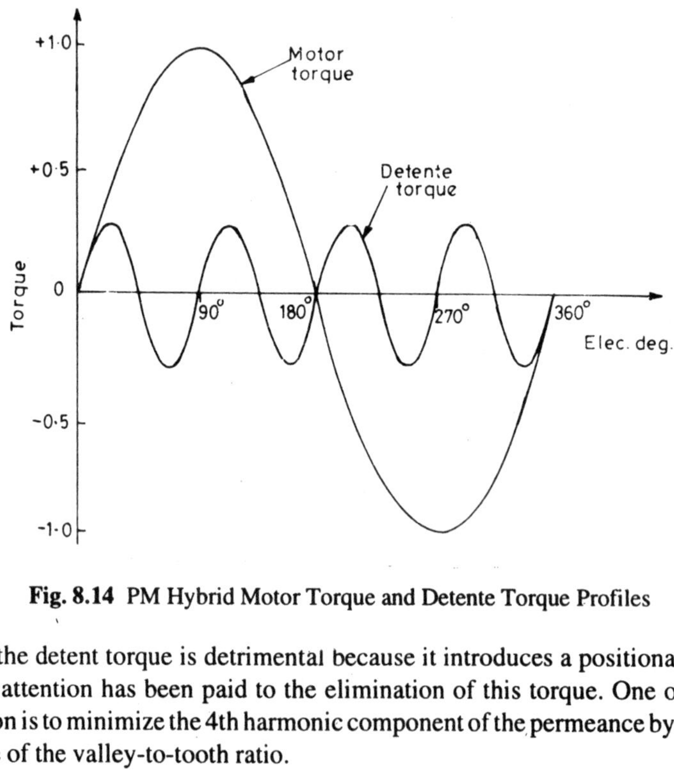


**Fig. 8.14** PM Hybrid Motor Torque and Detente Torque Profiles

In practice, because of manufacturing tolerances of motor parts the air gap permeances (Eq. 8.5) do not differ only in phase angles but also in magnitudes. Therefore, we can expect that other torque harmonics can be present.

## 8.10 VARIABLE RELUCTANCE MOTOR

An obvious difference between the PMH motor and the VR motor is the absence of the permanent magnet for the latter. In the PMH motor the torque is dependent on the direction of flux by *NI*. In the VR motor, the torque is independent of the direction of flux. For torque production, it needs a winding arrangement such as that shown in Fig. 8.15. Each phase or pole-pair has its own winding. As a result of these differences, torque, inductance, and speedance have significant differences.

### 8.10.1 Inductance

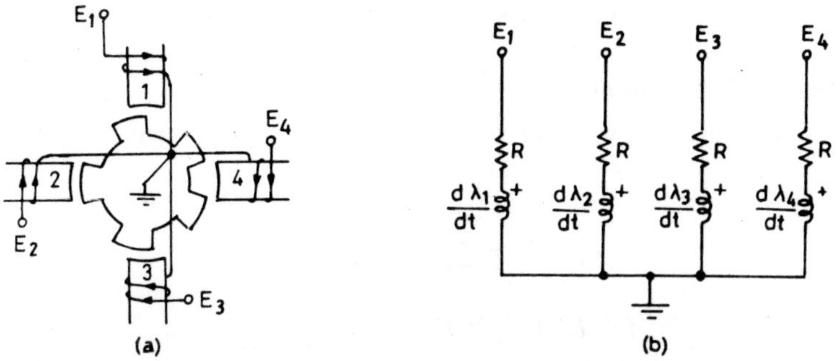


**Fig. 8.15** VR Motor Winding Arrangement and its Electrical Equivalent Circuit

Because each pole pair has its own winding, the flux linkage for each winding contains all the three mutual inductance terms, and no cancellation takes place, in contrast to the case with the PMH motor. Thus the flux linkage for winding 1 is

$$\lambda_1 = L_{11} I_1 + L_{12} I_2 + L_{13} I_3 + L_{14} I_4 \tag{8.41}$$

where

$$L_{11} = L_0 + L_1 \cos \theta_e \tag{8.42a}$$

$$L_{12} = -\frac{L_0}{3} - \frac{L_1}{\sqrt{2}} \sin (\theta_e + 45^\circ) \tag{8.42b}$$

$$L_{13} = -\frac{L_0}{3} \tag{8.42c}$$

$$L_{14} = -\frac{L_0}{3} + \frac{L_1}{\sqrt{2}} \sin (\theta_e - 45^\circ) \tag{8.42d}$$

In contrast to the PMH motor, the mutual coupling is quite strong and the first harmonic term is large.

### 8.10.2 Back EMF Constants

In the PMH motor, the only speedance terms is the one due to the permanent magnet, and all the other terms are zero. In the VR motor all the terms are present. They are, from Eq. (8.21).

$$K_{11} = -L_1 \left[ \sin \theta_e - \frac{\rho_1}{2 \rho_0} \sin 2 \theta_e \right] \tag{8.43a}$$

$$K_{12} = \frac{L_1}{2}\left[\sqrt{2}\,\sin\,(\theta_e - 45^\circ) - \frac{\rho_1}{\rho_0}\cos\,2\,\theta_e\right] \tag{8.43b}$$

$$K_{13} = -\frac{L_1\,\rho_1}{2\,\rho_0}\sin\,2\,\theta_e \tag{8.43c}$$

$$K_{14} = \frac{L_1}{2}\left[\sqrt{2}\,\sin\,(\theta_e + 45^\circ) + \frac{\rho_1}{\rho_0}\cos\,2\,\theta_e\right] \tag{8.43d}$$

### 8.10.3 Voltage Equation

Since there are four winding, there are four voltage equations to solve. They are

$$E_i = RI_i + \sum_{n=1}^{4}\left(L_{in}\frac{dI_n}{dt} + K_{in}\frac{d\,\theta_e}{dt}\right) \tag{8.44}$$

for $i = 1, 2, 3, 4$

Note the strong coupling in inductance and speedance among the windings.

### 8.10.4 Torque

Let us excite the motor with one phase such that

$$F_1 = NI \text{ and } F_2 = F_3 = F_4 = 0 \tag{8.45}$$

By solving Eq. (8.22)

$$T = -K_t\,I^2\left[\sin\,\theta_e - \frac{\rho_1}{3\,\rho_0}\sin\,2\,\theta_e\right] + \nabla T \tag{8.46a}$$

where the torque constant is

$$K_t = \frac{9}{32}N_R\,\rho_1\,N^2 \tag{8.46b}$$

Fig. 8.15 (c) shows the torque profile for the VR motor. The presence of the second harmonic term is easily noted. For this particular example, the mag-

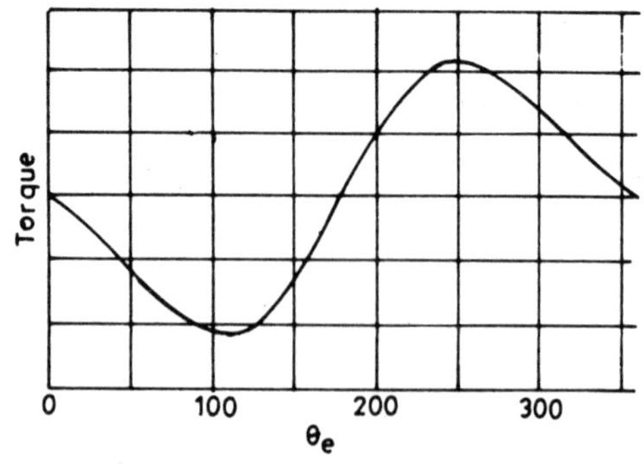


**Fig. 8.15 (c)** Torque Profile for VR Motor

nitude of the second harmonic is 16 per cent of the first harmonic, and this percentage does not change with a change in ampere-turns. This is in contrast to the second harmonic of the PMH motor, which is proportional to *NI*. For small value of *NI*, the VR motor has much less torque the PMH counterpart. But because the torque is proportional to $(NI)^2$, its value becomes bigger at large values of *NI* than the PMH motor, whose torque is proportional to *NI*. In practical motors, however, the saturation limits the increase in torque.

## 8.11 ILLUSTRATIVE EXAMPLES

The following numerical example is meant to illustrate the magnetic equivalent circuit, inductance, and torque calculations for both PMH and VR stepper motors.

The data for a *PMH stepper motor* are as follows:

Step angle = 1.8 mech. deg.
Number of poles = 4
Number of rotor teeth, $N_R = 50$

Permanent magnet

Diameter = 25 mm
Thickness = 3 mm
Flux density = 0.8 Tesla
Incremental permeability $\approx 4\pi \times 10^{-7}$ H

From the above, we obtain

$P_m = 0.206$ μh
$F_m = 1911$ amp-turn
Number of turns, $N = 100$ turns
Current, $I = 1$ amp
Tooth width, $W_t = 0.8$ mm
Valley width, $W_v = 1.2$ mm
Air gap, $l_g = 0.067$ mm
Stack thickness, $t = 10$ mm
Number of teeth/pole = 10

*Permeances.* Using the above values and the permeance data in Table 8.1 we find first five Fourier coefficients in Eq. (8.3) for 10 teeth per pole:

$$\rho_0 = 1.178 \ \mu h$$

$$\rho_1 = 0.576 \ \mu h$$

$$\rho_2 = 0.015 \ \mu h$$

$$\rho_3 = 0.028 \ \mu h$$

$$\rho_4 = 0.012 \ \mu h$$

*Inductances.* For $N = 100$ turns and the above permeance coefficients, we get, for the PMH motor,

$$L_0 = 8.84 \text{ mH and } L_i = 2.88 \text{ mH}$$

Using Eq. (8.26) with the above values, we get

$$L_{aa} = \frac{8}{3} L_0 = 23.57 \text{ mH and } L_{ab} = 0$$

*Back EMF Constants.* Using Eq. (8.27), $K_g = 9.62 \text{ mV/(rad/s)}_{\text{elec}}$ whereas $K_{aa} = K_{bb} = 0$ and $K_{am} = K_g \sin \theta_e = 9.62 \sin \theta_e$.

*Static Torque with 1-phase Energization.* From Eq. (8.37), we get

$$T = -4.81\,(NI)\left[\sin \theta_e - \frac{(1.46)\,(NI)}{1000} \sin 2\,\theta_e\right]$$

For $NI = 100$ amp-turns, $T = -481\,[\sin \theta_e - 0.146 \sin 2\,\theta_e]$

$$\approx -481 \sin \theta_e \text{ (mN-m)}$$

Note that $K_a = 0.146$ is << 1 and hence the effect of the second harmonic term on the static torque can be neglected.

*Static Torque with 2-Phase Energization.* Using Eq. (8.33) along with the above numerical values yields static torque with 2-phase energization as

$$T_{2ph} = \sqrt{2}\, T_1 = 680\,[\sin (\theta_e - 45^\circ) - 0.146 \sin 2\,(\theta_e - 45^\circ)] \quad \text{(nN-m)}$$

*Cogging Torque.* Substituting numerical values in Eq. (8.40) yields

$$T_{detent} = -33 \sin 4\,\theta_e \text{ (mN-m)}$$

This is approximately 7 per cent of the fundamental torque.

**Variable Reluctance (VR) Stepper Motor.** With the same numerical data as above except for absence of permanent magnet, we get Eqs. (8.47).

*Inductances.* Putting the values in Eqs. (8.47)

$$L_{11} = 8.84 + 2.88 \cos \theta_e$$

$$L_{12} = -2.95 - 2.04 \sin (\theta_e + 45^\circ)$$

$$L_{13} = -2.95$$

$$L_{14} = -2.95 + 2.04 \sin (\theta_e - 45^\circ)$$

in milli-henries. Other inductance terms can be similarly obtained.

*Back EMF Constants.* Back EMF constants are obtained from Eqs. (8.43)

$$K_{11} = -2.88\,[\sin \theta_e - 0.24 \sin 2\,\theta_e]$$

$$K_{12} = 1.44\,[\sqrt{2} \sin (\theta_e - 45^\circ) - 0.49 \cos 2\,\theta_e]$$

$$K_{13} = -0.70 \sin 2\,\theta_e$$

$$K_{14} = 1.44\,[\sqrt{2} \sin (\theta_e + 45^\circ) + 0.49 \cos 2\,\theta_e)]$$

*Torque.* From Eq. (8.46) we get

$$T = -(8.1 \times 10^{-3}) - (NI)^2\,[\sin \theta_e - 0.16 \sin 2\,\theta_e] \text{ (mN-m)}$$

For $NI = 100$ amp-turns

$$T = -81\ [\sin \theta_e - 0.16 \sin 2\,\theta_e]\ \text{(mN-m)}$$

We thus see that the torque output of VR motor is much smaller than PMH motors for low amp-turns. However, as $NI$ increase, $T$ for PMH motor increases linearly with $NI$, where it increase as $(NI)^2$ for VR motor.

## 8.12 DYNAMIC PULL-OUT TORQUE

Until now we have considered the steady state operation of the stepper motor. In this section, we turn our attention to dynamic operation of the stepper motor, when it is running at $F_s$ steps/s. We consider the most popular permanent magnet hybrid (PMH) stepper motor having a step angle of 1.8°. Such a motor could be viewed as a 100-pole 2-phase synchronous motor, and can therefore be represented by the simple model of Fig. 8.16 [4, 5]. The angle between the two phases is $(\pi/2\,p)$ (mechanical) corresponding to $(\pi/2)$ (electrical) where $p$ = no. of pole pairs. One step of the motor corresponds to a movement of $(\pi/2\,p)$ (mech.). Thus, for a 100-pole machine, $p = 50$ and one step becomes 1.8°.

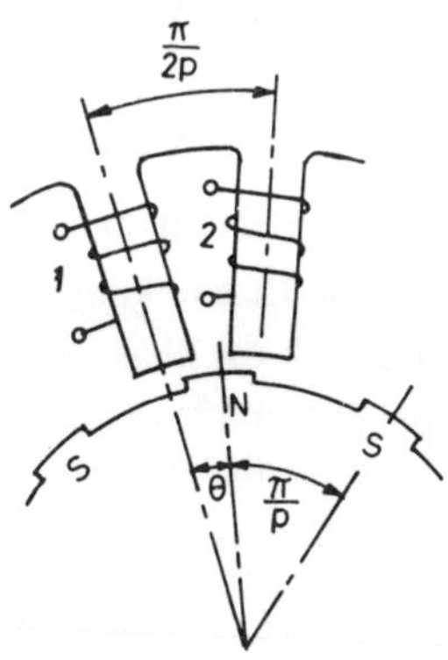


**Fig. 8.16** Simple Model of 2p-Pole Motor

We assume that the two phases of the stepper motor are energized by bi-polar square waves having 90° (electrical) phase difference, as shown in Fig. 8.17. The motor speed of $F_S$, steps/s corresponds to angular speed

$$\omega = 2\,\pi f = 2\,\pi\,(F_s/4)\ \text{(rad/s)} \tag{8.47}$$

Hence the square wave voltages applied to the two phases may be expanded into Fourier series. The fundamental components of the phase voltages are shown by dotted lines in Fig. 8.17. These fundamental voltages are given by

$$V_1 = V \cos \omega t \tag{8.48a}$$

$$V_2 = V \cos (\omega t - \pi/2) \tag{8.48b}$$

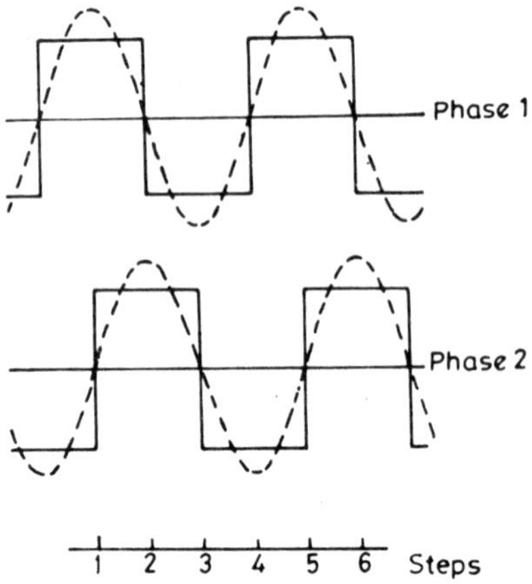


**Fig. 8.17** Voltage Waveforms, showing Fundamental Component

The phase currents $I_1$ and $I_2$ are then given by

$$V_1 = RI_1 + L\,(dI_1/dt) + d\,(N\,\phi_m \cos p\,\theta)/dt \qquad (8.45a)$$

$$V_2 = RI_2 + L\,(dI_2/dt) + d\,(N\,\phi_m \cos (p\,\theta - \pi/2)/dt \qquad (8.45b)$$

where $R$, $L$ are winding resistance and inductance, while $\phi_m$ is the flux due to the permanent magnet. $N\,\phi_m$ is the flux linking a phase having $N$ turns when the rotor teeth are fully aligned with the phase winding. When the rotor tooth is displaced from fully aligned position by an angle $\theta$, as shown in Fig. 8.16, the permanent magnet flux linking the phase is $\phi = N\,\phi_m \cos p\,\theta$. Then the fundamental component of the torque is given by

$$T = -\,pN\,\phi_m\,[I_1 \sin (p\,\theta) + I_2 \sin (p\,\theta - \pi/2)] \qquad (8.49)$$

Equations (8.44), (8.45) and (8.46) can be solved by means of a $d - q$ transformation, which is a popular technique of synchronous motor analysis. The resulting expression for the torque produced by the motor at a constant speed of $\omega$ rad/s is given by

$$T = (pN\,\phi_m/Z)\,[V \sin (\delta + \phi_0)] - (pN^2\,\phi_m^2\,\omega R/Z^2) \qquad (8.50)$$

where $Z = \sqrt{R^2 + \omega^2 L^2}$ = impedance of motor winding at an angular speed of '$\omega$' rad/s (i.e. stepping rate $F_s$ rad/s)

$\delta$ = rotor load angle

and $\phi_0 = \tan^{-1}(\omega L/R)$ = phase angle at speed $\omega$ (rad/s)

Torque $T$ will be a maximum when $\delta + \phi_0 = \pi/2$. This maximum torque is called pull-out torque, and is given by

$$T_m = \frac{PN\,\phi_m \,.\, V}{Z} - \frac{pN^2\,\phi_m^2\,\omega R}{Z^2} \tag{8.51}$$

$$T_s = pN\,\phi_m\,(V/R) = p\,.\,\phi_m\,(NI) \tag{8.52}$$

Then $T_m/T_s = [1/\sqrt{1 + (\omega^2 L^2/R^2)}\,] - K_p\,[(\omega\, L/R)\,/\,(1 + (\omega^2 L^2/R^2)]$ (8.53a)

$= [1/\sqrt{1 + \omega^2\,\tau_e^2}\,] - K_p\,\omega\,\tau_e/[1 + \omega^2\,\tau_e^2]$

$= \cos\phi_0\,[1 - K_p\,\sin\phi_0]$ (8.53b)

where $K_p = N\,\phi_m/[L\,(V/R)] = N\,\phi_m/(LI) = N\,\phi_m\,/(V_0\,\tau_e)$ (8.53c)

and $\tau_e = L/R$ (8.53d)

Equation (8.53) shows that the pull-out torque at a given speed $\omega$ is determined by two factors: (i) electrical time constant, $\tau_e$, and

$$\text{(ii) } K_p = \frac{N\,\phi_m}{LI} = \frac{\text{flux linkages due permanent magnet}}{\text{flux linkages due to phase currents}} \tag{8.54}$$

'$K_p$' is thus similar to 'short circuit ratio' used to characterize large synchronous machines.

The effects of $\tau_e$ and '$K_p$' on the pull-out torque of the motor are shown in Fig. 8.18. It is clear that as $\tau_e$ increases, the pull-out torque decreases. Similarly, there is a fall in the pull-out torque as '$K_p$' increases. For most PMH motors, $K_p$ lies in the range 0.2 to 0.6, the optimum value being 0.25. Secondly, we see that, by employing *R/L* drive, we obtain increased pull-out torque inasmuch as the effective $\tau_e$ decreases.

The pull-out power of the motor at a specified frequency $\omega$ (rad/s) is obtained as $P_0 = T\,\omega$ [6] where $T$ is given by Eq. (8.48). Thus

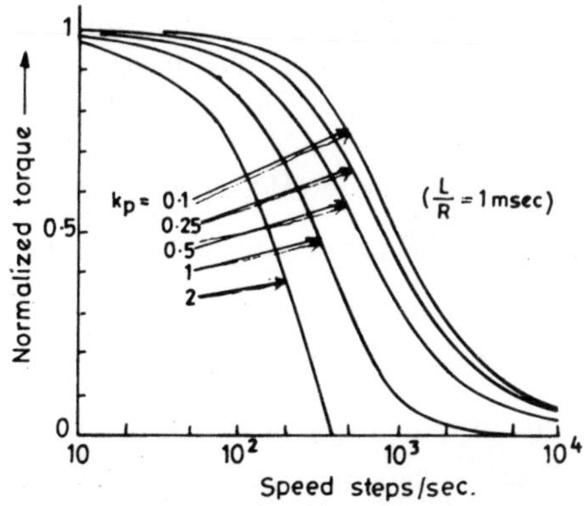


**Fig. 8.18 (a)** Effect of $K_p$ on Pull-Out Torque

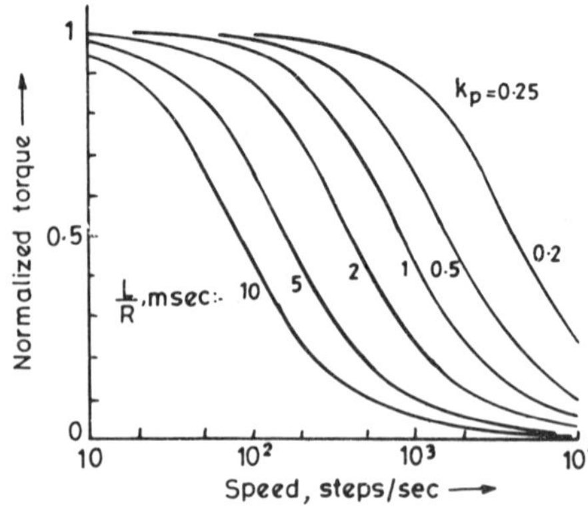


**Fig. 8.18 (b)** Effect of L/R on Pull-Out Torque

$$P_0 = \frac{\omega N \phi_m V}{\sqrt{R^2 + \omega^2 L^2}} - \frac{\omega^2 N^2 \phi_m^2 R}{\sqrt{R^2 + \omega^2 L^2}} \tag{8.55a}$$

$$= \frac{\omega N \phi_m I}{\sqrt{1 + \tau_e^2}} - \frac{\omega^2 N^2 \phi_m^2}{\sqrt{R\,[1 + \omega^2 \tau_e^2]}} \tag{8.55b}$$

## 8.13 ELECTROMAGNETIC DAMPING

Suppose that the stepper moot is at rest in its stable equilibrium condition $\theta = 0$. When we go to the next step in the excitation sequence, the motor will go through one step. The typical motion of the rotor is shown in Fig. 8.19, which is immediately recognized as oscillatory response of an underdamped mechanical system. O'Donahue [7] was the first to model this oscillatory motion of the rotor by a second order transfer function. Kieburtz [8], Robinson and Taft [9, 10] have also derived similar transfer functions. However, such a simplistic transfer function is not at all satisfactory. We, therefore, derive below a more accurate transfer function of the steeper motor [11].

### 8.13.1 Transfer Function of the PMH Stepper Motor

We have shown above that the torque produced by current $I_1$ flowing through phase winding 1 is given by

$$T_1 = -(N_R/2)\,\phi_m \,.\, NI_1 \sin p\,\theta \tag{8.56a}$$

whereas the torque due to current $I_2$ in phase 2 is given by

$$T_2 = -(N_R/2)\,\phi_m\, NI_2 \sin (p\,\theta - \lambda) \tag{8.56b}$$

where $\lambda$ = pole pitch as shown in Fig. 8.16, and $p$ = no. of pole pairs.

Let $J$ be the moment of inertia of the rotor and $B$ be the viscous damping coefficient. The equation of motion of the rotor with one phase excitation is given by

$$J \frac{d^2 \theta}{dt^2} + B \frac{d\theta}{dt} = \phi_m N [I_1 \sin p\,\theta + I_2 \sin (p\,\theta - \lambda)] \tag{8.57}$$

Neglecting hysteresis and eddy current losses, the voltage equations for the phase winding are given by

$$V = RI_1 + L \frac{dI_1}{dt} + M \frac{dI_2}{dt} - \frac{d}{dt} (N\,\phi_m \cos p\,\theta) \tag{8.58a}$$

$$V = RI_2 + L \frac{dI_2}{dt} + M \frac{dI_1}{dt} - \frac{d}{dt} (N\,\phi_m \cos p\,(\theta - 90°)) \tag{8.58b}$$

Using the small signal linearization method about the operating point $\theta_0 = 0$, $I_{10} = I_{20} = I_0$, we get linearized equations

$$J \frac{d^2}{dt^2} (\delta\,\theta) + B \frac{d}{dt} (\delta\theta) = 2\,p^2\,\phi_m N I_0 \cos (p\,\lambda/2)\,.\,(\delta\theta) + p\,\phi_m N \sin (p\,\lambda/2)\,.\,(\delta\,I_1 - \delta\,I_2) \tag{8.59a}$$

$$R\,(\delta\,I_1) + L \frac{d}{dt} (\delta\,I_1) + M \frac{d}{dt} (\delta\,I_2) - p\,\phi_m N \sin (p\,\lambda/2) \frac{d}{dt} (\delta\,\theta) = 0 \tag{8.59b}$$

$$R\,(\delta\,I_2) + L \frac{d}{dt} (\delta\,I_2) + M \frac{d}{dt} (\delta\,I_1) + p\,\phi_m N \sin (p\,\lambda/2) \frac{d}{dt} (\delta\,\theta) = 0 \tag{8.59c}$$

where $\delta\,\theta = \theta - \theta_0$, $\delta\,I_1 = I_1 - I_{10}$ and $\delta\,I_2 = I_2 - I_{20}$.

Taking Laplace transform of Eqs. (8.56) and eliminating all the intermediate variables, we get the motor transfer function as

$$\delta\,I_1\,(s) = -\,\delta\,I_2\,(s) = \frac{p\,\phi_m N \sin (p\,\lambda/2)\,[s\,\theta\,(s) - \theta_1\,(s)\,]}{(R + L_p\,s)} \tag{8.60}$$

$$\delta\,\theta\,(s) = \frac{\left[s^2 + \left(\frac{R}{L_p} + \frac{B}{J}\right)s + \left(\frac{R}{L_p}\frac{B}{J} + K_p\,\omega_{np}^2\right)\right]\theta_i\,(s)}{s^3 + \left(\frac{R}{L_p} + \frac{B}{j}\right)s^2 + \left(\frac{R}{L_p}\frac{B}{J} + \omega_{np}^2\,(1 + K_p)\right)s + \left(\frac{R}{L_p}\right)\omega_{np}^2} \tag{8.61}$$

where

$$L_p = L - M \tag{8.62a}$$

$$K_p = \frac{N\,\phi_m}{L_p\,I_0}\frac{\sin^2 (p\,\lambda/2)}{\cos (p\,\lambda/2)} \tag{8.62b}$$

and

$$\omega_{np}^2 = [2p^2\,\phi_m N I_0 \cos (p\,\lambda/2)]/J \tag{8.62c}$$

### 8.13.2 Characteristic Equation of Rotor Oscillations

From Eq. (8.57b), we obtain the characteristic equation of motion of the rotor as:

$$s^3 + \left(\frac{R}{L_p} + \frac{B}{J}\right)s^2 + \left[\frac{R}{L_p} \cdot \frac{B}{J} + (1 + K_p)\,\omega_{np}^2\right]s + \frac{R}{L_p}\,\omega_{np}^2 = 0 \quad (8.63)$$

In the following analysis, our main interest centers on the electro-magnetic damping. We, therefore, neglect the mechanical damping term, $B/J$. The characteristic equation thereupon simplifies to

$$s^3 + (R/L_p)\,s^2 + (1 + K_p)\,\omega_{np}^2\,s + (R/L_p)\,\omega_{np}^2 = 0 \quad (8.64)$$

Factorizing the l.h.s. yields

$$(s + \alpha)\,[(s + \beta)^2 + \Omega^2] = 0 \quad (8.65)$$

Hence, the transient response of the rotor will be of the form:

$$\delta\,\theta\,(t) = Ae^{-\alpha t} + Be^{-\beta t}\sin\,(\Omega t + \psi) \quad (8.66)$$

The two components of $\delta\,\theta\,(t)$ are shown in Fig. 8.19 (a, b), and their sum is shown in Fig. 8.19 (c).

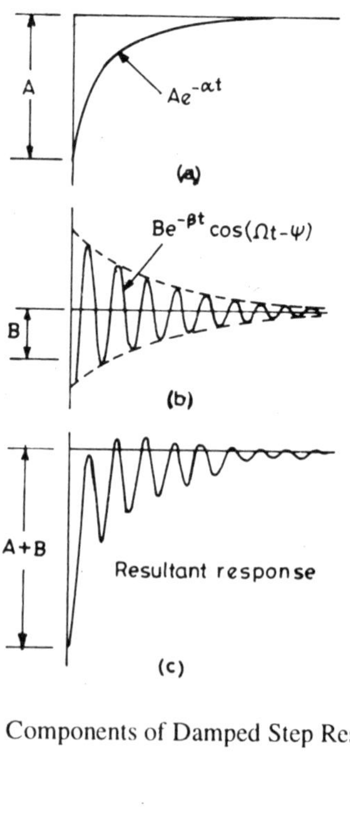


**Fig. 8.19** Components of Damped Step Response

Equating coefficients of equal powers of $s$ in Eqs. (8.61) and (8.62) yields

$$\alpha + 2\beta = R/L_p;\ 2\alpha\beta + \beta^2 + \Omega^2 = (1 + K_p)\,\omega_{np}^2;$$

$$\alpha(\beta^2 + \Omega^2) = (R/L_p)\,\omega_{np}^2 \tag{8.67}$$

We now normalize the coefficients in (8.67) w.r.t. $\omega_{np}$, yielding

$$\alpha' = \alpha/\omega_{np};\ \beta' = \beta/\omega_{np};\ \Omega' = \Omega/\omega_{np};\ (R/L)' = \frac{R/L}{\omega_{np}} \tag{8.68}$$

Then the normalized coefficient relations become

$$\alpha' + 2\beta' = (R/L)';\ 2\cdot\alpha'\beta' + \beta'^2 + \Omega'^2 = 1 + K_p;\ \alpha'(\beta'^2 + \Omega'^2) = (R/L_0)' \tag{8.69}$$

The dependance of $\alpha'$ and $\beta'$ on motor parameters $K_p$ and $(R/L_p)'$ is shown in Fig. 8.20. In order to appreciate the significance of this figure, we note that $\alpha'$ and $\beta'$ values have the same meaning as damping ratio $\zeta$ of a second order oscillatory system. Thus $\beta' = 0.1$ would lead to an oscillatory response similar to that of a second order system with $\zeta = 0.1$.

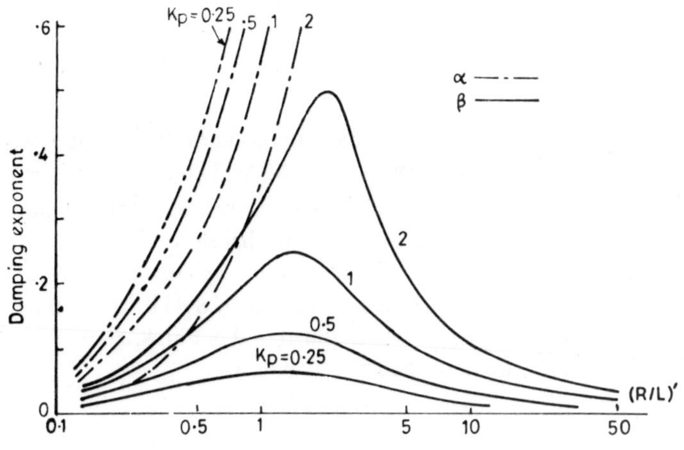


**Fig. 8.20** Dependence of Damping Exponents of Motor Parameters

Examination of Fig. 8.20 shows that in the range of $K_p$ values encountered in practice, viz. 0.2 to 0.6, $\alpha'$ is greater than $\beta'$. Hence the condition for $\beta'$ to have its maximum value can, therefore, be taken as the condition for optimum damping. Now, the conditions for $\beta'$ to be maximum can be derived as follows:

(i) Value of $(R/L)'$ to yield $\beta'_{max} = 1 + K_p/2$ (8.70a)

(ii) $\beta'_{max} = K_p/4$ (8.70b)

(iii) Corresponding value of $\alpha' = 1$ (8.70c)

This shows that, values of $\beta'_{max} \rightarrow 1$, which imply good damping, require very high value of $K_p \rightarrow 4$. However, in practice, $K_p$ ranges from 0.2 to 0.6. This corresponds to damping ratio $\zeta = 0.05$ to 0.15. The rotor is thus very poorly damped, resulting in highly oscillatory response.

This brings us to one of the basic conflicts in PMH stepper motor design viz. high pull-out torque at high frequency requires low values of $K_p$, while good damping demands high vaiues of $K_p \rightarrow 4$.

On delving deeper into $K_p$, we notice that it is the ratio of flux linkages ($N\,\phi_m$) produced by the permanent magnet to the flux linkages ($L_p\,I$) due to current $I$ flowing through the phase winding. There are very many ways of dividing the total flux linkages, needed to produce the specified static torque, into $N\,\phi_m$ and $L_p\,I$ i.e. between the permanent magnet and the phase windings. Each combination of $N\,\phi_m$ and $L_p\,I$ resultants in a different value for $K_p$, and consequently to damping ratio $\beta'$ and pull-out torque characteristics. We have to trade-off pull-out torque against $\beta'$.

One way of resolving the conflict is to alter $(R/L)'$ ratio by increasing $R'$. This can be accomplished by connecting an external resistance in series with the motor winding [24]. It then becomes possible to meet the requirements of high pull-out torque and good damping simultaneously.

## 8.14 METHODS OF DAMPING

We have seen above that, in order to obtain good running torque, we have to set the parameter $K_p$ in the range 0.2 to 0.6. As a consequence, the damping ratio $\beta'$ is very low. Consequently, the single step response of the motor is highly oscillatory as can be seen from Fig. 8.21. It, therefore, becomes necessary to employ special methods for damping oscillations of the rotor. Several methods of damping have been suggested in literature [28-41]. These may be conveniently divided into three classes as illustrated in Fig. 8.22. A few important methods of damping are described briefly below.

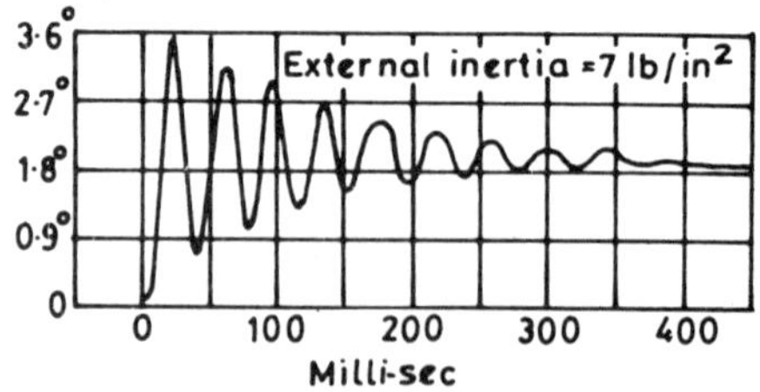


**Fig. 8.21** Single Step Response

- Damping Methods
  - Electro-mechanical
    - Viscous Inertia Damping
    - Eddy Current Damping
  - Electrical
    - Resistive
    - Capacitive
  - Electronic
    - Reverse Last Pulse
    - Delayed Last Step
    - High Frequency Pulsing

**Fig. 8.22** Methods of Damping

## 8.14.1 Viscous-Inertia Damping [31]

In this method, an inertia-friction disk is mounted on the stepper motor shaft as shown in Fig. 8.23 (a). It consists of a hollow cylinder filled with a viscous fluid such as silicone fluid or transformer oil. In this fluid is immersed damping inertia which often takes the form of two or four fan-like blades. As long as the motor shaft is at rest or is rotating at a constant speed, both the housing and the damping inertia rotate together freely; there is no damping. However, when the rotor begins oscillating in response to an input pulse, there is relative motion between damping inertia and the housing containing viscous fluid. Viscous friction is consequently introduced, which helps in damping out the rotor oscillation. Fig. 8.23 (b) illustrates this effect vividly.

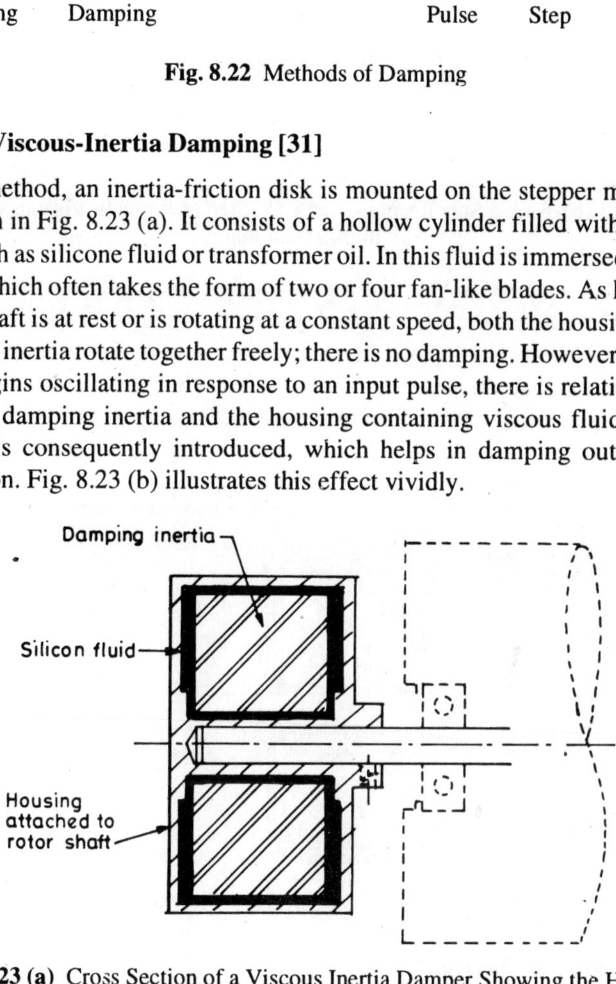


**Fig. 8.23 (a)** Cross Section of a Viscous Inertia Damper Showing the Housing Fixed to the Step Motor Shaft and the Viscously Coupled Inertia

## 8.14.2 Eddy Current Damping

In this method, a thin aluminium drag cup is mounted on the motor shaft as shown in Fig. 8.24. The drag cup rotates in the magnetic field set up a permanent

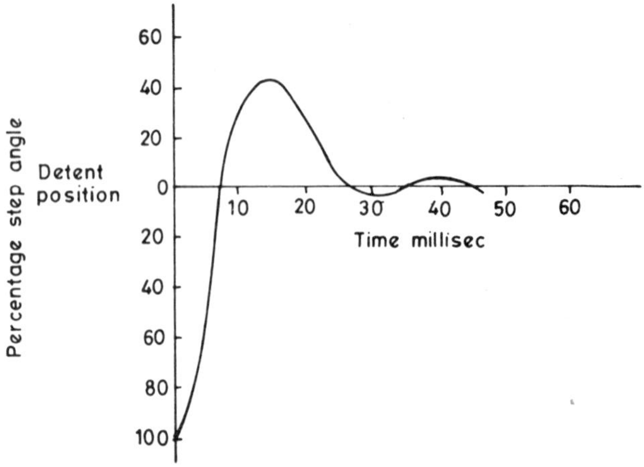


**Fig. 8.23 (b)** Single Step Response for a 15° Step Motor with Viscous Coupled Inertia Damping

magnet. The magnet and soft iron poles pieces for providing magnetic flux return path make up the inertia which is free to rotate on bearings. When the motor shaft begins to oscillate, there is relative motion between the drag cup and the permanent magnet. Eddy currents are induced in the drag cup which produces a damping torque. The motor oscillations are consequently quickly damped out.

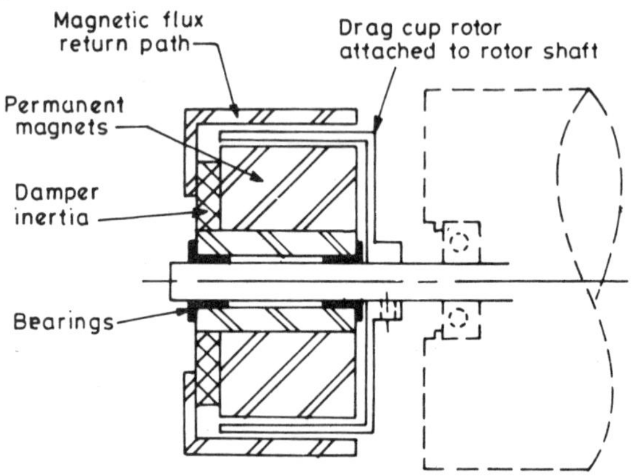


**Fig. 8.24** A Cross Section of an Eddy-Current Inertia Damper

### 8.14.3 Resistive Damping

Fig. 8.25 (a) illustrates this method of damping. Herein Q1-Q4 are driver transistors which are turned on when the corresponding phase winding is to be energized. When this phase winding, say phase 1, is to be de-energized, the corresponding drive transistor, $Q1$, is turned off. Simultaneously $Q5$ is turned on. The damping resistor $R_D$ is introduced into the circuit. This causes oscillations to be damped out, as shown in Fig. 8.25 (b). For best results, $Q5$ is turned on at the last but one step and switched off immediately after the step in order to reduce motor heating.

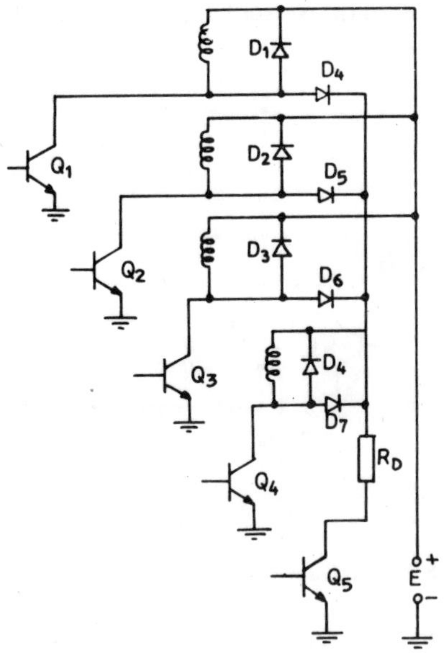


**Fig. 8.25 (a)** Resistance Damping

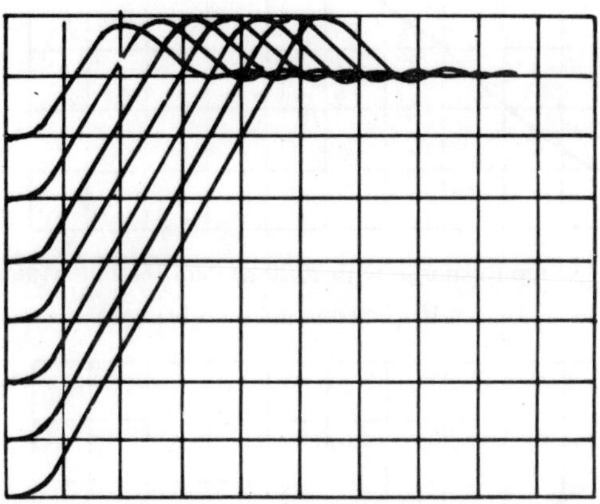

**Fig. 8.25 (b)** Rotor Position Vs. Time Using Resistive Damping. The Resistor is Switched in when Stopping. Set is Switched Out After a Short Time Delay, to Reduce Motor Heating

### 8.14.4 Capacitive Damping

This scheme is often adopted in bifilar wound stepper motors. Fig. 8.26 (a) shows the typical capacitive damping scheme, in which a capacitor $C$ is connected across the bifilar windings: Ph1 + Ph3 and Ph2 + Ph4. When a phase winding, say Ph1, is de-energized by switching TR 1 off, capacitor *C* provides a low impedance path for the AC back emf induced in it due to oscillation of the permanent magnet rotor. The current flowing through the capacitor in the closed loop shown in Fig. 8.26 (a) is oscillatory in nature. This causes dissipa-

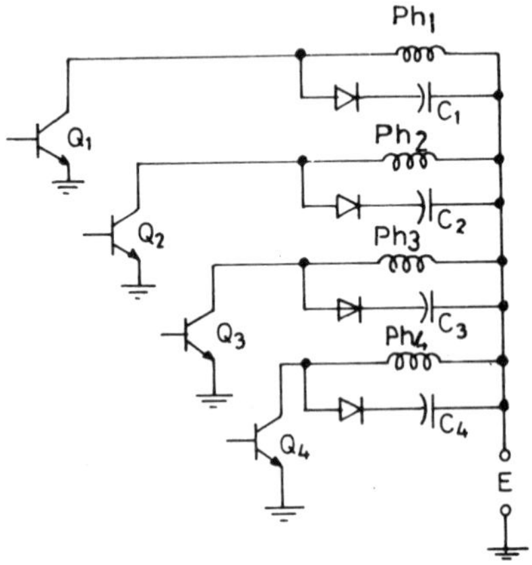


**Fig. 8.26 (a)** Capacitive Damping Circuit

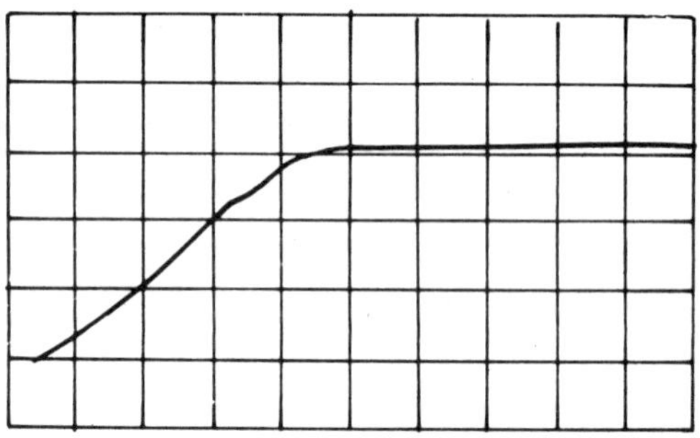

**Fig. 8.26 (b)** Single Step Response with 2200 μ*f* Parallel with Motor Winding Load J $1.7 \times 10^{-4}$ oz-in-sec$^2$ – no Friction

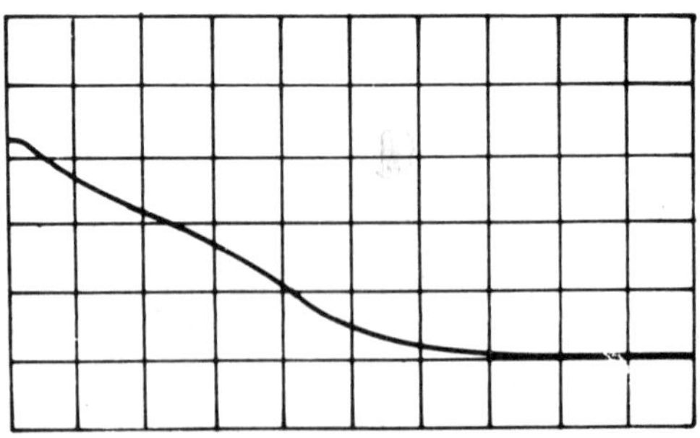

**Fig. 8.26 (c)** Current decay with capacitive damping SM 072-0060 RA step motor driven 2 phases on 24 volts @ 1.7 amps/phase 7.8 Ω resistor in series with each phase Scale Horizontal 5 msec/div Vertical 0.5 amp/div

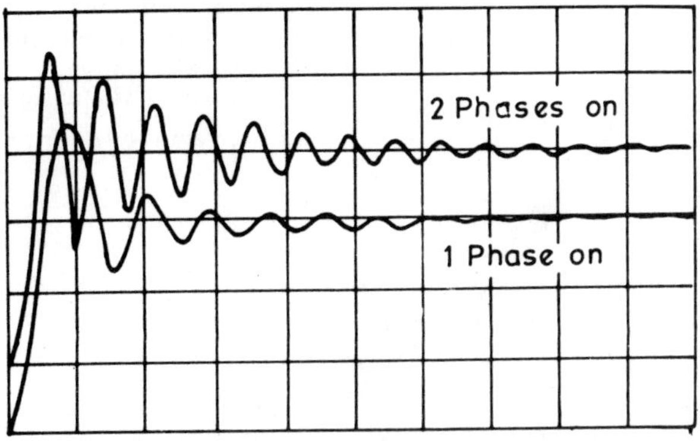


**Fig. 8.26 (d)** 1-phase on Damping Compared to Normal 2-Phase on Single-Step Response Walner SM-024-0030-RA Step Motor Driven 24 Volt 1.6 Amps/Phase with 9 Series Resistor in each Return Lead 8 Ω Resistor Diode Suppression Load. Inertia $1.85 \times 10^4$. Friction 0 Vertical 5 Degrees/cm; Horizontal 10 msec/cm

tion of kinetic energy of the oscillating rotor and hence to damping out of these oscillations. Typical pull-out currents for a stepper motor with capacitive damping are shown in Fig. 8.26 (b).

Capacitive damping arrangement for a four phase permanent magnetic stepper motor is shown in Fig. 8.27 (a) and pull-out torques for various values of $C$ are shown in Fig. 8.27 (b).

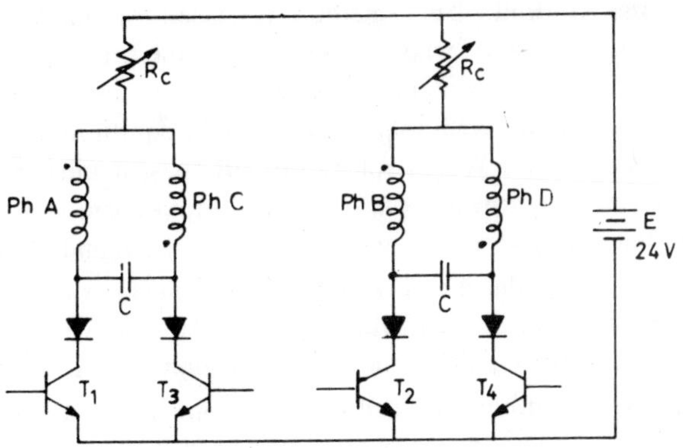


**Fig. 8.27 (a)** Four-Phase Driver with Condenser Suppressor. External Resistors Denoted by $R$ are adjusted so that the Current is at Rating

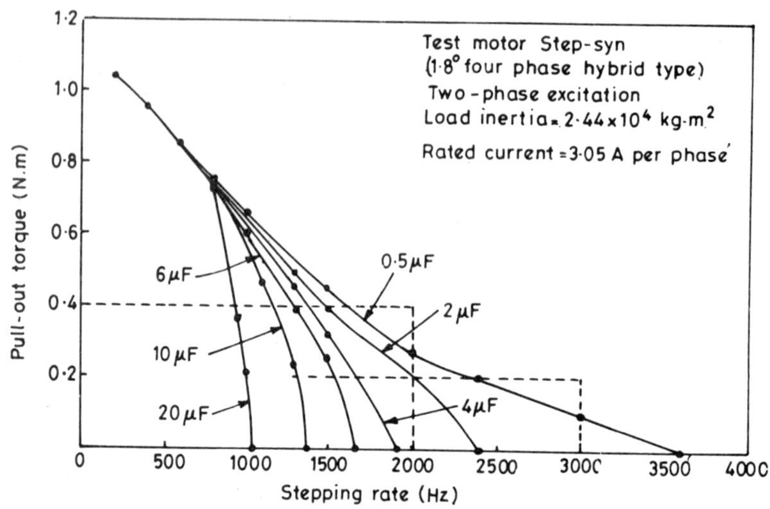


**Fig. 8.27 (b)** Variation of Pull-out Torque Curve with Capacitor connected between Phase-measured on the Circuit of Fig. 5.22 (from Ref. 2)

### 8.14.5 Electronic Damping Methods

These are active damping schemes in contrast to passive damping schemes studied so far. They involve a variation in the normal pattern of energization of stepper motor windings. Among the multitude of methods of electronic damping, we study two popular methods: reverse last pulse and delayed last step methods.

**Reverse Last Pulse Method.** This method is based on negative torque produced by the stepper motor when we go back to the previous step in the switching sequence of the motor. Figure 8.28 (a) illustrates the principle of 'back-phasing'. Suppose we wish to go from phase *A* equilibrium position to phase *B* equilibrium position. We, therefore, turn off phase *A* and turn on Phase *B*. The rotor starts moving towards phase *B* equilibrium position as shown in Fig. 8.28. At an intermediate time $t_1$, we switch off phase *B* and switch on the previous phase *A*. This produces a reverse torque which slows down the rotor and causes the rotor to come to rest when it equals the positive torque due to phase *B*. Now $t_1$ is so selected that the rotor will momentarily come to rest exactly at the phase *B* equilibrium position. At this instant $t_2$ we de-energize phase *A* and re-energize phase *B*. All of this calls for a delicate balance between switching on and off of phase *B* and phase *A* windings, but the results are much better than passive damping schemes.

**Delayed Last Step Damping.** This scheme becomes operative in the final three-steps of an *N*-step move. In the last three steps, if input pulses are applied at regular intervals, we obtain oscillatory motion of the rotor as shown in Fig. 8.21 (a).

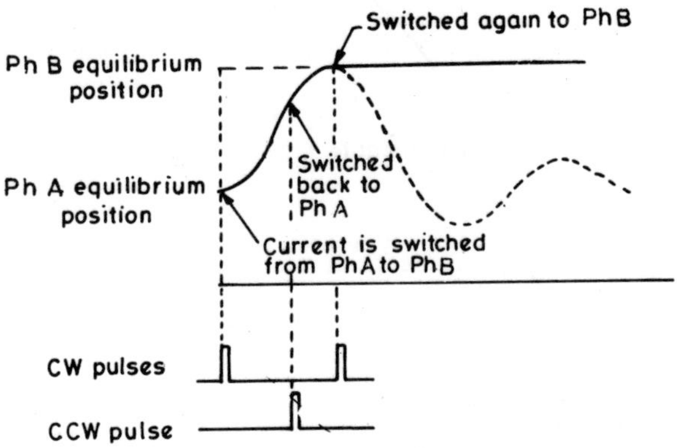


**Fig. 8.28 (a)** Rotational Angle and Pulse Timings in Back-Phasing Damping

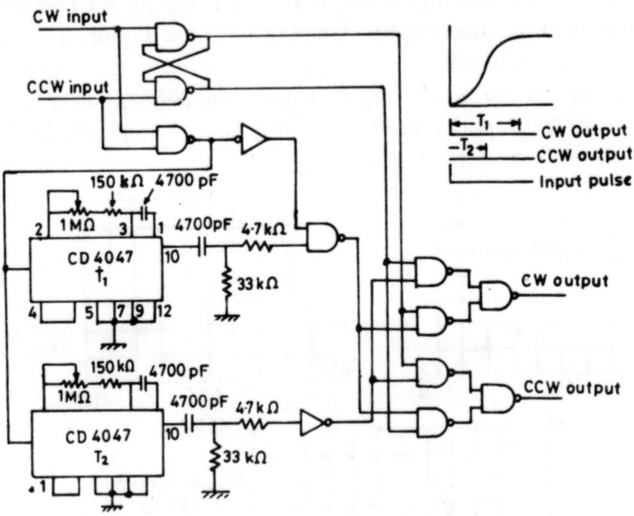


**Fig. 8.28 (b)** An Import Controller for a Back-Phasing Damped Single-Step Motion

However, in the delayed last pulse scheme, the second pulse is applied earlier as shown in Fig. 8.29. The second is purposely timed such that it produces 100% overshoot. This 100% overshoot takes the rotor to equilibrium position for the third pulse.We delay application of the third and the last pulse such that the rotor has just reached equilibrium position for the third pulse. When we now apply the third pulse, the rotor will be held at the third and last equilibrium position. The success of this method depends upon preponing the second pulse and delaying the last pulse by just the right time intervals so that the desired result is obtained.

**High Frequency Pulsing or Dithering.** It is well known in non-linear control theory that low frequency oscillations in a dynamic system can be quenched

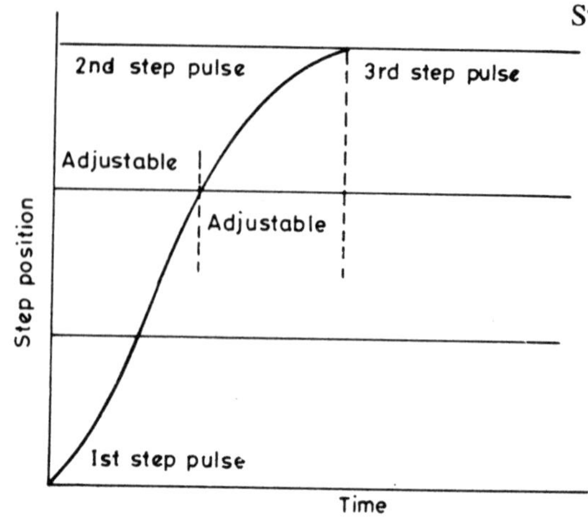


**Fig. 8.29** Three Steps Using the Delayed Last Step Method of Electronic Damping

by applying the so-called high frequency 'dither' signal. We take recourse to this phenomenon of dithering for damping rotor oscillations out. Instead of applying the last single pulse of an $N$-step move, we apply 3 to 6 high frequency pulses as shown in Fig. 8.30. This quenches rotor oscillations as can be seen from Fig. 8.30 (b). Input controller circuit meant to generate high frequency dithering pulses is shown in Fig. 8.30 (c).

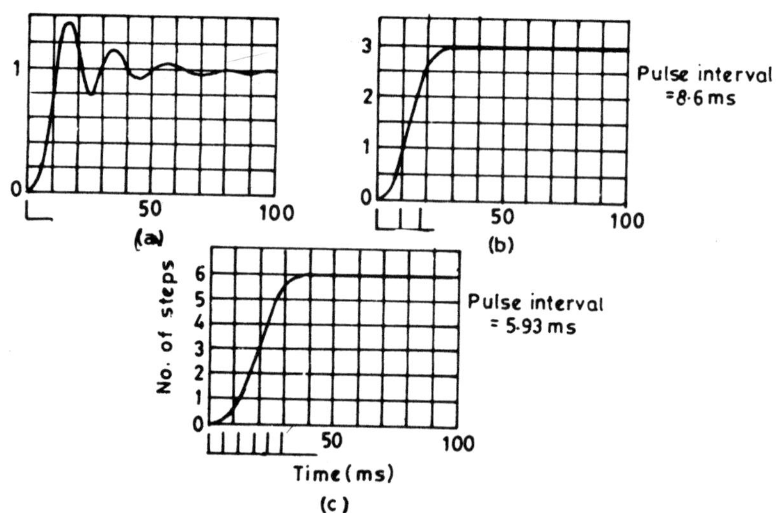


**Fig. 8.30** Single-Step Motion and Non-Oscillatory Motions with Several Pulses of Equal Interval

## 8.15 MIDFREQUENCY RESONANCE

Midfrequency or midrange resonance is a form of instability in stepper motors. This phenomenon was mentioned when we studied the dynamic characteristics of stepper motors in Chapter 3. Typical dynamic characteristics of a stepper

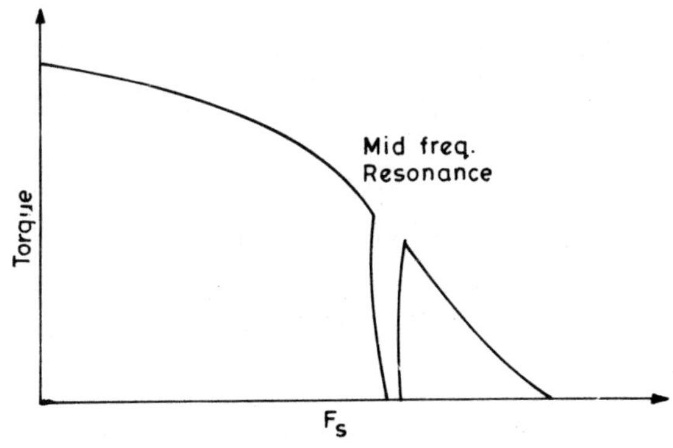


**Fig. 8.31** Mid-Frequency Resonance

motor are shown in Fig. 8.31. Observe that there is a range of stepping rates, and corresponding input pulsing frequencies, in which there is a sudden drop in the torque output of the motor. This range of frequencies is defined as *resonance frequency range*. We must guard against resonance, and avoid operation of our stepper motor in this frequency range when we design our incremental motion control system (IMCS).

This phenomenon of resonance in stepper motor operation was recognized quite early in development of stepper motors [ ]. This phenomenon has been investigated by several investigators [42-52]. Our explanation below closely follows the paper by Verghese, et al. [53].

### 8.15.1 Stepper Motor Model Used

We use the state space model of the stepper motor characterised by state equations

$$d\,\theta/dt = \omega \tag{8.71a}$$

$$d\,\omega/dt = [-(K/J)\, i_a \sin(N\,\theta) + (K/J)\, i_b \cos(N\,\theta) - (B/J)\,\omega] \tag{8.71b}$$

$$di_a/dt = (-1/L)\,[v_a - i_a R + K\,\omega \sin(N\,\theta)] \tag{8.71c}$$

$$di_b/dt = (1/L)\,[v_b - i_b R - K\,\omega \cos(N\,\theta)] \tag{8.71d}$$

where $v_a$, $i_a$, $v_b$, $i_b$ are voltages and currents; $R$, $L$ are phase winding resistance and inductance; $N$ = number of teeth; $J$, $B$ are moment of inertia and coefficient of viscous friction of motor + load; $K$ is the torque constant (Nm/A) of the motor.

When the motor is operating at a constant speed $\omega$, it is possible, to transform the above state equation into a synchronously rotating rotor frame, consisting of direct and quadrature axes. On carrying out such a Park transformation, we obtain the following transformed equations:

$$d\,\theta/dt = \omega \tag{8.72a}$$

$$d\,\theta/dt = [KNi_2 - B\,\omega]/J \tag{8.72b}$$

$$\begin{bmatrix} di_1/dt \\ di_2/dt \end{bmatrix} = \begin{bmatrix} -R/L & N\omega \\ -N\omega & -R/L \end{bmatrix} \begin{bmatrix} i_1 \\ i_2 \end{bmatrix} + \begin{bmatrix} \cos(N\theta)/L & \sin(N\theta)/L \\ -\sin(N\theta)/L & \cos(N\theta)/L \end{bmatrix} \cdot \begin{bmatrix} v_a \\ v_b \end{bmatrix} - \begin{bmatrix} 0 \\ KN\omega/L \end{bmatrix} \quad (8.72c)$$

where $i_1$, $i_2$ are the direct and quadrature axis currents.

Since these non-linear equations are difficult to handle, we take recourse to the well-known technique of small signal linearization about the steady state operating condition defined by

$$v_{1n} = V\cos\omega t, \qquad v_{2n} = V\sin\omega t \quad (8.74a)$$

$$\theta_n = \omega t + \theta_0, \qquad \omega_n = \omega \quad (8.74b)$$

$$\theta_0 = [\cos^{-1}(-P/Q) + \tan^{-1}(R/N\omega L)/N \quad (8.74c)$$

$$i_{1n} = [-KN^2\omega^2 L \pm \sqrt{Q^2 - P^2}]/z^2 \quad (8.74d)$$

$$i_{2n} = B\omega/KN \quad (8.74e)$$

$$P = (B\omega Z^2/KN) + RKN\omega \quad (8.74f)$$

$$Q = VZ \quad (8.74g)$$

$$Z = \sqrt{R^2 + N^2\omega^2 L^2} \quad (8.74h)$$

where the principal angle from $\tan^{-1}(.)$ is assumed in (8.74 c). Equation (8.74 d) shows that a meaningful solution is possible only when $Q^2 - p^2 \geq 0$. This condition requires that the applied voltages $v_1$, $v_2$ be sufficiently large for the motor torque developed to overcome friction torque $\beta$ at speed $\omega$. Observe that two solutions for $i_{1n}$ result depending on the sign of the second term in Eq. (8.74d). The positive sign is of interest as it can lead to stable operation.

Carrying out the small signal linearization, we obtain

$$\frac{d}{dt}\begin{bmatrix} \delta\theta \\ \delta\omega \\ \delta i_1 \\ \delta i_2 \end{bmatrix} = \begin{bmatrix} 0 & 1 & 0 & 0 \\ 0 & -B/J & 0 & KN/J \\ -(NV/L)\sin(N\theta_0) & Ni_{2n} & -R/L & N\omega_n \\ -(NV/L)\cos(N\theta_0) & -N(i_{1n} + K/L) & -N\omega_n & -R/L \end{bmatrix} \begin{bmatrix} \delta\theta \\ \delta\omega \\ \delta i_1 \\ \delta i_2 \end{bmatrix} \quad (8.75)$$

where $\delta\theta = \theta - \theta_n$, etc.

The eigenvalue of the $A$ matrix in Eq. (8.75) for various values of $\omega$ will reveal the instability in the operation of the motor.

### 8.15.2 Illustrative Example*

Let us take a numerical example with a view to illustrating the above concepts. We consider the permanent magnet stepper motor, model no. 2235 D200–F2.5, manufactured by M/s. Sigma Instruments, Inc., Braintree, Massachussettes, USA. The parameters of this motor are given in Table 8.1. Substituting these parameters in Eq. (8.75), we may obtain eigenvalues of the motor for various speeds ω. The eigenvalues so obtained for speed ω ranging from 5 to 55 rad/s are also shown in Table 8.1.

**Table 8.1** Analysis of Eigenvalues of a PM Stepper Motor at Various Speeds

**Stepper Motor Data**

Manufacturer : Sigma Motors Model No. 20-2235 D 200 – F 2.5
Resistance/Phase, $R = 7.35$ Ohms
Inductance/Phase, $L = 10.7$ mH
Rated Voltage, $V = 12.05$ V
Torque Constant, $K = 9.386 \times 10^{-3}$ Nm/A
Moment of Inertia, $J = 5.415 \times 10^{-3}$ kg-m$^2$
Coefficient of Friction, $B = 1.6 \times 10^{-3}$ Nm/(rad/s)
Number of Rotor Teeth, $N = 50$

Eigenvalues at various speeds

| *Stepping Rate (Steps/s)* | *Speed, ω (rad/s)* | *Eigenvalues of A Matrix in Eq. (8.75 )* | |
|---|---|---|---|
| 159 | 5 | – 685 ± j 252 | – 2.0200 ± j 81.04 |
| 318 | 10 | – 686 ± j 502 | – 0.7132 ± j 73.44 |
| 477 | 15 | – 687 ± j 751 | – 0.0417 ± j 65.57 |
| 636 | 20 | – 687 ± j 1001 | + 0.1690 ± j 58.69 |
| 796 | 25 | – 687 ± j 1251 | + 0.1964 ± j 52.85 |
| 955 | 30 | – 687 ± j 1500 | + 0.1657 ± j 47.76 |
| 1273 | 40 | – 687 ± j 2000 | + 0.0828 ± j 38.65 |
| 1592 | 50 | – 687 ± j 2500 | + 0.0195 ± j 28.05 |
| 1751 | 55 | – 687 ± j 2750 | – 0.0041 ± j 15.15 |

We observe that the first pair of eigenvalues is given by $(-R/L \pm j\,\omega N)$, and is stable throughout the range of speeds of interest. These eigenvalues also show that monotonically decaying phase currents appear oscillatory when viewed from the synchronously rotating frame attached to the rotor.

The second pair of eigenvalues is due to electromechanical factors. It is these eigenvalues which exhibit instability in a certain range of speeds. We notice that these eignevalues are in the left half of the *s*-plane (LHP) at speed upto 15

* Source : Verghese, et. al., Ref. No. 53

rad/s. They cross over to the right half of the $s$-plane (RHP) at 16 rad/s and stay in RHP for $\omega = 16 - 54$ rad/s.They return to LHP for $\omega > 55$ rad/s, as shown in Fig. 8.33.

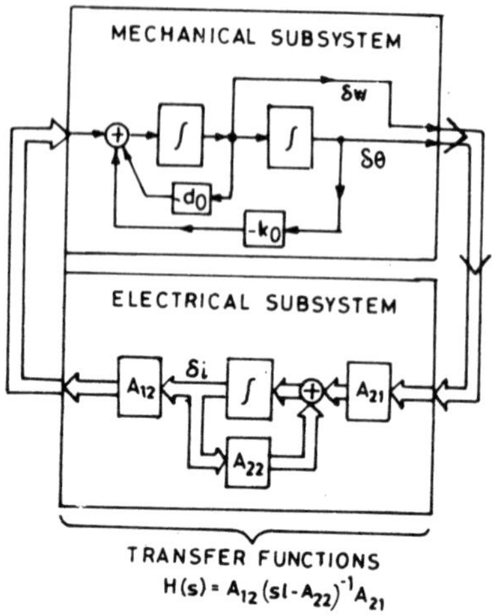


**Fig. 8.32** Interconnection of Mechanical and Electrical Subsystems in [7]

In this way, the second pair of eigenvalues is in RHP for $\omega = 16 - 54$ rad/s, indicating instability in motor operation. This instability is termed as *mid-range resonance.* Our object is to investigate this phenomenon of mid-range instability.

### 8.15.3 Selective Mode Analysis

Observation of the state equation (8.75) of the stepper motor reveals that the state variable can be grouped into (a) mechanical system state variables $\theta$ and $\omega$, and (b) electrical states $i_a$ and $i_b$. Accordingly, the system matrix $A$ in Eq. (8.75) can be partitioned its four sub matrices, as shown below:

$$\begin{bmatrix} \theta \\ \omega \\ i_a \\ i_b \end{bmatrix} = \begin{bmatrix} A_{11} & A_{12} \\ A_{21} & A_{22} \end{bmatrix} \begin{bmatrix} \theta \\ \omega \\ i_a \\ i_b \end{bmatrix}$$

where $A_{11}$ and $A_{12}$ represent the mechanical and electrical subsystems of the motor; $A_{12}$ and $A_{22}$ represent interactions between the two sub-systems. This concept of partitioning of a matrix is illustrated by the following example:

**Example 8.4*.** Consider the same stepper motor as in Table 8.1.For $\omega = 30$ rad/sec. the system matrix $A$ becomes

* Source : Verghese, et. al., Ref. No. 53

$$A = \begin{bmatrix} 0.0 & 0.0 & 0.0 & 0.0 \\ 0.0 & 0.295 & 0.0 & 86.7 \\ 54.4\times10^3 & 0.005\times10^3 & -0.687\times10^3 & 1.500\times10^3 \\ 1.45\times10^3 & -0.033\times10^3 & -1.500\times10^3 & -0.687\times10^3 \end{bmatrix}$$

The eigenvalues of the whole of A matrix are $0.657 \pm j\,47.76$ and $-687 \pm j\,1500$. The eigenvalues of $A_{11}$ are 0 and 0.295, while the eigenvalues of $A_{22}$ are $-678 \pm j\,1500$.

This example shows that the electrical subsystem is not much affected by the mechanical subsystem. However, the mechanical subsystem is critically affected by the electrical subsystem.

The effect of interaction between the electrical and mechanical subsystems is illustrated in Fig. 8.32. The transfer function $H(s)$ of the electrical subsystem, as seen by the mechanical subsystem, is given by

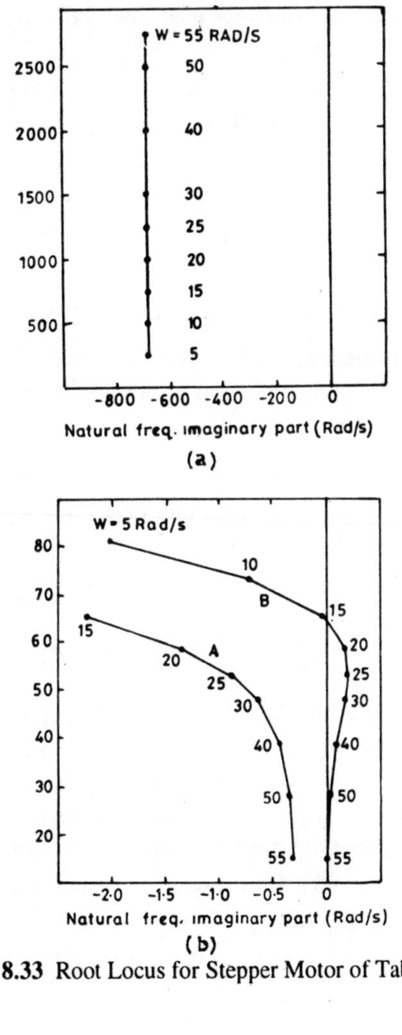


**Fig. 8.33** Root Locus for Stepper Motor of Table 8.1

$$H(s) = A_{12}\,[sI - A_{22}]^{-1}\,.\,A_{21} = \begin{bmatrix} 0 & 0 \\ h_\theta(s) & h_\omega(s) \end{bmatrix} \tag{8.77}$$

Various approximation, such as singular perturbations (SP), derivative damping correction (DDC), etc. have been tried. As a result, the following simple, yet effective, approximation has been derived:

$$\begin{bmatrix} \dot{\theta} \\ \dot{\omega} \end{bmatrix} = \begin{bmatrix} 0 & 1 \\ -K_4 & -d_4 \end{bmatrix} \begin{bmatrix} \theta \\ \omega \end{bmatrix} \tag{8.78a}$$

where $$K_4 = (KN^2/JZ^2)\sqrt{Q^2 - P^2} \tag{8.78b}$$

and $$d_4 = (B/J) + K^2 N^2 R\,(R^2 - N^2\,\omega^2 L)/(JZ^4) \tag{8.78c}$$

and $$Z^2 = (R^2 + N^2\,\omega^2 L^2) \tag{8.78d}$$

### 8.15.4 Stability Analysis

The origin of instability, or resonance in stepper motor operation can be traced to the damping coefficient '$d_4$' of Eq. (8.78c). For low values of $\omega$, $d_4$ is positive; hence motor operation is stable, since the spring constant '$K_4$' of Eq. (8.78b) is always positive. Similarly for sufficiently large values of $\omega$, '$d_4$' is again positive and the motor operation is stable. It is the intermediate range of $\omega$ that '$d_4$' becomes negative, and leads to unstable operation of the motor.

A simple stability test can be derived from Eq. (8.78c). The motor operation will be stable at an operating speed $\omega$ if and only if

$$K^2 N^2 R\,(N^2\,\omega^2 L^2 - R^2)/[B\,(R^2 + N^2\,\omega^2 L^2)^2] < 1 \tag{8.79}$$

Note that this is only quadratic in $\omega^2$; hence, existence and limits of instability (i.e., resonance) can be predicted from Eq. (8.79). In particular, there will be *no unstable operation* if and only if

$$8BR/K^2 N^2 > 1 \tag{8.80}$$

If this condition is not satisfied, instability exists; the limits of instability are given by

$$\omega^2 = (K^2 R\,/2BL^2)\,[1 - (2BR/K^2 N^2 \pm \sqrt{1 - (8BR/N^2 K^2)}] \tag{8.81}$$

Let us illustrate this simple test of stability of operation in the case of the stepper motor we have been studying.

**Example 8.6.** Determine the stability of the stepper motor of Table 8.1. If instability exists, determine the limits of unstable operation.

In our case, Eq. (8.80) yields $8\,BR/K^2 N^2 = 0.09408/0.22024 = 0.4272 < 1$. This shows that the motor does exhibit unstable operation. Applying Eq. (8.81) yields limits of unstable operation as $\omega_1 = 15.6$ rad/s (497 steps/s) and $\omega_2 = 54.0$ rad/s (1719 steps/s). These results agree with those obtained from the full 4th order system of Eq. (8.75).

In fact eigenvalue of the subsystem model of Eq. (8.78a) have been calculated for the same values of ω as in Table 8.1. These points are plotted in Fig. 8.33. Again the agreement between reduced and full order stepper motor mode is remarkable.

In this way, we have presented a simple test for instability of operation and a simple calculation of the limits of unstable operation of a PMH stepper motor. The results so obtained agree remarkably with those of the original fourth order model of the motor.

## REFERENCES


### Magnetic Circuit Analysis

1. Mukherji, K.C. and Neville, S., 'Magnetic permeance of identical double slotting: deductions from analysis by F.W. Carter', Proc IEE, Vol. 118, pp. 1257-1268, 1971.
2. Harris, M.R. and Andjargholi, V., 'Torque production in hybrid motors', Int. Conf. on Stepping Motors & Systems, Leeds, pp. 148-157, 1974.
3. Harris, M.R., Andjargholi, V., Hughes, A., Lawrenson, P.J., Ertan, B., 'Limitation on specific torque in stepping motors', Proc. 3rd IMCSD Symp., pp. P1-P10, 1974.
4. Sinha, N.K., Elliot, A.R., Wong, R.C.S., 'A realistic mathematical model for PM step motors', IEEE Trans. Vol. IECI-21, No. 3, pp. 168-173, 1974.
5. Harris, M.R., Hughes, A., Lawrenson, P.J., 'Static torque production in saturated doubly salient machines', Proc. IEE, Vol.122, No. 10, pp. 1121 - 1127, 1975.
6. Bakhuizen, A.J.C., 'On optimal torque production in doubly slotted structures', Proc. 4th IMCSD Symp. pp. 01-012, 1975.
7. Harris, M.R., Andjargholis, V., Lawrenson, P.J., Hughes, A., Ertan, B., 'Static torque in PM and VR stepping motors', Proc. IEE Conf. on Small Elect. Machines, London, pp., 1976.
8. Harris, M.R., Andjargholis, V., Lawrenson, P.J., Hughes, A., Ertan, B., 'Unifying approach to static torque of stepping motor structures', Pro. IEE, Vol. 124, No. 12, pp. 1215-1224, 1977.
9. Athani, V.V. and Khurana, S.K., 'Torque optimization of a VR stepping motor', Proc. IEE, Vol. 123, No. 11, pp. 1271-1272, 1978.

### Permeance Models of Stepping Motors

10. Kuo, B.C. and Chen, I.J., 'Permeance model of low resolution VR step motors', Proc. 10th IMCSD Symp., pp. 159-163, 1981.
11. Gao, F.A. and Kuo, B.C., 'Permeance model of saturated tooth structure and its utilization in step motor design', Proc. 11th IMCSD Symp., pp. 233-240, 1982.
12. Kuo, B.C. and Chen, Y.J., 'A nonlinear magnetic circuit model and its application to holding torque production of hybrid step motors', 13th IMCSD Symp., pp. 303-313, 1984.
13. Athani, V.V., 'A new theory of development of force and torque in VR stepping motors', Proc. Indian Acad. of Sciences, Part IV: Sadhana, pp. 329-350, 1984.
14. Kuo, B.C. and Hugh, U.V., 'Permeance models and their applications in step motor design', Proc. 15th IMCSD Symp., pp. 351-370, 1986.
15. Chai, H.D., 'Magnetic circuit and formulation of static torque for single stack PM and VR step motors', Proc, 2nd IMCSD Symp. pp. E1-E18, 1973.

16. Chai. H.D., 'Permeance model and reluctance force between toothed structures', ibid, pp. K1-K12, 1973.
17. Chai. H.D., 'Permeance based step motor model revisited', Proc. 14th IMCSD Symp., pp. 399-410, 1985.
18. Chai. H.D., 'A mathematical model for single stack step motors', IEEE Trans., Vol. PAS-94, No. 5, pp. 1508-1517, 1975.

## Dynamic Analysis of Stepper Motors

19. Kieburtz, K.R., 'The step motor : the next advance in control systems', IEEE Trans., Vol. AC-9, pp. 98-104, 1964.
20. Robinson, D.J. and Taft, C.K., 'Dynamic analysis of magnetic stepping motors', IEEE Trans., Vol. IECI - 16, pp. 111-125, 1969.
21. Nigam, M.M., 'Studying single step operation in PM step motors', Electomech Design: System Designers Handbook, pp. 234-241, 1973/74.
22. Hughes, A., Lawrenson, P.J., Davies, T.S., 'Factors determining high speed torque in hybrid motors', Proc. Int. Conf. Stepping Motors & Systems, Leeds, pp. 150-157, 1976.
23. Hughes, A., 'Parameters governing dynamic performance of PM stepping motors', Proc. 6th IMCSD Symp., pp. 39-47, 1977.
24. Pulle, D.W., Hughes, A., 'Normalized high speed performance analysis of small hybrid stepping motors', Proc. IEE. Vol. 134, Part B, No. 6, pp. 333-338, 1987.
25. Wang, X., Eichenwald, R., 'Torque vs. speed analysis and simulation for PM step motors', Proc. 15th IMCSD Symp., pp. 241-250, 1986.
26. Russell, A.P., and Pickup, I.E.D., 'Torque calculations for hybrid step motors under dynamic conditions', Proc. 18th IMCSD Symp., pp. 271-292, 1989.
27. Lawrenson, P.J. Hughes, A. and Acarnley, P.P., 'Starting/stopping rates of stepping motors: improvements and prediction', Proc. Int. Conf. on Stepping Motors & Systems, pp. 54-60, 1976.

## Damping Methods

28. Kuo, B.C. and Singh, G., 'Damping methods for step motors', Proc. 2nd IMCSD Symp., pp. H1-H13, 1973.
29. Cassat, A., 'Higher permeance active suppression driver for VR step motors', Proc. 5th IMCSD Symp., pp. 195-202, 1976.
30. Kent, A.J., 'Investigation into the use of inertia dampers on step motors', Proc. 2nd IMCSD Symp., pp. G1-G38, 1973.
31. Lawrenson, P.J., and Kingham, I.E., 'Design of viscously coupled inertia dampers', Proc. Int, Conf. on Stepping Motors & Systems, Leeds, pp. 169-174, 1974.
32. Hughes, A. and Lawrenson, P.J., 'Introduction to electromagnetic damping in stepping motors', ibid, pp. 135-147, 1974.
33. Hughes, A. and Lawrenson, P.J., Electromagnetic damping in stepping motors', Proc. IEE, Vol. 122, No. 8, pp. 819-825, 1975.
34. Godijin, B.H.A., 'Analog electronic damping of stepping motors', Proc. Int. Conf. on Stepping Motors & Systems, pp. 61-67, 1976.
35. Unger, J.D., 'Adaptive step motor damping using current feedback', Proc. 6th IMCSD Symp, pp. 5-18, 1977.
36. Kordic, K.S., 'Improved damping for step motors', ibid, pp. 1-4, 1977.
37. Leenhouts, A.C.. and Singh G., 'An active stabilization technique for open loop PM step motor drive system, ibid, pp. 19-24, 1977.

38. White, G. and Kuo, B.C., 'A method for controlling damping of step motors', Proc. 11th IMCSD Symp., pp. 158-164, 1982.
39. Tal, J., Antogini, L., Gandel, P., Veignat, N., 'Damping a two phase step motor with velocity coils', Proc. 14th IMCSD Symp., pp. 305-311, 1985.
40. Squire, J.S., 'Electronic step motor damping using bipolar chopper drive circuit', ibid, pp. 233-245, 1985.
41. Srinivas, K., Brown, R.H., and Ventola, C., 'A damping method for bifilar hybrid step motors using phase lead compensation', Proc. 18th IMCSD Symp., pp. 259-266, 1989.


### Resonance in Stepper Motors


42. Venkataraman, V. and Mouli, E.C., 'Stability analysis of a stepping motor', Proc. IEE, Vol. 118, No. 6, pp. 808-812, 1971.
43. Singh, G., Leenhouts, A.C. and Mosel, E.F., 'Electromagnetic resonance in PM step motor drive systems', Int. Conf. on Stepping Motors & Systems, Leeds, pp. 115-124, 1976.
44. Word, P.A. and Lawrenson, P.J., 'Backlash resonance and instability in stepping motors', Proc. 6th IMCSD Symp., pp. 73-88, 1977.
45. Lawrenson, P.J. and Kingham, I.F., 'Resonance effects in stepping motors', Proc. IEE, Vol. 124, No. 5, pp. 445-448, 1977.
46. Russell, A.P. and Pickup, I.E.D., 'Parametric oscillatory motion electromechanical devices', Proc. IEE, Vol. 125, No. 4, pp. 269-277, 1978.
47. Hughes, A. and Lawrenson, P.J., 'Simple theoretical stability criteria for 1.8° hybrid stepping motors', Proc. Int. Conf. on Stepping Motors and Systems, Leeds, pp. 127-135, 1979.
48. Pollack, S.H., 'Analysis and prediction of the mid-frequency resonance phenomena in PM step motors', Proc. 8th IMCSD Symp., pp. 29-54, 1979.
49. Pickup, I.E.D. and Russell, A.P., 'Parametric instability in stepping motors', Proc. 8th IMCSD Symp., pp. 1-28, 1979.
50. Hair, V.D., 'Constant speed stability analysis in VR step motors', Proc. 11th IMCSD Symp., pp. 259-270, 1982.
51. Russell, A.P. and Pickup, I.E.D., 'Non-linear resonance phenomena in stepping motors', pp. 259-270, 1982.
52. Taft, C.K. and Harned, T.J., 'Mid-frequency resonance in step motors', Proc. 14th IMCSD Symp., Proc. 11th IMCSD Symp., pp. 87-111, 1985.
53. Verghese, G.C., Lang, J.H., Casey, L.F., 'Analysis of instability in electrical machines', IEEE Trans., Vol. 1A-22, No. 5, pp. 853-864, 1986.


### Additional References


54. Jenkins, M., Brich, T.S., Howe, D., 'The influence of the magnet on static torque production in hybrid stepping motors', Proc. Int. Conf. on Elec. Machines & Drives, IEE Conf. Publn. pp. A1.3.1-A1.3.12, 1986.
55. Jenkins, M., Birch, T.S., Howe, D., 'Static torque production in hybrid stepping motors', Proc. IEE Int. Conf. on Elec. Machines and Drives, IEE Publn. No., pp. 270-274, 1987.
56. Hashen, A.M., El Shanawany, M., Abignoli. M., 'Complete model for transient analysis of the stepping motor', ibid, pp. 325-329, 1987.
57. Ward, E.D., Raider, J.W., 'An approach to step motor understanding', Proc. 15th IMCSD Symp., pp. 145-165, 1986.

**Books on Stepper Motors**


58. Kuo, B.C., 'Theory and Application of Step Motors', West Pub. Co., St. Paul (USA), 1974.
59. Kuo, B.C., 'Step Motors and Control Systems', SRL Pub. Co., Champaign, IL, 1979.
60. Kenjo, T., 'Stepping Motors and Their Microprocessor Controls', Clarendon Press, Oxford, 1985.
61. Acarnley, P.P., 'Stepping Motors : A Guide to Modern Theory and Practice', 3rd Edn., Peter Peregrinus, London, 1992.

# CHAPTER - 9

# *Design of Stepper Motors*

This chapter is meant to explain the principles of design of stepper motors. Various factors which affect stepper motor design are explained in the beginning. Certain guidelines on the design are given next. Finally step by step design of stepper motors is explained. A few illustrative examples of design are given at the end.

## 9.1 INTRODUCTION

When we survey literature on stepper motors, we come across a peculiar situation. There is no lack of references on stepper motors in the form of books [1-4], proceedings of annual symposia on incremental motion control systems and devices (IMCSD) held by Prof. B.C. Kuo since 1972; three conferences on stepping motors and systems held at University of Leeds (UK) in 1974, 1976 and 1979; as well as papers published in journals like Proceedings of IEE (UK). However, most of these papers deal with characteristics and applications of stepper motors. There are few papers discussing design of stepper motors. Whatever few papers are available, deal with the design of a particular part of stepper motors. For example, Oliferenko [5] and Kura [6] have discussed the design of the rotor permanent magnet of a PMH stepper motor. Kuo [7] has presented the design of the rotor of the PMH stepper motor. Design of the stator of the PMH stepper motor is covered by a US patent [8]. Two papers by Kuo and his associates [9, 10] on computer aided design and simulation are available. They are, however, more simulation, rather than design, oriented. Recently, Kuo [11] has come out with a book on stepper motor design.

There is thus very little material available on the design of the stepper motor. We have, therefore, to develop our own design of stepper motors. The design procedure given below is based on the author's paper [12].

## 9.2 FACTORS AFFECTING STEPPER MOTOR DESIGN

Several factors such as (i) air gap geometry, (ii) materials used, and (iii) production technology employed, have a profound effect on stepper motor design. These factors are discussed below.

### 9.2.1 Geometric Factors

The gross geometric factors affecting the design are stator OD, ID and stack length; rotor OD, ID and stack length; permanent magnet OD, ID and length; and number of teeth on the rotor and the stator.

It is, however, the air gap geometry, shown in Fig. 9.1 that has a crucial effect on the design of stepper motor. The main air gap geometry factors are tooth pitch $\lambda$, tooth thickness $t$, slot width $s$, tooth height $h$ and length of the air gap $g$. The ratio of (i) tooth thickness to tooth pitch ($t/\lambda$); and (ii) tooth pitch to air gap ($\lambda/g$) are of vital importance inasmuch as they determine air gap permeances $P_1$, $P_2$ and $P_0$ as well as their space harmonics. Graphs showing variation of $P_1$, $P_2$, $P_0$ with $t/\lambda$ and $\lambda/g$ have been presented by Mukherji and Nevil [13], and Harris and Finch [14].

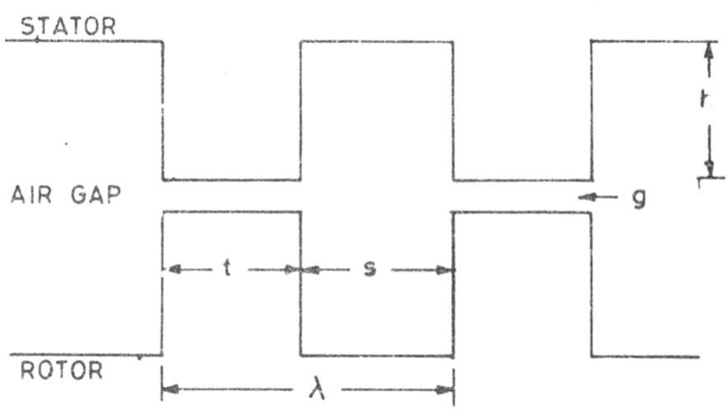


**Fig. 9.1** Air Gap Geometry of a Stepper Motor

A list of factors pertaining to the geometry is given in Table 9.1.

## 9.3 MATERIALS FACTORS

The principal materials influencing stepper motor design are (i) magnetic materials, (ii) conductor materials and (iii) insulation materials. These are discussed below in brief.

### 9.3.1 Magnetic Materials

Stator poles and yokes of both permanent magnet hybrid (PMH) and variable reluctance (VR) stepper-motors are made up of soft magnetic materials. The rotor disks in both of these motors are also made of soft iron materials. PMH

**Table 9.1** Geometric parameters affecting PMH stepper motor design

| *Stator* | *Air Gap Geometry* |
|---|---|
| Outer Dia, $D_{so}$ | *Stator* |
| Inner dia, $D_{si}$ | No. of teeth, $N_s$ |
| Axial length, $L$ | Tooth pitch, $Y_{st}$ |
| No. of Poles, $N_p$ | Tooth width, $W_{st}$ |
| Pole pitch, $P_p$ | Tooth height, $H_{st}$ |
| Pole height, $H_p$ | Stator slot width, $W_{ss}$ |
| Pole width, $W_p$ | Ratio, $R_{swy} = W_{st}/Y_{st}$ |
| Pole shoe height, $H_{ps}$ | |
| Pole arc | *Airgap*: |
| Yoke Width, $W_y$ | Lenth, of airgap, $L_g$ |
| Cross section, $W_a$ | |
| | *Rotor* |
| *Rotor* | No. of teeth, $N_R$ |
| Outer dia, $D_{ro}$ | Tooth pitch, $Y_{rt}$ |
| Inner dia, $D_{ri}$ | Tooth width, $W_{rt}$ |
| Stack length, $L_r$ | Tooth height, $H_{rt}$ |
| *Rotor Permanent Magnet* | Rotor Slot width, $W_{rs}$ |
| Outer dia, $D_m$ | Ratio, $R_{rwy} = W_{rt}/Y_{rt}$ |
| Inner dia, $D_{mi}$ | *Stator Phases Winding* |
| Axial length, $L_m$ | No. of turns, $N$ |
| Cross section, $A_m$ | Rated current, $I$ |
| | Rated Voltage, $V$ |

motors carry a cylindrical permanent magnet on the rotor. Hence the design of stepper motors is affected by selection of both soft and hard (i.e. permanent magnet) materials.

### 9.3.2 Hard (i.e. Permanent Magnet) Materials

Hard magnetic materials available are of three types: (i) ceramic, (ii) Alnico alloys, and (iii) the modern high energy density materials like rare earth cobalt (REC) and NdFeB. The characteristics of these hard magnetic materials are summarized in Table 9.2 [15-17]. Demagnetization curves for these materials are shown in Fig. 9.2.

Ceramic permanent magnets are employed in low cost, low end stepper motors wherein cost is the most important consideration. Alnico magnets are most popular for medium performance, cost effective designs. Alnico magnets are employed in stepper motors manufactured in India. REC and NdFeB, being new and more expensive, are presently restricted to high end applications in which performance, rather than cost, is the deciding factor. However, it is expected that the cost of NdFeB magnets will come down in the near future. Consequently, PMH stepper motors of the next decade may employ NdFeB rather than Alnico magnets.

**Table 9.2** Properties of Permanent Magnet Materials

| *Material* | | $B_r$ | *Coercivity* | | $(BH)_{max}$ | $B_m$ | $H_m$ | *Temp. Coeff of* $\mu_{recoil}$ | | | *Density* | $\alpha$ |
|---|---|---|---|---|---|---|---|---|---|---|---|---|
| | | | $bH_c$ | $iH_c$ | | | | $B$ | $iH_c$ | | | |
| | | *(KG)* | *(KOe)* | *(KOe)* | *(MGOe)* | *(KG)* | *(KOe)* | *(%/°C)* | *(%/°C)* | | *(g/cm³)* | (× $10^{-7}$/°C) |
| Ceramic | 1 | 2.15 | 1.75 | 3.5 | 0.95 | | | –0.18 | 0.20 | 1.2 | 4.90 | 99 |
| | 2 | 2.9 | 2.45 | 3.25 | 1.90 | | | | | 1.2 | 4.85 | 99 |
| | 3 | 3.8 | 2.2 | 2.3 | 3.0 | | | | 0.43 | 1.2 | 4.95 | 110 |
| • | 7 | 3.75 | 3.4 | 4.2 | 3.25 | | | | 0.29 | 1.1 | 4.80 | 130 |
| | 8 | 3.95 | 3.5 | 3.75 | 3.6 | | | | 0.33 | 1.1 | 4.85 | 130 |
| Alnico | 5 | 12.8 | 0.66 | | 5.5 | 10.1 | 0.54 | 0.021 | | 3.6 | 7.3 | |
| | 5DG | 13.0 | 0.69 | | 6.1 | 10.8 | 0.57 | | | 3.0 | 7.3 | |
| | 5Col | 13.5 | 0.73 | | 7.8 | 11.6 | 0.67 | | | 2.5 | 7.3 | |
| | 7 | 6.9 | 1.05 | | 2.3 | 3.8 | 0.6 | –0.02 | | 3.3 | 7.3 | |
| | 8 | 9.0 | 1.50 | | 5.5 | 5.7 | 0.96 | –0.02 | | 2.4 | 7.3 | |
| | 9 | 11.0 | 1.50 | | 10.0 | 8.6 | 1.16 | –0.02 | | 1.3 | 7.3 | |
| $SmCO_5$:REC | 16 | 8.2 | 7.5 | 30 | 16 | 4.0 | 4.0 | | | 1.05 | 8.2 | |
| | 18 | 8.7 | 8.2 | 15 | 18 | 4.25 | 4.25 | –0.04 | –0.3 | 1.05 | 8.25 | 6.5 |
| | 20 | 9.0 | 8.4 | 15 | 20 | 4.48 | 4.48 | –0.04 | –0.3 | 1.05 | 8.25 | 6.5 |
| $Sm_2CO_{17}$:REC | 22 | 9.4 | 8.8 | 15 | 22 | 4.60 | 4.78 | | | | | |
| | 24 | 10.1 | 9.1 | 10 | 24 | | | –0.03 | –0.02 | 1.06 | 8.45 | 6.5 |
| | 26 | 10.4 | 10.0 | 20 | 26 | 5.3 | 4.9 | –0.089 | –0.57 | 1.08 | 7.55 | –3.0 |
| | 27 | 10.7 | 9.7 | 10 | 27 | | | –0.03 | –0.2 | 1.05 | 8.45 | 6.5 |

*(Contd.)*

**Table 9.2** *(Contd.)*

| *Material* | | $B_r$ | *Coercivity* | | $(BH)_{max}$ | $B_m$ | $H_m$ | *Temp. Coeff of* $\mu_{recoil}$ | | | *Density* | α |
|---|---|---|---|---|---|---|---|---|---|---|---|---|
| | | | $bH_c$ | $iH_c$ | | | | $B$ | $iH_c$ | | | |
| | | *(KG)* | *(KOe)* | *(KOe)* | *(MGOe)* | *(KG)* | *(KOe)* | (%/°C) | (%/°C) | | (g/cm³) | (× 10⁻⁷/°C) |
| NdFeB:Neomax* | 27H | 10.6 | 10.1 | 17 | 27 | | | –0.11 | –0.58 | 1.05 | 7.35 | 5.8 |
| | 30 | 11.2 | 10.5 | 12 | 30 | | | –0.11 | –0.60 | 1.05 | 7.35 | 5.8 |
| | 32 H | 11.6 | 11.1 | 17 | 32 | | | –0.12 | –0.58 | 1.05 | 7.50 | 5.8 |
| | 33 | 11.7 | 11.1 | 15 | 33 | | | –0.12 | –0.60 | 1.05 | 7.50 | 5.8 |
| | 27 SH | 10.6 | 10.1 | 21 | 27 | | | –0.11 | –0.55 | 1.05 | 7.45 | 5.8 |
| | 30 H | 11.2 | 10.7 | 17 | 30 | | | –0.11 | –0.58 | 1.05 | 7.35 | 5.8 |
| | 35 | 12.1 | 11.5 | 12 | 35 | | | –0.11 | –0.60 | 1.05 | 7.35 | 5.8 |
| | 35 H | 12.1 | 11.6 | 17 | 35 | | | –0.12 | –0.58 | 1.05 | 7.50 | 5.8 |
| | 37 | 12.4 | 11.8 | 15 | 37 | | | –0.11 | –0.60 | 1.05 | 7.50 | 5.8 |
| | 30 SH | 11.2 | 10.7 | 21 | 30 | | | –0.11 | –0.55 | 1.05 | 7.45 | 5.8 |

* Trademark of Sumitomo Metals, Japan

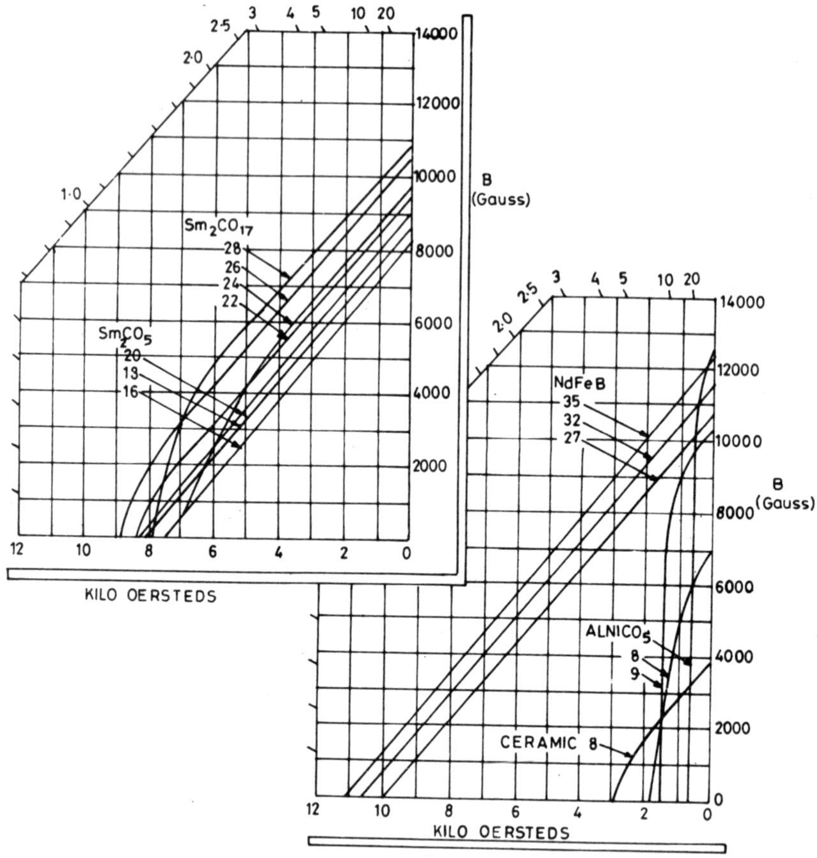


**Fig. 9.2** Demagnetization Curves for Permanent Magnet Materials*

### 9.3.3 Soft Magnetic Materials

Cold rolled non-oriented (CRNO) silicon steel laminations constitute the most common soft magnetic materials. Properties of these steels are governed by Indian, British, American standard specifications. For example, properties of CRNO steels, as per Indian standard specifications IS 640 (1980), are given in Table 9.3. Similarly, CRNO steels,* as per American ASTM specifications, are to be found in Table 9.4.

For small, low end applications, solid rotor disks are sometimes employed for sake of ease of manufacture. Such solid rotor disks are made of electrolytic iron or cast steel. Properties of such materials are to be found in Table 9.5. B-H curves for soft magnetic materials are shown in Fig. 9.3.

* Source : Permanent Magnets, Sumitomo Special Metals Co., Japan

**Table 9.3** Characteristics of CRNO electrical steel sheets* as per IS 640 (1980)

| *Length (mm)* | *Width (mm)* |
|---|---|
| 3000 | 1000 |
| 2500 | 1000 |
| 2000 | 1000 |
| 1500 | 750 |

| | *Grade as per IS:648* | *Density (g/cm³)* | *Silicon content (%)* | *Thickness (mm)* | *Mass (kg/m²)* | *Maximum iron* losses at 50 Hz* | | *B/H characteristics*** | | *Resistivity (mm²/m)* | *Temperature coefficient of resistance* | *Ageing*** (%)* |
|---|---|---|---|---|---|---|---|---|---|---|---|---|
| | | | | | | *1.0 T (W/kg)* | *1.3 T (W/kg)* | *H A/m* | *B T* | | | |
| *(1)* | | *(2)* | *(3)* | *(4)* | *(5)* | *(6)* | *(7)* | *(8)* | *(9)* | *(10)* | *(11)* | *(12)* |
| | Group A | | | | | | | | | | | |
| | | | | | | | | 400 | 1.31 | | | |
| | | | | 0.40 | 3.12 | – | 4.62 | 800 | 1.46 | | | |
| 1 | 360 | 7.80 | 0.30 | 0.50 | 3.90 | 3.60 | 5.58 | 1600 | 1.54 | 0.15 | $33.8 \times 10^{-4}$ | 5.0 |
| | | | | 0.63 | 4.91 | 4.30 | 6.50 | 4000 | 1.67 | | | |
| | | | | 1.00 | 7.80 | 5.50 | – | 8000 | 1.78 | | | |
| | | | | | | | | 24000 | 1.98 | | | |

*(Contd.)*

**Table 9.3** *(Contd.)*

| | | | | | | | | | | | | |
|---|---|---|---|---|---|---|---|---|---|---|---|---|
| | | | | | | | | 400 | 1.27 | | | |
| | | | | 0.40 | 3.10 | – | 4.12 | 800 | 1.38 | | | |
| 2 | 300 | 7.75 | 0.85 | •0.50 | 3.88 | 3.00 | 4.76 | 1600 | 1.50 | 0.21 | $25.0 \times 10^{-4}$ | 5.0 |
| | | | | 0.63 | 4.88 | 3.59 | 5.64 | 4000 | 1.64 | | | |
| | | | | 1.00 | 7.75 | 4.62 | – | 8000 | 1.76 | | | |
| | | | | | | | | 24000 | 1.96 | | | |
| | | | | | | | | 400 | 1.30 | | | |
| | | | | 0.40 | 3.08 | – | 3.70 | 800 | 1.38 | | | |
| 3 | 260 | 7.70 | 1.75 | 0.50 | 3.85 | 2.60 | 4.12 | 1600 | 1.48 | 0.33 | $16.5 \times 10^{-4}$ | 5.0 |
| | | | | 0.63 | 4.85 | 2.84 | 4.70 | 4000 | 1.60 | | | |
| | | | | 1.00 | 7.70 | 3.94 | – | 8000 | 1.72 | | | |
| | | | | | | | | 24000 | 1.94 | | | |
| | | | | | | | | 400 | 1.30 | | | |
| | | | | 0.40 | 3.06 | – | 3.40 | 800 | 1.38 | | | |
| 4 | 230 | 7.65 | 2.50 | 0.50 | 3.82 | 2.30 | 3.75 | 1600 | 1.48 | 0.41 | $13.7 \times 10^{-4}$ | 5.0 |
| | | | | 0.63 | 4.82 | 2.51 | 4.21 | 4000 | 1.60 | | | |
| | | | | 1.00 | 7.65 | 3.08 | – | 8000 | 1.72 | | | |
| | | | | | | | | 24000 | 1.92 | | | |
| | | | | | | | | 400 | 1.28 | | | |
| | | | | 0.40 | 3.04 | – | 2.93 | 800 | 1.37 | | | |
| 5 | 180 | 7.60 | 3.00 | 0.50 | 3.80 | 1.80 | 3.22 | 1600 | 1.46 | – | – | 5.0 |
| | | | | 0.63 | 4.79 | 2.13 | 3.64 | 4000 | 1.58 | | | |
| | | | | 1.00 | 7.60 | – | – | 8000 | 1.70 | | | |
| | | | | | | | | 24000 | 1.90 | | | |

*(Contd.)*

**Table 9.3** *(Contd.)*

| | | | | | | | | | | | | |
|---|---|---|---|---|---|---|---|---|---|---|---|---|
| | Group B | | | | | | | | | | | |
| | | | | | | | | 400 | 1.28 | | | |
| | | | | 0.35 | 2.64 | 1.40 | 2.36 | 800 | 1.36 | | | |
| 6 | 140 | 7.55 | 3.50 | 0.40 | 3.02 | – | 2.51 | 1600 | 1.44 | – | – | 2.0 |
| | | | to | 0.45 | 3.40 | – | 2.67 | 4000 | 1.56 | | | |
| | | | 4.00 | 0.50 | 3.78 | – | 2.82 | 8000 | 1.67 | | | |
| | | | | | | | | 400 | 1.28 | | | |
| | | | | 0.35 | 2.64 | 1.30 | 2.20 | 800 | 1.36 | | | |
| 7 | 130 | 7.55 | 4.00 | 0.40 | 3.02 | – | 2.36 | 1600 | 1.44 | – | – | 2.0 |
| | | | | 0.45 | 3.40 | – | 2.51 | 4000 | 1.56 | | | |
| | | | | 0.50 | 3.78 | – | 2.67 | 8000 | 1.67 | | | |
| | Group C | | | | | | | | | | | |
| | | | | | | | | 400 | 1.30 | | | |
| | | | | | | | | 800 | 1.41 | | | |
| 8 | 120 | 7.55 | 4.00 | 0.35 | 2.64 | 1.20 | 2.03 | 1600 | 1.49 | 0.60 | $7.5 \times 10^{-4}$ | 1.0 |
| | | | | 0.50 | 3.78 | 1.54 | 2.51 | 4000 | 1.59 | | | |
| | | | | | | | | 8000 | 1.70 | | | |
| | | | | | | | | 24000 | 1.90 | | | |

*(Contd.)*

**Table 9.3** *(Contd.)*

| | | | | | | | | | | | | |
|---|---|---|---|---|---|---|---|---|---|---|---|---|
| | | | | | | | | 400 | 1.26 | | | |
| 9 | 108 | 7.55 | 4.00 | 0.35 | 2.64 | 1.08 | 1.90 | 800 | 1.35 | | | |
| | | | | 0.50 | 3.78 | – | – | | | | | |
| | | | | | | | | 1600 | 1.43 | 0.60 | $7.5 \times 10^{-4}$ | 1.0 |
| | | | | | | | | 4000 | 1.55 | | | |
| | | | | | | | | 400 | 1.26 | | | |
| 10 | 99 | 7.55 | 4.00 | 0.35 | 2.64 | 0.99 | 1.76 | 800 | 1.35 | 0.60 | $7.5 \times 10^{-4}$ | 1.0 |
| | | | | 0.50 | 3.78 | – | – | 1600 | 1.47 | | | |
| | | | | | | | | 4000 | 1.55 | | | |
| | | | | 0.35 | 2.64 | 0.92 | 1.63 | | | | | |
| 11 | 92 | 7.55 | 4.00 | 0.50 | 3.78 | – | – | – | – | 0.60 | $7.5 \times 10^{-4}$ | 1.0 |

* Underlined values determine the grade of that material (100 × Max iron loss).

** For B/H characteristics, also Ref. Figs. 2.2(a), 2.2(b) and 2.3.

*** Permissible deterioration in core loss due to ageing.

**Table 9.4** American Standard Grades of Electrical Steels

**(a) Fully Processed Non-Oriented Steels (as per ASTM A677)**

| *ASTM* | *Former AISI Type* | *Nominal Thickness* | | *Max core Loss at 1.5T* | | *Si+Al Content (%)* | *Density $g/cm^3$* | *Resistivity Ω-cm × $10^6$* | *Saturation Flux Density (Tesla)* | *Characteristics* | *Application* |
|---|---|---|---|---|---|---|---|---|---|---|---|
| | | *in* | *mm* | *W/lb* | *W/kg* | | | | | | |
| 36F145 | M15 | 0.0140 | 0.36 | 1.45 | 2.53 | 3.5 | 7.65 | 52 | 1.98 | 1. Lowest core loss | 1. Small power transformers |
| 47F168 | M15 | 0.0185 | 0.47 | 1.68 | 2.93 | | | | | 2. Excellent permeability at low *B* | High efficiency small machines |
| 36F158 | M19 | 0.0140 | 0.36 | 1.58 | 2.75 | | | | | Low core loss<br>Good permeability at low and intermediate *B* | • High reactance cores<br>• Generators, stators of high efficiency rotating machines |
| 47F174 | M19 | 0.0185 | 0.47 | 1.74 | 3.03 | 3.3 | 7.65 | 50 | 1.99 | | |
| 64F208 | M19 | 0.0250 | 0.64 | 2.08 | 3.62 | | | | | | |
| 36F168 | M22 | 0.0140 | 0.36 | 1.68 | 2.93 | | | | | | |
| 47F185 | M22 | 0.0185 | 0.47 | 1.85 | 3.22 | 3.2 | 7.65 | 48 | 2.00 | | |
| 64F218 | M22 | 0.0250 | 0.64 | 2.18 | 3.80 | | | | | | |
| 36F180 | M27 | 0.0140 | 0.36 | 1.80 | 3.13 | | | | | | |
| 47F190 | M27 | 0.0185 | 0.47 | 1.90 | 3.31 | 2.8 | 7.70 | 45 | 2.02 | | |
| 64F225 | M27 | 0.0250 | 0.64 | 2.25 | 3.92 | | | | | | |
| 36F190 | M36 | 0.0140 | 0.36 | 1.90 | 3.31 | | | | | • Good core loss<br>• Good permebility• all *B*'s | • Small generators<br>• High efficiency continous duty rotating DC and AC machines |
| 47F205 | M36 | 0.0185 | 0.47 | 2.05 | 3.57 | 2.65 | 7.70 | 44 | 2.02 | | |
| 64F240 | M36 | 0.0250 | 0.64 | 2.40 | 4.18 | | | | | | |

*(Contd.)*

**Table 9.4** *(Contd.)*

| | | | | | | | | | | | |
|---|---|---|---|---|---|---|---|---|---|---|---|
| 47F230<br>64F270 | M43<br>M43 | 0.0185<br>0.0250 | 0.47<br>0.64 | 2.30<br>2.70 | 4.01<br>4.70 | 2.35 | 7.70 | 40 | 2.04 | • Low exciting current<br>• Good stamping properties | |
| 47F290<br>64F340 | M45<br>M45 | 0.0185<br>0.0250 | 0.47<br>0.64 | 2.90<br>3.40 | 5.05<br>5.92 | 1.85 | 7.75 | 34 | 2.07 | • Ductile<br>• Good stamping properties | • Small motors<br>• Ballasts |
| 47F380<br>64F470 | M47<br>M47 | 0.0185<br>0.0250 | 0.47<br>0.64 | 3.80<br>4.70 | 6.62<br>8.19 | 1.05 | 7.80 | 24 | 21.1 | • Good permeability at high B's | • Relays |
| 47F450<br>64F550 | –<br>– | 0.0185<br>0.0250 | 0.47<br>0.64 | 4.50<br>5.50 | 7.84<br>9.58 | 0.80 | 7.80 | 21 | 2.12 | | |
| 47F490<br>64F600 | –<br>– | 0.0185<br>0.0250 | 0.47<br>0.64 | 4.90<br>6.00 | 8.53<br>10.45 | 0.50 | 7.85 | 18 | 2.13 | | |

**(b) Fully Processed Non-Oriented Steels (as per ASTM A677)**

| *ASTM* | *Former AISI Type* | *Nominal Thickness* | | *Max. core* | | *Induction B (Tesia)* | *Si+Al Content (%)* | *Density* $(g/cm^3)$ | *Resistivity* $(\Omega\text{-}cm \times 10^6)$ | *Saturation Flux Density B (Tesla)* | *Characteristics* | *Application* |
|---|---|---|---|---|---|---|---|---|---|---|---|---|
| | | *ub* | *mm* | *W/lb* | *W/kg* | | | | | | | |
| 23G048<br>27G053<br>30G058<br>35G066 | –<br>M-4<br>M-5<br>M-6 | 0.087<br>0.106<br>0.118<br>0.138 | 0.22<br>0.27<br>0.30<br>0.35 | 0.48<br>0.53<br>0.58<br>0.66 | 0.80<br>0.89<br>0.97<br>1.11 | 1.5<br>1.5<br>1.5<br>1.5 | 3.15 | 7.65 | 48 | 2.00 | • High directional properties due to grain orientation | • Highest efficiency power & distribution transformers with low Wt./KVA |
| 27H076<br>30H083<br>35H094 | M-4<br>M-5<br>M-6 | 0.106<br>0.118<br>0.138 | 0.27<br>0.30<br>0.35 | 0.76<br>0.83<br>0.94 | 1.27<br>1.39<br>1.57 | 1.7<br>1.7<br>1.7 | 3.15 | 7.65 | 48 | 2.00 | • Very low core loss, and Very high permeability in rolling direction | • Small generators and transformers |
| 27P066<br>30P070<br>35P076 | –<br>–<br>– | 0.106<br>0.118<br>0.138 | 0.27<br>0.30<br>0.35 | 0.66<br>0.70<br>0.76 | 1.11<br>1.17<br>1.27 | 1:7<br>1.7<br>1.7 | 2.90 | 7.65 | 45 | 2.01 | | |

**Table 9.5** Characteristics of soft solid core materials

| *Materials* | *Density* $(g/cm^3)$ | *Silicon content (%)* | *Resistivity* $(mm^2/m)$ | *Relative permability* | | *Saturation (flux density)* $(T)$ | *Ultimate strength* $(MN/m^2)$ | *Applications* |
|---|---|---|---|---|---|---|---|---|
| | | | | *Initial* | *Maximum* | | | |
| 1 Pure iron | 7.85 | Low | 0.107 | 275 | 2500 | 2.16 | 275 | Pole pieces, relays |
| 2 Low carbon sheets or shapes | 7.85 | Low | 0.130 | 250 | 2500 | 2.12 | 310 | Fields and frames of DC and synchronous machines |
| 3 Cast steel (annealed) | 7.80 | 0.4 | 0.150 | 175 | 1500 | 2.10 | 415 | Frames of solid poles |
| 4 Cast iron (annealed) | 7.00 | 2.0 | 1.000 | 125 | 500 | 1.40 | 172 | Frames |
| 5 Mumetal | 8.00 | – | 0.600 | 40000 | 120000 | 0.80 | – | Instrument Tranformers |
| 6 Permendur | 8.05 | – | 0.470 | 1000 | 7000 | 2.36 | – | Electromagnets |
| 7 Permalloy | 8.60 | – | 0.220 | 9000 | 100000 | 1.10 | – | Telephone Equipments |
| 8 Hipernik | 8.30 | – | 0.450 | 6000 | 90000 | 1.50 | 450 | Instrument Transformers |

(For B/H characteristics ref. Fig. 2.1)

**Table 9.6** Properties of insulating materials*

| *Class* | *Tempe-rature °C* | *Principal/ subsidiary* | *Insulating materials* | *Bonding, impregnating or coating substances* used in the manufacture of the material in Col. 3.* | *Impregnating substances* which may be used in the treatment of the insulated assembly* |
|---|---|---|---|---|---|
| (1) | (2) | (3) | (4) | (5) | (6) |
| Y | 90 | Principal | Cotton, natural silk, regenerated cellulose fibre, cellulose acetate fibre, polyamide fibre, paper and paper products, pressboard, vulcanised fibre, wood, aniline-formaldehyde resins, urea formaldehyde resins. | None | None required |
| | | Subsidiary | Polyacrylates, polyethylene, polystyrene (may be limited to less than 90°C by softening temperature), polyvinyl chloride with or without plasticizer, vulcanized natural rubber. | None | None required |
| A | 105 | Principal | Cotton, natural silk, regenerated cellulose fibre, cellulose acetate fibre, polyamide fibre, paper and paper products, pressboard, vulcanised fibre (when impregnated or when immersed in a liquid dielectric) wood. | None | Drying oil-modified natural resins; shellac, copal and other natural resins; solutions or suspensions of cellulose esters and ethers. Those listed in higher temperature classes. |
| | | | Varnished textile based on cotton, natural silk*, regenerated cellulose, cellulose acetate or polymide fibre, varnished paper. | Drying oil-modified natural or synthetic resin varnish | Insulating oil synthetic dielectric liquids. |

* Source : Indian Standard No. 1271 (1958)

*(Contd.)*

**Table 9.6** *(Contd.)*

| | | | | | |
|---|---|---|---|---|---|
| A | 105 | Principal | Laminated wood | Phenol-formaldehyde resin | |
| | | | Cellulose acetate film, cellulose acetate butyrate film, cross-linked polyester resins, wire enamel based on polyamide resin. | None | |
| | | Subsidiary | Polychloroprene elastomers, butadiene acrylonitrile elastomers. | None | Those listed above and in higher temperature classes. |
| A | 120 | Principal | – | – | – |
| | | Subsidiary | Wire enamels based on polyvinyl-formal, polyurethane or epoxy resins | None | Oil-modified asphalt and synthetic resins; cross linked polyester resins; epoxy resins |
| | | | Mouldings with cellulose filters, cotton fabric, laminates, paper laminates. | Melamine – formaldehyde, phenol formaldehyde and phenol-furfural resins. | Those linked in higher temperature classes. |
| | | | Cross linked polyester resins, cellulose triacetate film, polyethylene terephthalate film, polyethylene terephthalate fibre. | | |
| | | | Varnished polyethylene temperature terephthalate textile. | Oil modified alkyd resin varnish. | |
| B | 130 | Principal | Glass fibre asbestos | None | Oil modified asphalt and synthetic resins; cross-linked polyester resins; |

*(Contd.)*

**Table 9.6** *(Contd.)*

| | | | | | |
|---|---|---|---|---|---|
| B | 130 | Principal | Glass fibre asbestos | None | Oil-modified asphalt and synthetic resins; cross-linked polyester resins; epoxy resins (under severe mechanical stress, materials above may prove to be inadequate, and unmodified phenolic resins may be needed) |
| | | | Varnished glass fibre textile, varnished asbestos | Oil-modified synthetic resin varnishes, Shellac, asphalt or bituminous compounds | |
| | | | Built-up mica (with or without supporting materials) | Oil modified synthetic resins | |
| | | | | Alkyd resins, crosslinked polyester resins, epoxy resins | Those listed in higher temperature classes. |
| | | | Glass fibre laminates, asbestos laminates, mouldings with mineral filters | Melamine-formaldehyde resins, phenol-formaldehyde resins. | |
| | | | Mouldings with mineral filters. | Cross-linked polyester resins | Those listed, in this class than those listed in higher temperature classes |
| | | | Polymonochlorofluoro-ethylene | None | |

*(Contd.)*

**Table 9.6** *(Contd.)*

| | | | | | |
|---|---|---|---|---|---|
| B | 155 | Principal | – | – | – |
| | | Subsidiary | Glass fibre, asbestos | None | Alkyl, epoxy cross-linked polyester and polyurethane resins with superior thermal stability |
| | | | Varnished glass fibre textile, varnished asbestos, built-up mica (with or without supporting materials). | Alkyd, epoxy, cross-linked polyester and polyurethane resins with superior thermal stability, silicon-alkyd resins. | Silicon-alkyd and silicon phenolic resins. Those listed in higher temperatures classes. |
| H | 180 | Principal | Glass fibre, asbestos | None | Appropriate silicon resins |
| | | | Varnished glass fibre textile, varnished asbestos | Appropriate silicon resisns, silicon elastomers. | |
| | | | Built-up mica (with or without supporting materials); glass fibre laminates. | Appripriate silicon resins | |
| | | | Silicon elastomer | None | |
| | | Subsidiary | – | – | – |

*(Contd.)*

**Table 9.6** *(Contd.)*

| | | | | | |
|---|---|---|---|---|---|
| C | Above 180 | Principal | Mica, porcelain and other ceramics, glass, quartz.<br>Note: Maximum operating temerature may be listed by physical, chemical or electrical properties at operating temperature | None | Inorganic binder, such as glass or cement. |
| | | Subsidiary | Treated glass fibre textile, treated asbestos, built-up mica. | Silicon resins possessing superior thermal stability (limited stability above 225°C) | Silicon resins possessing superior thermal stability (limited stability above 225°C) |
| | | | Polytetrafluoroethylene (limited stability above 250°C) | None | |

* Bonding and impregnating substances may often be limited by factors other than thermal stability such as mechanical properties at operating temperatures. For example, some epoxy and polyester resins under severe mechanical stress may be limited to class *A* temperature.

**Notes**

(1) For the purpose of these general recommendations, the various materials are classified under temperature limits that will give an acceptable life under usual industrial conditions of service. However, actual life in service depends upon particular service conditions, which may vary widely with environmental exposure, duty cycles and type of apparatus. Further the acceptable length of life in service varies greatly, depending upon the relative importance of weight, reliability, desired period of use of associated equipment and other economic considerations.

(2) It is assumed that except where otherwise specified, insulating materials are employed in air. In the absence of oxygen, however, considerable increase in maximum temperature may be permissible for some materials insofar as their thermal stability is concerned.

(3) Only experience or adequate acceptable tests provide bases for rational temperature limits. Such experience and tests are recognized in establishing temperature limits for insulation. Lists of materials given in the tabulation are intended to be useful as a guide but are not mandatory in setting temperature limits.

(4) Two lists of materials in each class, viz. principal list and subsidiary list are given. The principal list comprises materials generally accepted in the class under consideration. The subsidiary list comprises materials of which some experience is available but whose introduction into the class under consideration is not universally accepted.

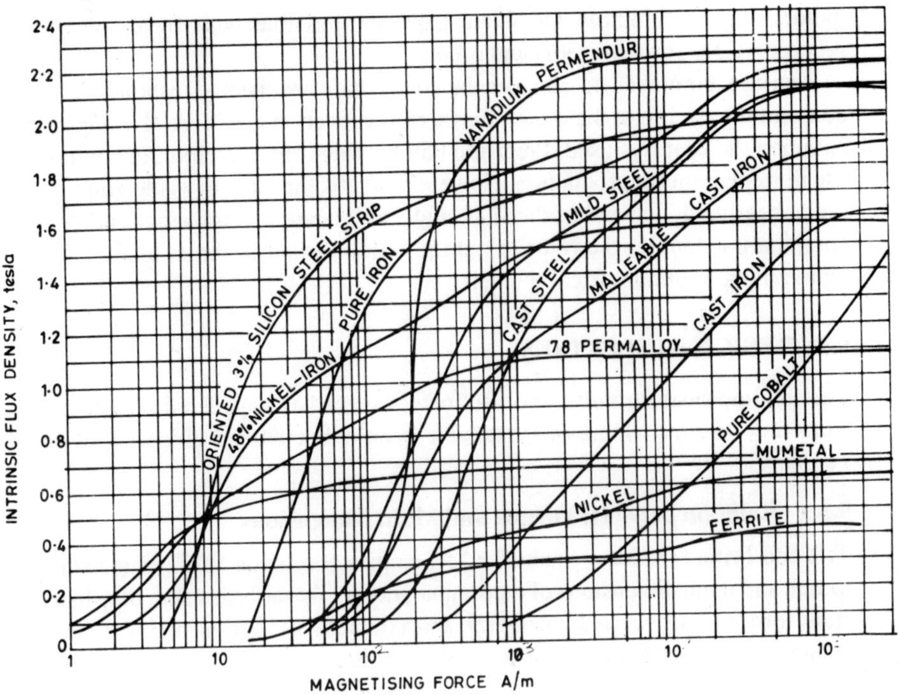


**Fig. 9.3** B-H Curves for Soft Magnetic Materials*

### 9.3.4 Insulating Materials*

Properties of common insulating materials are to be found in Table 9.6. Of these materials, class *B* is most common. High performance, highly compact stepper motors employ class *F* insulations material

## 9.4 PRODUCTION TECHNOLOGY FACTORS

Fine workmanship and accuracies in machining, assembling and aligning play a crucial role in the performance of the stepper motors produced. Air gap between rotor and stator teeth is of prime importance, because the torque produced by the stepper motor is inversely proportional to the air gap. Consequently, for the same dimensions of the stator and the rotor, it is possible to obtain double the torque by halving the air gap (to first approximation). Now the air gap that can be maintained is squarely determined by techniques used for machining aligning and assembling, as well as the manufacturing tolerances. Air gaps of the order of 1 mm are quite standard in stepper motors of upto 40 kg-cm torque rating. Smaller air gaps, in the range 0.5 to 1 mm, are employed in stepper motors for floppy disk drive application. Certain Japanese manufacturers have gone down to 0.1 mm air gap for their premium grade stepper

* Source : Permanent Magnets, Sumitomo Special Metals Co., Japan

motors! Such incredibly small air gaps are possible only by employing precision CNC machine tools and robots.

Bearings employed to support the rotor shaft are mainly responsible for determining the life of the motor. Furthermore, friction levels are also dependent upon the bearings used. Precision ball bearings are, therefore, in common use in stepper motor production, However, of late, the tendency is to employ a thrust bearing at one end of the shaft and a ball bearing at the other end. This combination enables the rotor to put up with unbalanced thrust loads, while maintaining minimum friction levels.

## 9.5 DESIGN GUIDELINES

Certain empirical formulae and parameter ranges have appeared in literature from time to time. Some of these have been collected and given below for guidance.

### 9.5.1 Relation between Torque and Main Dimensions

Taft and Prina [18] have established an empirical relation between the static torque and main dimensions of the stepper motor. Towards this end, they listed static torque ($T_s$), overall diameter ($D$) and axial length ($L$) from manufacturers' catalogs. A representative table used by them is given as Table 9.7. Then they assumed a relation between torque, diameter and length as

$$T_s = KD^{\alpha} L^{\beta} \tag{9.1}$$

or

$$\log T_s = \log K + \alpha \log D + \beta \log L \tag{9.2}$$

**Table 9.7** Data on 1.8° PM Stepper Motors*

| *Motor No.* | *Holding Torque oz – in* | *Dia D (in)* | *Axial Length L (ins)* | $K = \dfrac{T_s}{D^{1.7} L^{1.34}}$ |
|---|---|---|---|---|
| 1 | 57.5 | 2.25 | 2 | 5.72239 |
| 2 | 120 | 2.25 | 3 | 6.93631 |
| 3 | 168 | 2.25 | 4 | 6.60448 |
| 4 | 188 | 3.38 | 2.44 | 7.17624 |
| 5 | 336 | 3.38 | 3.7 | 7.34160 |
| 6 | 496 | 3.38 | 5.06 | 7.12462 |
| 7 | 650 | 4.25 | 5.39 | 5.81197 |
| 8 | 1150 | 4.25 | 7.56 | 6.53453 |

The 'best' value of $K$, $\alpha$ and $\beta$ were determined employing multi-linear regression method. This 'best' values of these parameters, so obtained, are

* Source : Taft and Prina, Ref. No. 18

$$K = 6.49573, \alpha = 1.7, \beta = 1.34$$

As a result, the empirical relation of Eq. (9.1) becomes

$$T_s = 6.49573\, D^{1.7}\, L^{1.34} \pm 13\% \qquad (9.3)$$

This empirical relation is useful to the designer as a guideline in the selection of motor main dimensions.

### 9.5.2 Acceptable Ranges of Parameters

In addition, several empirical relations have been established amongst parameters in stepper motor design. A set of such empirical ranges of parameters are given in Table 9.8. These data have been taken from sources like Kuo, et. al. [9, 10].

**Table 9.8** Acceptable Ranges of Stapper Motor Parameters*

| | | |
|---|---|---|
| For | 1.8° PM stepper motors | |
| | rotor teeth $N_R$ = 50 | |
| No. of | stator pulses = 8 | |
| No. of | teeth per poles = 5 | |
| **Stator** | tooth width/tooth pitch | : 0.034-0.60 (0.38) |
| | tooth pitch/air gap | : 10-200 |
| | tooth height/tooth pitch | : 0.4-0.6 |
| | pole width/pole length | : 0.3-0.6 (0.33) |
| **Stator** | Pole width/yoke width | : 0.9-1.0 |
| | Pole length/yoke width | : 3-4 (4) |
| | ID/OD | : 0.4-0.6 (0.45) |
| | L/OD | : 4-0.6 |
| **Rotor** | tooth width/tooth pitch | : 0.35-0.6 (0.38) |
| | tooth height/tooth pitch | : 0.4-0.6 (0.5) |
| | tooth width/stator tooth width | : 0.75-1.20 (1) |
| | tooth height/stator tooth height | : 1 |
| | tooth pitch/stator tooth pitch | : 1 |
| **Rotor Permanent Magnet** | | |
| | OD/rotor OD | : 0.5-0.8 (0.667) |
| | ID/OD | : 0.5-0.75 |
| | length/rotor stack length | : 0.3-0.6 (0.333) |
| **Flux Densities** in stator and rotor teeth | | : 1.2-1.5 Tesla |
| | $B_{pole}/B_{teeth}$ | : 0.75-0.9 |
| | $B_{yoke}/B_{pole}$ | : 1 |
| Leakage flux between poles/total pole flux | | : 0.04-0.06 |
| Solid stack length/hollow slack length | | : 0.95-1.0 |
| **MMF:** $F_m \approx 2\,F_e$ | | |

where $F_m$ = *mmf* provided by rotor permanent magnet

$F_e$ = $NI$ = *mmf* due to energization of stator winding.

* Source : Kuo, et. al., Ref. No. 9

The empirical relations are again meant for guidance of the designer, so that his/her design conforms to current technological practice.

## 9.6 STEPPER MOTOR DESIGN EQUATIONS

The main equations, governing the design of permanent magnet hybrid (PMH) stepper motors are given below [9]:

(a) Step Angle $\theta_s = 360°/(N_R \, . \, n)$ (9.4)

where $N_R$ = no. of teeth on the rotor disks and

$n$ = no. of steps per tooth pitch (= 4)

(b) Pole pitch $P_p = (m \pm (l/n)) \, . \, T_p$ (9.5)

where $T_p$ = tooth pitch

$m$ = positive integer.

Values of $m$ and $n$ are so selected as to result in a well-balanced, symmetrical magnetic circuit; otherwise, unbalanced magnetic pulls result. For the common 1.8° stepper motor, $n = 4$ and $m = 6$ represent suitable choices.

(c) Static torque, with single phase energization, is given by

$$T_{s1} = (N_R/2)\,(NI)\,(P_m\,F_m)\,(\rho_1/\rho_0)\,\sin\theta_e + \Delta T \qquad (9.6)$$

where $NI$ = amp-turns provided by the energized stator winding

$P_m$ = permeance of the rotor permanent magnet.

$F_m$ = mnf produced by rotor permanent magnet.

$\rho_0, \rho_1$ = coefficients in Fourier series expansion of air gap permeance.

$\theta_e$ = rotor displacement from fully aligned position in deg. (elect).

and $\Delta T$ = torque due to higher order harmonics.

(d) Permanent magnet permeance and mnf are given by

$$P_m = \mu_m \cdot A_m/L_m \qquad (9.7a)$$

and

$$F_m = B_d \, . \, L_m/b_m \qquad (9.7b)$$

where $A_m, L_m$ = area of cross section and length of the rotor permanent magnet.

$B_d$ = operating point flux density on the demagnetization curve of the permanent magnet used.

$\mu_m$ = permeability of the permanent magnet material.

$\mu_r$ = relative permeability

$\mu_0$ = permeability of free space = $4^{\pi} \times 10^{-7}$ (H/m)

(e) Static Torque with *Two Phase Energization*

$$T_{s2} = \sqrt{2}\,T_{s1} \, . \, \sin(\theta_e + 45°) + \Delta T \qquad (9.8)$$

(f) Detente or Cogging Torque available when

$$T_{cog} = -\,(N_R/2) \, . \, (P_m F_m)^2\,(\rho_4/\rho_0^2)\,\sin 4\theta_e \qquad (9.9)$$

where $\rho_4$ = Coefficient of 4th harmonic component of air gap permeance.

In the above formulae, the Fourier series expansion coefficients, $\rho_0$, $\rho_1$, $\rho_4$ are estimated with the help of Table 9.9 provided by Chai [20].

**Table 9.9** Fourier Coefficients for Normalized Permanence for One Tooth*

| $T_p$ | 20 | 20 | 20 | 40 | 40 | 40 |
|---|---|---|---|---|---|---|
| $W_v/W_t$ | 1 | 1.5 | 2 | 1 | 1.5 | 2 |
| $\alpha_{max}$ | 12.1 | 10.22 | 8.953 | 22.54 | 18.66 | 16.06 |
| $\alpha_{min}$ | 6.609 | 4.616 | 3.757 | 8.345 | 4.928 | 3.949 |
| $\beta_{max}$ | 0.671 | 0.736 | 0.760 | 0.864 | 0.891 | 0.900 |
| $C_0$ | 9.363 | 7.333 | 6.085 | 15.36 | 11.3 | 8.989 |
| $C_1/C_0$ | 0.2696 | 0.3642 | 0.4181 | 0.4143 | 0.5732 | 0.6522 |
| $C_2/C_0$ | 0.0008835 | 0.0044288 | 0.03452 | 0.004341 | 0.01996 | 0.08269 |
| $C_3/C_0$ | 0.01698 | 0.01559 | 0.003558 | 0.0323 | 0.02899 | 0.005899 |
| $C_4/C_0$ | −0.0004757 | 0.0005337 | 0.0009972 | 0.0009965 | 0.01456 | 0.0258 |
| $C_5/C_0$ | 0.00373 | 0.0005754 | 0.002737 | 0.00837 | 0.001454 | 0.007256 |

| $T_p$ | 20 | 20 | 20 | 40 | 40 | 40 |
|---|---|---|---|---|---|---|
| $W_v/W_t$ | 1 | 1.5 | 2 | 1 | 1.5 | 2 |
| $\alpha_{max}$ | 17.36 | 14.48 | 12.54 | 27.69 | 22.8 | 19.54 |
| $\alpha_{min}$ | 7.614 | 4.808 | 3.863 | 8.944 | 5.054 | 4.066 |
| $\beta_{max}$ | 0.799 | 0.845 | 0.865 | 0.893 | 0.912 | 0.914 |
| $C_0$ | 12.45 | 9.376 | 7.518 | 18.2 | 13.17 | 10.36 |
| $C_1/C_0$ | 0.3553 | 0.4886 | 0.557 | 0.4576 | 0.6334 | 0.7195 |
| $C_2/C_0$ | 0.003434 | 0.01267 | 0.06101 | 0.004584 | 0.02606 | 0.1006 |
| $C_3/C_0$ | 0.02538 | 0.02352 | 0.005032 | 0.03772 | 0.03275 | 0.006202 |
| $C_4/C_0$ | 0.0004927 | 0.01016 | 0.01871 | 0.001263 | 0.01838 | 0.03148 |
| $C_5/C_0$ | 0.006087 | 0.001044 | 0.005006 | 0.01029 | 0.001704 | 0:009443 |

$$\alpha \equiv \frac{P}{\mu_0 t} = C_0 + C_1 \cos \theta_e + C_2 \cos 2\theta_e + \ldots \qquad \theta = \frac{2X}{T_p}\pi$$

$$T_p = \frac{(W_v + W_t)}{l_g}$$

$$\beta = \left(\frac{l_g}{\mu_0 t}\right)\frac{dP}{dx} \qquad \mu_0 = 4\pi \times 10^{-7} \text{ hen/n}$$

## 9.7 DESIGN PROCEDURE

Flow chart for PMH stepper motor design is shown in Fig. 9.4. There are two phases in the design procedure.

### 9.7.1 Phase 1

The starting point for the design consists of the set of specifications for the motor: step angle (deg), the static torque (N-m), no. of phases on, length of the air gap (mm), rated phase current (A), etc.

---

* Source : Chai, H.D., Ref., No. 20

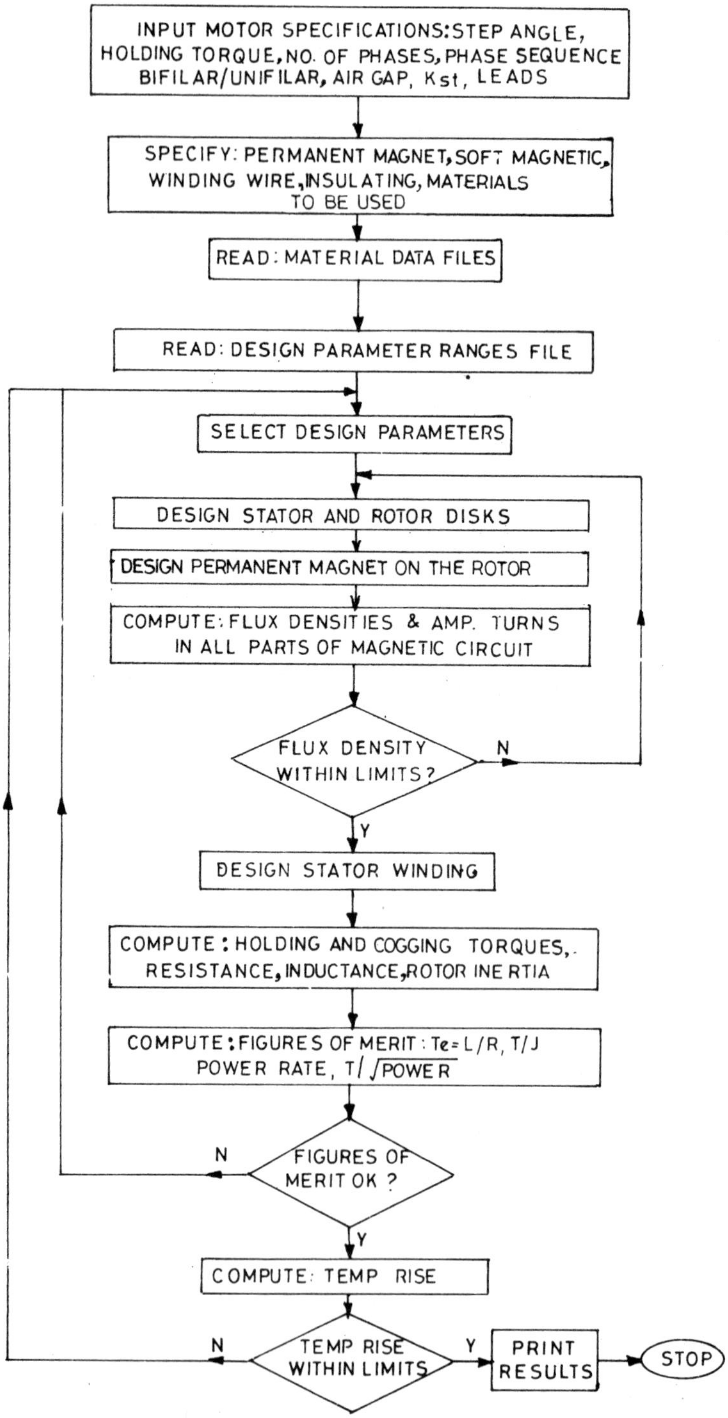


**Fig. 9.4** Stepper Motor Design Flowchart

Specification of the materials to be used viz. permanent magnet material, soft magnetic material, class of insulation etc. also need to be specified.

The overall dimensions, such as dia. $D$ (mm) and stack length $L$ (mm) are sometimes specified with a view to conforming with standard practice or constraints imposed by the applications.

From these basic data, the design procedure computes:

(i) stator pole and yoke dimensions
(ii) rotor disc dimensions
(iii) rotor permanent magnet dimensions
(iv) stator and rotor teeth and slot dimensions as well as length of the air gap.

This completes the first phase of design.

### 9.7.2 Phase 2

This phase consists of design verifications. In this phase detailed magnetic circuit computations are performed with a view to ensuring that flux densities, especially in the teeth are within limits imposed by the materials selected. These computations also yield the ampereturns required. This enables the design of the phase windings to be carried out.

Thereafter, the motor static torque and detente torque, as well as phase winding resistance ($R_m$) and inductance ($L_m$) are computed. The moment of inertia ($J$) is also calculated. Figures of merit such as acceleration ($T/J$), power rate and torque/power ratio are also computed, to ensure that the motor design is satisfactory.

Finally temperature rise calculations are performed to ensure that the temperature rise is within permissible limits.

## 9.8 COMPUTER AIDED DESIGN PROGRAM

A CAD program, called PCSMD, has been developed to implement the above design procedure on a PC/AT or XT computer. It is an interactive, user friendly program written in PASCAL. It permits the user t

(i) set input specifications
(ii) specify materials to be used
(iii) set and modify design parameters.

The results are basically displayed on the CRT monitor, and later printed to get a hard copy output.

## 9.9 DESIGN EXAMPLES

A number of PMH stepper motors of various ratings have been designed with the help of PCSMD program. The results compare well with those published in Kuo et. al. [9]. Later on, motors were designed using our PCSMD to meet the same specifications as those of well-known commercial motors. Our designs compare well with commercial designs.

As examples, design sheets generated for a few PMH motors are given in Table 9.10.

**Table 9.10** Details of PHM Stepper Motor Using PCSMD Soctware

| *Make Model No.* | *Kuo, et al. [9]* | *Kuo and Hunter [10]* | *Srijan Control Drives Srisyn STM 1101A* | *Sigma Instrument* | | | *Superior Electric Co. Slosyn MO61* | *15-4415-30* | *Units* |
|---|---|---|---|---|---|---|---|---|---|
| | | | | *20-2220* | *20-3437* | *22-4247* | | | |
| Rated current | 1.5 | 0.35 | 3.30 | 1.00 | 4.00 | 3.10 | 1.00 | 0.40 | A |
| Holding torque | 0.055 | 0.04 | 2.88 | 0.42 | 2.21 | 3.68 | 0.67 | 4.415 | N-m |
| No. of Phases On | 1 | 1 | 2 | 2 | 2 | 2 | 2 | 2 | |
| Step angle | 1.8 | 1.8 | 1.8 | 1.8 | 1.8 | 1.8 | 1.8 | 0.5 | Deg. |
| Stator OD | 47.60 | 37.97 | 102.00 | 56.00 | 87.00 | 107.50 | 57.15 | 150.99 | mm |
| ID | 20.65 | 17.37 | 59.78 | 32.82 | 50.99 | 63.00 | 33.97 | 120.37 | mm |
| Stack length | 25.40 | 12.70 | 42.50 | 51.00 | 95.00 | 120.00 | 45.72 | 30.00 | mm |
| Air gap | 0.05 | 0.05 | 0.05 | 0.05 | 0.01 | 0.01 | 0.05 | 0.10 | mm |
| Rotor OD | 20.55 | 17.27 | 59.65 | 32.72 | 50.86 | 62.87 | 33.87 | 120.17 | mm |
| ID | 19.26 | 16.19 | 55.90 | 30.67 | 47.66 | 58.92 | 31.31 | 40.50 | mm |
| Rotor cap length | 10.80 | 4.45 | | | | | 19.87 | 10.29 | mm |
| PM OD | 13.46 | 10.03 | 41.75 | 21.92 | 34.07 | 42.12 | 23.71 | 120.17 | mm |
| ID | 6.50 | 6.50 | 16.70 | 8.77 | 13.63 | 16.85 | 16.59 | 40.50 | mm |
| Length | 3.80 | 3.80 | 21.25 | 25.50 | 47.50 | 60.00 | 0.97 | 4.43 | mm |
| Electrical time const. | 6.39 | 3.57 | 6.90 | 3.40 | 5.40 | 4.60 | 98.125 | 65.18 | msec |
| MI of Rotor | $2.76 \times 10^{-6}$ | $2.181 \times 10^{-7}$ | $3.547 \times 10^{-5}$ | $3.917 \times 10^{-5}$ | $4.258 \times 10^{-4}$ | $1.26 \times 10^{-3}$ | $2.24 \times 10^{-7}$ | $7.38 \times 10^{-3}$ | kg-$m^2$ |
| T/J Ratio | 20,000 | 180,000 | 8,109.5 | 10,832 | 5,191 | 2,911 | 31,959 | 636 | Rad/sec |
| Power rate | 1,095 | 7,336 | 23,325,129 | 45,967,250 | 114,779,935 | 107,098,218 | 229,169 | 2,991 | Watts/sec |

## 9.10 CONCLUSION

A procedure for designing PMH stepper motors has been presented. A CAD program called PCSMD, has been developed for this design procedure. The program has been validated by comparing our designs with known and commercial designs. The interested reader is welcome to contact the author for further details.

## REFERENCES


1. Kuo, B.C., 'Theory and applications of stepper motors', West Pub. Co., St. Paul, 1974.
2. Kuo, B.C., 'Stepper motors and control systems', SRL Publ. Co., Champaign, IL., 1979.
3. Kenjo, T., 'Stepping motors and their microprocessor controls', Oxford University Press, Oxford, 1984.
4. Accarnley, P.P., 'Stepping motors : a guide to modern theory and Practice' (3/e), Peter Peregninus Ltd., London 1992.
5. Yu. N. Oliferenko, 'Determination of optimum dimensions of permanent magnet in electromagnetic induction stepper motors', Electromechanics (in Russian), 1977 pp. 1117-1124.
6. Takura, T., 'A method for determining appropriate dimensions of permanent magnet in HS type step motors', Elect. Engg. in Japan, Vol. 100, No. 1, 1990 pp. 921-928.
7. Kuo, B.C., and Chen, Y.J., 'Design consideration of the rotor of hybrid step motors', Proc. 17th Annual Symp. on IMCSD, 1988, pp. 335-341.
8. Johnson, M.H., 'High torque stepper motor', US Patent 4 127 802 dated Nov. 28, 1978.
9. Kuo, B.C., West, P.J., Yeadon, W., Meyerson, S. and Brodsky, P., 'Computer aided design of stepper motors', Proc. 11th Symp. on IMCSD, 1982, pp. 251-254.
10. Kuo, B.C., and Hunter, D., 'How to use IBM PC for stepper motor design and simulation', Proc. 13th Annual Symp. on IMCSD, 1984, pp. 187-213.
11. Kuo, B.C., Design of Step motors', SRL Pub. Co., Champaign, IL, 1993.
12. Athani, V.V., 'Design of permanent magnet hybrid stepper motors', Proc. 3rd Intl. Conf. on Elect. Rotating Machines, Bombay, 1992, Vol. 2, pp. VA 8-VA 13.
13. Mukherji, K.C., and Neville, S., 'Magnetic permeances of identical double slotting', Proc. IEE, Vol. 118, No. 9, 1971, pp. 965-974.
14. Harris, M.R., and Finch, J.W., 'Estimation of static characteristics in the hybrid stepper motors', Proc. 8th Annual Symp. on IMCSD, 1979, pp. 293-306.
15. 'Permanent Magnets', Sumitomo Special Metals Co. Ltd., Osaka (Japan).
16. 'Permanent Magnets Handbook', Hitachi Magnetics Corp.' Edmore, Michigan, USA.
17. 'Technical Guidance Mannual', TDK Magnets.
18. Taft, C.K., and Prina, S.R., 'Motor figures of merit as a function of motor size', Proc. 18th Annual Symp. on IMCSD, 1989, pp. 158-161.
19. Taft, C.K., 'The application of motors using figures of merit as a function of continuous and size', Proc. Motorcon Intl. Conf., 1990.
20. Chai, H.D., 'Permeance based step motor model revisited', Proc. 14th Annual Symp. on IMCSD, 1985, pp. 399-410.